Frank Wisbar

Frank Wisbar

The Director of Ferryman Maria,
from Germany to America and Back

Henry Nicolella

McFarland & Company, Inc., Publishers
Jefferson, North Carolina

LIBRARY OF CONGRESS CATALOGUING-IN-PUBLICATION DATA

Names: Nicolella, Henry author.
Title: Frank Wisbar : the director of Ferryman Maria, from Germany to America and back / Henry Nicolella.
Description: Jefferson, North Carolina : McFarland & Company, Inc., Publishers, 2018. | Includes bibliographical references and index.
Identifiers: LCCN 2017046876 | ISBN 9781476666884 (softcover : acid free paper) ∞
Subjects: LCSH: Wisbar, Frank—Criticism and interpretation.
Classification: LCC PN1998.3.W5687 N53 2018 | DDC 791.4302/33092—dc23
LC record available at https://lccn.loc.gov/2017046876

BRITISH LIBRARY CATALOGUING DATA ARE AVAILABLE

ISBN (print) 978-1-4766-6688-4
ISBN (ebook) 978-1-4766-2976-6

© 2018 Henry Nicolella. All rights reserved

No part of this book may be reproduced or transmitted in any form or by any means, electronic or mechanical, including photocopying or recording, or by any information storage and retrieval system, without permission in writing from the publisher.

Front cover: Frank Wisbar illustration by Helmuth Ellgaard, 1961 (Ellgaard family archives)

Printed in the United States of America

McFarland & Company, Inc., Publishers
  Box 611, Jefferson, North Carolina 28640
  www.mcfarlandpub.com

For E.J. O'Hagan
Che la vita ti sorrida sempre

Table of Contents

Acknowledgments ix

Introduction 1

Biography: The Stranger from the Other Shore 4

The Films and Television Programs

Im Bann des Eulenspiegels
  (Under the Spell of the Owl Mirror) (1932)   23
Anna und Elisabeth (Anna and Elisabeth) (1933)   29
Rivalen der Luft (Rivals of the Air) (1934)   48
Hermine und die seiben Aufrechten
  (Hermine and the Seven Upright Men) (1935)   56
Die Werft zum Grauen Hecht (The Grey Pikes Wharf) (1935)   62
Fährmann Maria (Ferryman Maria) (1936)   65
Die Unbekannte (The Unknown) (1936)   82
Ball im Metropol (Ball in Metropol) (1937)   94
Petermann ist dagegen! (Petermann Is Against It!) (1937)   98
Women in Bondage (1943)   104
Strangler of the Swamp (1946)   112
Devil Bat's Daughter (1946)   120
Secrets of a Sorority Girl (1946)   129
Lighthouse (1947)   134
The Prairie (1948)   140
Madonna of the Desert (1948)   147
The Mozart Story (1948)   149
Rimfire (1949)   153
Fireside Theater (1949)   156
Haie und kleine Fische (Sharks and Little Fish) (1957)   166
Nasser Asphalt (Wet Asphalt) (1958)   170

Hunde, wollt ihr ewig leben?
    (*Dogs, Do You Want to Live Forever?*) (1959)   178
Nacht fiel über Gotenhafen
    (*Darkness Fell on Gotenhafen*) (1960)   183
Fabrik der Offiziere (*The Officer Factory*) (1960)   192
Barbara (1961)   196
Commando (1962)   205
Durchbruch Lok 234 (*Breakthrough Locomotive 234*) (1963)   209
West German TV   212

Bibliography   221

Index   223

Acknowledgments

This book would not have been possible without the help of André Stratmann. I've never had the pleasure of meeting André in person but we've been corresponding for well over a decade and he's contributed greatly to my other strange projects as well.

For this volume, André tracked down rare German films done by Frank Wisbar, found articles about the director and translated them, and displayed saint-like patience in answering all of my questions and requests. I began to feel like Columbo: "Oh, there's just one more thing." And André always responded and gave me even more than what I had asked him for. I can't thank him enough.

Hey, André, isn't it about time you did your own book? Heidelinde Weis is waiting!

I would like to thank the following good people for their help. In alphabetical order:

Bill Chase, pride of the Cleveland Public Library, who generously sent some reviews and articles my way.

The indispensable Steve Joyce, writer and master of fine details who once again took on the task of putting the illustrations together. And of course did a slam-bang job.

Rosemary Hanes of the Library of Congress.

The expert's expert, Dr. Robert Kiss, who found many invaluable articles on Herr Wisbar and his movies from the German press of the '30s.

Alexander Kogan of Films Around the World for sending me a copy of *Secrets of a Sorority Girl* after I had given up trying to find one.

Joan McDonald, Carl de Vogt's biggest fan. Okay, maybe his only fan but who is someone writing a book on Frank Wisbar to judge?

Gary Don Rhodes, one of today's most meticulous and prolific film scholars, for offering encouragement on this project from the get-go.

John Soister, my former partner-in-crime, who did some proofing and translating. Time for us to do another book together, Juan!

Tania Wisbar, daughter of the director. I had a very enjoyable correspondence with her when I first began this book. Tania, 80 years old, is a published author and playwright herself and has worked for decades providing services to the handicapped. She also has done a play on the troubled relationship between her mother and father.

Introduction

This book on the career of Frank Wisbar owes its existence almost entirely to one movie, *Fährmann Maria* (*Ferryman Maria*). As per William K. Everson's description: "It is a great film by any standards, needing neither explanation nor apology."

I first came by the film indirectly via its semi-remake *Strangler of the Swamp* wherein Frank Wisbar tried to refashion his moody romantic masterpiece as a straight-out horror film. I was a teenager when I caught it on the late show. I was—and am—a diehard horror buff and had already seen quite a few monster movies by this time. It didn't strike me as a great film by any means, but it *was* different. It certainly wasn't scary but it had an odd, unique look to it and was unsettling in a way that was hard to pin down. Was the dry ice swamp phony-looking? Perhaps, but it seemed to fit very well. And that ending! No mob of villagers bearing torches, no Prof. Van Helsing and his wolfbane, no mammoth fusillade from the army. Instead a young girl offers her life willingly and the monster is defeated. Much later I would see *Nosferatu* and realize that *Strangler*'s ending had its predecessors.

The first time I read of *Fährmann Maria* was in 1974 in William K. Everson's book *Classics of the Horror Film*. Everson was writing primarily about *Strangler of the Swamp* but naturally *Ferryman* was described as well. Many years later, by the time I caught up with it, I had become an admirer of silent films, especially German ones from the Expressionist era. The mysticism and strangeness of *Fährmann*, while not a silent, fit right in with those earlier classics. The copy I watched was of poor quality with bad sound and no English subtitles. Yet the lack of subtitles didn't matter at all as I was completely drawn into this visually fascinating tale of "death and the maiden." I was also quite taken with the film's star, the tragic Sybille Schmitz, who had provided *Vampyr* with its most terrifying moment.

Later I became curious about the man who directed *Fährmann Maria*. Had he done other great films that had not come to light? At that time, the '80s and '90s, there was very little information out there on Frank Wisbar.

He had done many of his movies during the Third Reich and I assumed that most of the films made during that period, in addition to being impossible to see, were merely propaganda pieces for the Nazis. David Hull Stewart's *Film in the Third Reich* (1969) disabused me of that notion and had appreciative words for Wisbar and *Fährmann Maria*. In 1986 came Frederick Ott's *The Great German Films*, which devoted a chapter to *Fährmann Maria*.

Little by little over a long period of time, I learned more about Wisbar and his films. A mediocre copy of his *Anna und Elisabeth*, only partly subtitled in English, was available from a variety of sources. It was curious and without a clear meaning but hypnotic. I had also read that Wisbar fled the Third Reich because he had a Jewish wife. Much later I discovered that this wasn't the whole truth.

When I first considered writing a book on Wisbar's career, I had only seen a few of his movies. Some of the films he did in Germany during the '30s never made it to America and those that did got very little play. Today, they can be found in archives and in the collections of a few German film buffs. I was eventually able to find copies of most of them though Wisbar's

Frank Wisbar seems captivated by his star Sybille Schmitz on the set of *Fährmann Maria*.

very first feature, *Under the Spell of the Owl Mirror*, still eludes me. Most of the low-budget films he did in the '40s weren't hard to locate though *Secrets of a Sorority Girl* proved a challenge. Wisbar had done a popular but now largely forgotten TV series, *Fireside Theater*, in the late '40s and early '50s but there seemed to be little interest in it among fans of vintage TV and few episodes have even made it to video. He did several pictures on his return to Germany in the mid–50s and many of them were both controversial and noteworthy but they rarely crossed the ocean. Obscure video outlets for German films provided a source for most of them. Wisbar's career ended with him doing movies for German TV. I managed to see only two out of the five he directed, though I expect they were the most interesting ones.

So, having viewed most of his work, would I call Frank Wisbar one of Germany's greatest directors? He certainly doesn't rank with Fritz Lang or F.W. Murnau. Comparisons with E.A. Dupont and particularly Edgar G. Ulmer seem more apt. Like Wisbar, Ulmer did one outstanding film, *The Black Cat* (1934). Ulmer's best work on Poverty Row in the '40s—*Detour*, *Strange Illusion* and *Bluebeard*—is overrated but definitely superior to Wisbar's films during that period. The scales tip the other way later with Ulmer doing dreck like *Daughter of Dr. Jekyll* and *The Amazing Transparent Man* while Wisbar directed the interesting and thoughtful films *Darkness Fell on Gotenhafen* and *Wet Asphalt*. One other difference between the two is that Ulmer has more credits in the low-budget horror-mystery department than Wisbar and is therefore more of a cult figure and easier to peg. Wisbar changed directions, decisively going from a largely apolitical director making attempts to "visualize the landscape of the soul" in pictures like *The Unknown* and *Anna and Elisabeth* to soldiering on Poverty Row and then finally doing films with a more commercial slant aimed at down-to-earth contemporary issues. He doesn't seem to fall squarely into any category or genre which is perhaps why he has less of a following than his very good work merits. In any event, *Ferryman Maria* provides more than enough justification for taking a serious look into Wisbar's career.

A final note, on the spelling of the director's name: Throughout the book, we will go with "Wisbar," the name he used for most of his professional career. We will note his birth name Wysbar only in the credits of his '30s German films.

Biography
The Stranger from the Other Shore

So, who was Frank Wisbar? I'm afraid this brief biographical sketch won't really answer that question. Like the hero in *Ferryman Maria*, he crosses over from the other shore pursued by mysterious forces and dependent on the love of another to survive while at the same time revealing very little of himself. It's tempting just to give a career overview of Wisbar's work and leave the personal and political out entirely, but they are unavoidable and must be touched upon. There are also many gaps in his history where we lack the information, and sources are often ambiguous or contradictory. A full-scale biography of the director—should anyone ever want to attempt it—would have to come from Germany.

Frank Wisbar had the misfortune to come into his own as director right as the Nazis were gaining ascendancy. Obviously, dishonesty was a matter of self-preservation during the Third Reich but he continued a dubious personal narrative after he fled to America and then later when he became a citizen of the Federal Republic of Germany. Articles about Wisbar in the German press of the '30s focused on his movies and his approach to directing. However, he did write a brief piece on his background (or granted an interview written up by others) for the *Hamburger Anzeiger* (March 5, 1937) and I will refer to it from time to time. There's also a questionnaire he was obliged to submit to the film division of the Reichskulturkammer (all movie people had to give a brief history and prove they were Aryan if they wanted to keep working). In 1993, 26 years after Wisbar's death, journalist-filmmaker-gossip monger Will Tremper wrote a book titled *Meine wilden Jahre* (*My Wild Years*) wherein he recalls a few of his experiences working with Wisbar on the film *Wet Asphalt* in 1958. The problem is that Tremper, a questionable though interesting character, is not the most trustworthy of reporters and Wisbar was apparently drinking heavily at the time, so it's hard to take as gospel the wine-fueled gabbing of one famous fibber reported by another famous fibber decades later. Nevertheless, they have to be discussed and might sometimes be closer to the truth than the "official" comments about his Third Reich days that Wisbar made for the American press in the '40s and the German papers in the '50s.

Other than a few scattered recollections by people who worked with him at the beginning of the '30s, the best source we have for the director's career at that time was written by his Jewish wife Eva Wisbar. After the whole family fled to America in 1938, Eva entered a lengthy essay about her experiences in a contest (run by Harvard University) about daily life right before and just after Hitler. Written in 1940, the essay was published as a book in 1980, *Hinaus aus Deutschland, irgendwohin* (roughly *Out of Germany—Anywhere!*), with a controversial afterword by scholar Detlef Garz whose appraisal of Frank Wisbar was so negative that the fourth Mrs. Wisbar sued the publisher and the book was withdrawn. Whatever one thinks of the afterword, Eva's book is the most reliable source for making sense of Frank Wisbar's struggles as a filmmaker in the Third Reich and will be frequently referenced throughout this book. However, it should be noted that she was very much in love with Wisbar and perhaps blind to his faults.

Frank Wisbar was born Franz Paul Wysbar on December 9, 1899. The 1940 U.S. census lists "about 1901" as the date and a brief piece on him in the September 10, 1947, *Film Daily* says 1900 but these are certainly errors. He was billed as Frank *Bentick* Wisbar in 1943's *Women in Bondage* but it's anyone's guess why unless Wisbar himself briefly adopted the moniker in tribute to his earlier film *The Unknown* whose hero is named Bentick. Wisbar, correctly referred to as Lithuanian, was born in Tilsit, then part of East Prussia but now Sovetz, Russia. Tilsit has two other claims to fame: Its cheese was internationally known and it was the setting of the short story "A Trip to Tilsit" which was the basis for the classic Murnau film *Sunrise*.

Frank's parents were Franz August Wysbar and Anna Tonat. His father may have been a minor local government employee. Frank had one brother, Fritz, who also ended up in film though his career was unimportant. Frank Wisbar later described the people of his region as "strong-willed and patriotic." We know nothing about these early years. Wisbar later said he completed his Abitur (basically a combination high school diploma-college entrance exam) but it's not certain he went on to University. The aforementioned 1947 *Film Daily* has him attending universities at Königsberg and Munich. This information presumably came from Wisbar but for the dates to work, he must have gone to those schools while he was in the army, and I'm not sure this would have been possible. He was definitely in those cities during his military service but one can't be certain about any university attendance. Higher education or no, he was obviously cultured and well-read.

Some sources say Frank was drafted into the German army in 1915 (he actually would have been underage) but Wisbar himself said that it wasn't until 1918, the last year of the Great War, that he joined the service. (Elsewhere he gave 1917 as the year.) At that point, the regular army was disbanding and its soldiers headed for home on their own, so Wisbar hooked up with one of the Freikorps, paramilitary groups comprised mostly of former soldiers. There were a number of different ones, many with reputations for brutality. Some were devoted to putting down the Communist uprisings that were springing up all over Germany and the surrounding areas. In the *Hamburger Anzeiger* piece cited earlier, Wisbar reported that his group functioned as a border patrol and he later described himself as a "private soldier." A December 16, 1953, article in the *San Mateo Times* had a brief description of one of Wisbar's military experiences:

> It was Christmas but there were few reasons to be happy. So, thought a young German soldier as he rode horseback along a German road headed for a small garrison town to be demobilized. As the procession of some 250 men rode along the streets of the town, Xmas trees could be seen through the windows and their spirits heightened. Just about the moment the feeling of Xmas built up, gunfire opened. Communists from rooftops were blasting away at those tired and homesick troops. Unable to move either way, the soldiers sat and tried to hide in the narrow street. The massacre cost 73 dead and wounded.

There are no details on where this happened or who these Communist sharpshooters were. Presumably, they were other Germans.

By 1920, the German army was reorganized as the Reichswehr and began absorbing the troops from most of the Freikorps. Wisbar reported that he became part of the Reichswehr in 1922 (serving in Artillery Regiment No. 1 Königsberg; Artillery Officers Academy, Jüterbog; Infantry School, Munich; War Academy, Ohdruf). He later claimed he had the special assignment of observing the development of glider flying; we will come to that in a bit.

Wisbar was at the Infantry School in Munich during Hitler's "beer hall putsch" fiasco on November 8 and 9, 1923. Hitler and his storm troopers, inspired by Mussolini's march on Rome, staged a coup against the Bavarian government and they hoped it would lead to widespread revolt. They enlisted the aid of General Ludendorff, commander of the German army during the last two years of the war, and a firm believer in the "stab in the back" theory as to why Germany had lost. (He preferred to blame Jews, Freemasons and intellectuals rather than admit his own incompetence.) The Infantry School cadets marched in support of the coup. The marchers were dispersed by the Bavarian police and a number of the Nazis were killed or wounded. Wisbar was there and told the *Hamburger Anzeiger* he "witnessed" this historic event. He said likewise on the Reichskulturkammer questionnaire. He described the incident to Will Tremper:

> In the night of the Hitler putsch 9 Nov 23 I was dining at the restaurant Boettners in the Theatiner Straße in Munich. When the SA started, marching people became curious and ran outside. I went outside, too, and became part of the undertow of the march. A lot of people just went with them. One was young and foolish. These were the days of inflation where a dinner (at Boettners) cost some million marks. The word "revolution" hung in the air. Then suddenly there was gunfire and panic. I helped to rescue the wounded, and put them against the walls of the buildings next to the Feldherrnhalle. Then I was arrested.

People who participated in the abortive coup were later given the Blutorden (the blood order) after Hitler came to power. Wisbar told Tremper he had received one himself, which he found ironic since he was married to a Jew, but it was useful whenever he got into trouble with Party officials. In his afterword to Eva Wisbar's book, Detlef Garz repeated the claim that Wisbar did indeed receive the award and that may be one reason why Annemarie, Wisbar's widow, sued the publisher. Eva herself says nothing about it. In any case, whatever Wisbar might have said to Tremper after a few beers can't be verified as Wisbar's name does not appear on any of the lists of recipients of the blood order. It also seems curious that if Wisbar did receive one—and it was the most prestigious award the Reich could give at the time—he didn't mention it either in the *Hamburger Anzeiger* article or the questionnaire. It would seem that Garz's only source may be the Tremper story. Of course, it could be that Wisbar figured he had only to say he was there during the putsch for Party members to assume he had gotten the medal.

Wisbar made lieutenant in 1925. In 1927, he went to Jüterbog where he was to work as a driving instructor. However, according to his account in the *Anzeiger*, something quite different developed:

> At that occasion I made my first contact with movies by coincidence. A (female) friend took me to Berlin-Weißensee [which is not too far away from Jüterbog]. There, at the old Joe May Studio, Carl Boese was directing *Weiße Spinne* (*White Spider*) with Maria Paudler. At this moment, I realized where I belonged. Film stretched out its tentacles and captured me. I abandoned my chosen career and spontaneously I applied for discharge from the service. Then I stood before Carl Boese again and said to him: "I hereby introduce myself as your new assistant." Boese was seemingly thunderstruck and hence he did not throw me out.

A good story but obviously oversimplified. After leaving the army, Wisbar initially occupied himself with a variety of pursuits, none of them very lucrative. He edited a literary magazine called *Stage and Art* and found employment writing advertising copy for Rothgiesser and Diesing, a publishing firm specializing in radio and technical journals. (Two of the magazines Wisbar worked on were *German Radio* and *Radio Post*.) He would stop at the Café Drobin and eat cookies and drink Steinhäger (a gin drink) with other writers and media people. The communist journalist Hans Tasiemka recalled him as quiet and polite and something of an outsider (there was some prejudice against him both because he was from the Baltics and had a military career). He would only join in the conversation when it was about the movies and frequently made the assertion that he was going to be a director. Though his modest circumstances made this sound farfetched, he spoke with such conviction that his companions didn't doubt he would achieve his goal.

One source says that Wisbar was an assistant director in the late silent era but this seems unlikely. While he did indeed work for Boese (though probably just part-time), his apprenticeship was much humbler. He acted as a "gopher," moved furniture around the sets and cleaned up. He did write scenarios but they were not accepted.

It wasn't until Wisbar met producer-director Carl Froelich that he achieved a firm hold in the film world. They were introduced by Eva Krojanker, who worked for Froelich in the script department and had a variety of good connections. Eva's brother was married to the daughter of the founder of Rothgeisser and Diesing (that's probably where Frank and Eva met) and her uncle started Tobis Klang-Film. Eva came from a very wealthy family that controlled the famous Conrad Tack shoe company. She and Frank married in 1932 and Tremper claims Wisbar boasted to him about his good fortune marrying into money even though things did not work out.

Wisbar's first big job for Froelich was working on the production team for the 1931 *Mädchen in Uniform*. Wisbar carefully observed each scene, memorized every line in the script and threw himself so wholeheartedly into its making that *Film-Kurier* assumed he was head of the production team. Wisbar was also determined to absorb everything there was to know about filmmaking. He made notes continually and even rescued trash from the wastebaskets to determine if it contained something useful. Such obsessive behavior caused Hugo Froelich, actor-brother of the director and himself a member of the production team, to label Wisbar a "spinner" (oddball).

Later in 1931, Wisbar served as production manager for two short films directed by actor Carl Behr, *Die schwarze Maske* (*The Black Mask*) and *Zwischen Zwölf und Viertel Eins* (*Between Twelve and a Quarter to One*). They were made for Deutsche Film Gemeinschaft, the same company that produced *Maidens in Uniform*. Other than a reference to *Zwischen Zwölf* being an "amusing sketch," no information on either film has turned up.

Wisbar also made the acquaintance of Dr. Herbert Ephraim, a businessman and an investor in the Ultraphon Record Company. Ephraim was interested in doing films and was willing to experiment. He got behind Wisbar's first feature as a director, *Under the Spell of the Owl Mirror* (1932), which, like *Maidens*, was funded on a collective basis (cast deferring full salaries until the film was released when it would presumably turn enough profits to pay everyone). Wisbar also planned it as a "paper film" which basically just means extensive storyboarding (see entry on *Spell*). Unfortunately, the film was a critical and financial flop.

Wisbar bounced back in 1933 with *Anna and Elisabeth*, reuniting Dorothea Wieck and Hertha Thiele, the stars of *Maidens in Uniform*. This too was partly financed on a collective basis. It did not match the substantial profits of *Maidens* but it was a critical success and led to Wisbar finding employment at Ufa. Propaganda minister Dr. Goebbels hated the film, which was released just after the Nazis took power.

The triumph of the Nazis in 1933 turned the film world and the lives of Frank and Eva Wisbar upside down. Later in America, Wisbar passed himself off as an ardent anti–Nazi but he may not have been so from the beginning, at least according to comments reported by Will Tremper:

> Who says I was against them? The whole country was enthusiastic. The way Hitler grappled things. How he took the unemployed off the streets. How he set upright the frustrated ones. And Jews supported him too. The German Jews did not think Hitler's anti–Semitism referred to them. They thought he meant the East European Jews who were coming from Poland and Galicia in the '20s. My Jewish friend Herbert Ephraim even read me a telegram to Hitler from the Association of Jewish War Veterans offering congratulations on his victory.

Eva Wisbar writes that Frank was certain the Nazi era wouldn't last long:

> Up to this point my husband had been convinced that a purifying storm would break above our heads and that afterward a new dawn would shine forth on Germany. Equally strong was his conviction—shared by a great many people—which every non–Nazi was doing his part to help prepare this dawn. How mistaken he was. The sun did not rise. It sank over Germany and the red glow of dusk meant blood.

Before long it became clear the Nazis had meant everything they said and Jews were purged from stage and screen. The loss was particularly hard on the film world since many Jews were prominent in directing, producing and acting. And soon a sinister eye would be cast at film people who had Jewish spouses.

Frank Wisbar ended up doing only one movie at Ufa, *Rivals of the Air*, a patriotic 1934 film about glider pilots. He became acquainted with Leni Riefenstahl who was fascinated by the World War 1 spy Elsbeth Schragmüller, also known as Fraulein Doktor, and wanted to star in a film about her with Wisbar directing. However, while Ufa thought the athletic Riefenstahl was fine striking picturesque poses against mountains and ice floes, they didn't feel she was a good enough actress to carry a dramatic film, so the project fell through. (Several movies were made much later about Schragmüller.) Wisbar also had to tolerate Nazi big shots who thought their positions merited special treatment in the film world. One such character drove on the lot in a huge Mercedes-Benz with his girlfriend in tow. He told Wisbar she was going to be a big star and demanded an immediate screen test for her. Wisbar quickly realized the girl was hopelessly untalented but had no choice but to get the cameras rolling. However, he found a good way of getting rid of her by asking her to sing the Horst Wessel Song. She tried stumbling through the lyrics but couldn't finish. Embarrassed that his girlfriend didn't know a tune that had become the Nazi national anthem, the official took his young lovely and left the studio.

Being part of the glamor of filmdom sometimes worked to Wisbar's advantage. He became friends with Gunter d'Alquen, a prominent Nazi journalist and Black Shirt who went on to become editor of the SS weekly *The Black Corps*. D'Alquen had a fondness for hanging around film people and thought he could make Wisbar a convert to the Nazi cause, probably because of the director's military background. An adjutant to Himmler, D'Alquen occasionally helped deflect anonymous denunciations of Wisbar, many of them no doubt made by rivals and enemies in the film world, especially as being married to a Jew left Wisbar particularly vulnerable. D'Alquen's friendship did not extend to the Jewish Eva and he encouraged Wisbar to separate from her.

Wisbar left Ufa perhaps hoping to work at a less important studio that might not be as carefully scrutinized by Dr. Goebbels. However, film world people were already being pressured to divorce their Jewish spouses. Dr. Goebbels is alleged to have said, "*We* decide who is Jewish," so exceptions, at least temporary ones, were possible. Comic Theo Lingen was so popular that Goebbels did not harass him for having a Jewish spouse out of fear that he would emigrate. On the other hand, Walter Supper, a writer who had worked on *Maidens in Uniform*, was able to stay married to his Jewish wife for quite a while—but in the end, he shot her and himself to avoid arrest. Eva found herself obliged to report to Gestapo headquarters twice a month. The Wisbars, according to Eva, decided they would have to eventually emigrate. The process was complicated and time-consuming. There were strict limits on how much money you could take with you, and Frank would have to find a film company willing to hire him. In the meantime, they dragged their feet on getting a divorce.

Dr. Goebbels seemed to be of two minds about Frank Wisbar. He rarely had anything good to say about his films but he still recognized his ability and perhaps was reluctant to lose still another "artistic" director to the hemorrhaging of talent that had flowed to other shores. But his patience had its limits.

Before Terra Film would hire him for his next movie, *Hermine and the Seven Upright Men*, Wisbar had to agree to divorce Eva. They separated with Eva living in the family home and Frank in a hotel. However, he often spent the night at home and returned to the hotel in the morning in time for the studio car to pick him up. *Hermine* was to be shot in Switzerland so the Wisbars considered moving there. At this point they had one child, Maria. During the filming, Frank looked for a suitable location for their new home. However, according to Will Tremper's account, Wisbar didn't spend all his free time house-hunting but went to a brothel in the city of Celle in the company of *Hermine*'s star, the massive Heinrich George. The brothel owner said he needed extra cash to keep things going so Wisbar and George, no doubt both very inebriated, contributed to the cause. Later in the year, they were much surprised to each receive 2400 marks from the brothel keeper; apparently, their investment had paid off.

There were some budget problems of another sort with *Hermine* and the crew had to return to Berlin to finish filming. The picture was one of the German entries in the 1935 Venice Film Festival and did well there. That put Wisbar in Dr. Goebbels's good graces, at least temporarily. However, paradoxically, it increased the pressure for the divorce since a filmmaker of any prominence must not be seen as flouting Third Reich policy. This was especially true after the Nuremberg laws were passed forbidding marriage or sexual relations between Jews and Aryans (though not automatically dissolving such marriages already in place).

After *The Grey Pikes Wharf*, a minor comedy romance, Wisbar directed his one truly great film, *Ferryman Maria* (*Fährmann Maria*). It was an extraordinary movie to come from Germany during the Third Reich and the very talented but troubled Sybille Schmitz was the star. She was good friends with Wisbar—and some would say they were more than that. Apparently Eva and Annemarie, the last Frau Wisbar, didn't think so. Tremper says Wisbar told him that he and Schmitz were indeed lovers "though she preferred women."

Critics were very enthusiastic about *Maria* though a few Nazi bluenoses had their objections. Goebbels despised the film's ambiguity and considered it a failed experiment. Nevertheless, the movie was awarded a financial prize to be put toward the next Wisbar film. Possibly Goebbels felt even an artistic misfire deserved some encouragement when so many German films were unadventurous pieces of celluloid cotton candy. However, Eva gives another reason for Goebbels' seeming about-face: Hitler saw the movie and pronounced it a "good German film." If true, this is surprising as *Ferryman Maria* would seem to be the kind of artsy film Hitler usually hated. He preferred movies like *King Kong* and *The Lives of a Bengal Lancer*. In any case, Wisbar and Schmitz used the money to re-team for *The Unknown*. When it proved to be neither a critical or box office success, Wisbar lost whatever traction he may have had with Goebbels.

Eva and Frank did what they could to slow down the divorce proceedings. She was entitled to a reconciliation hearing at which both parties had to be present. Wisbar found various excuses not to show up, often claiming he had to be on location for his job. Things got grimmer when Wisbar applied for a new passport, his old one having expired. It became clear that he was not going to get one until Eva was out of the picture completely. The birth of their second child, Tania, in 1936 showed how phony their separation was. However, now it was up to Eva, who still had a passport, to go abroad and try to find a new home for her family and a directing job for her husband. German directors were allowed to go abroad to film because their wages automatically went back to the Reich, which was always in need of foreign currency. If Frank received an offer, Goebbels would very likely let him accept.

Eva went from country to country looking for assistance. She was denied any help from Jewish sources because she was married to a Gentile. They suggested that she divorce Frank, causing her to remark that on the question of divorce, "at least my Jewish friends and Aryan enemies are of one mind." She was further hampered by the fact that her visa only permitted her two weeks in each country. She even approached the Ufa agent for South America who told her, "Your husband makes wonderful films but I can't sell them to my people. Too German and too highbrow." Eva returned to Germany very discouraged.

In spite of his shaky status with Goebbels, Wisbar was not entirely cut out of the film world. He worked on early television and experimental color and was allowed to direct the occasional movie (*Ball in Metropol, Petermann Is Against It!*) though he found he had to contend with Gestapo spies on the set (see the *Petermann* essay for an especially close call for the director). He was assigned the Heinz Rühmann comedy *Five Million in Search of an Heir* but Rühmann had some problem with Wisbar and complained to Goebbels, who promptly removed the director. (Wisbar's old boss Carl Boese replaced him.) One of the movie's stars, Vera von Langen, would soon play an important role in Wisbar's life.

Weary of the constant surveillance and threats, Wisbar had a falling out with d'Alquen, who was getting tired of waiting for him to see the light and become a good Nazi. In a rare fit of temper, Wisbar called him, amongst other things, "a filthy spy." D'Alquen denounced him as a traitor and threatened to arrest him on the spot but fortunately the argument took place in Sybille Schmitz's apartment. D'Alquen had a crush on the actress so he spared Wisbar at her request.

Wisbar was also fearful that his long periods of inactivity would result in his being drafted. As a former military officer, this was a serious possibility and would eliminate any chance of escaping Germany. According to Eva, Wisbar was increasingly despondent at his prospects:

> The constant life in the shadows, the relentless need to scheme and watch his step, to suppress his own opinion and to lead a double life—all of this is more than he could bear. When I saw him for the first time after many months, I knew this man

was doomed to destruction if we could not find a way to get him out of Nazi Germany.

In spite of his depression, Wisbar apparently found the energy to take up with Vera von Langen. Presumably, this happened during one of Eva's long absences during which she was desperately trying to find asylum for him and their daughters.

Then, as Eva put it, a miracle occurred: Casino, the New York film exchange that imported German films, cabled Wisbar inquiring about the rights to *Anna and Elisabeth* with the possibility of selling them to a Hollywood producer for a remake. For some reason, the Wisbars had not even considered America as a possible new home. In April 1938, Eva went to the U.S. and, to her amazement, she was able to procure the needed affidavits for immigration for herself, her two children and her brother. Frank Wisbar received two film invitations. He later told Will Tremper that he left Germany with a Hollywood contract in his pocket but that was hardly the case. There was certainly nothing firm or guaranteed about these offers. One apparently came from Monogram since Edward Golden, an executive at that company, was listed as a contact person for Wisbar on the ship's manifest when he came to New York. But Wisbar didn't do any work for that Poverty Row studio until 1943.

Things finally began to fall into place for the Wisbars. In June, their daughters left for Rotterdam with their nanny. Eva soon followed and they arrived in the U.S. in September. At about the same time, the divorce became final and Wisbar got his passport and a six-month vacation during which it was expected that he would be going to America to direct a film. In an effort to convince anyone who might be listening that he intended to return, Wisbar dropped hints that, while Eva had indeed left, the girls were still in Germany and would be living with him. Wisbar subsequently headed for Rotterdam, sailed from there on November 19 and arrived in the U.S. on November 23. The ship's manifest has his name as "Wisbar" rather than "Wysbar" (the same was true for Eva) but whether it was an error or not, Frank kept the Wisbar spelling and adopted that as his professional name.

We don't know what passed between Eva and Wisbar when he arrived in America but they did not stay together. Vera von Langen emigrated in January 1939 and subsequently she and Wisbar married. Wisbar later gave different reasons as to why he left Germany. He once said that it was "because of a woman." The natural assumption is that Eva was that woman but Detlef Garz thinks it may have been von Langen. Garz mistakenly states that Wisbar and von Langen came over together but their trips were actually a couple of months apart—though her coming to America hardly seems coincidental. Von Langen had a wealthy family and was just embarking on a promising film career in Germany so more likely she left because of Wisbar, not the other way around. Perhaps Wisbar only meant that Eva had shown him the wisdom of leaving the Third Reich, not that he left for love of her.

In America and then later back in Germany, Wisbar presented himself as anti-Nazi, even claiming Kristallnacht, when the Nazis rampaged against the Jews, was some sort of factor in his decision to leave Germany. However, that infamous night took place barely a week before Wisbar headed to Rotterdam and he had already been planning to emigrate for a long time. He told the American press that he had lectured against the Nazis in four universities but that was nonsense. He occasionally lectured about film but the subject was strictly aesthetics; anyone openly criticizing the Nazis in the mid-'30s would have been quickly arrested. In his infrequent comments to the press about his Third Reich days, Wisbar never mentioned Eva, the divorce or the success of some of his Nazi-era films.

No doubt Wisbar left Germany for a variety of motives but they were likely more personal than political. The atmosphere in the Third Reich was poisonous for him both as a man and an artist. The constant threat of informers, the harassment of his family, the lack of personal freedom, the suspicion by the powers-that-be that he was not committed to the Nazi cause, Goebbels' overall dislike of his work ... to remain under those conditions was too much of a risk. In America if your movies failed to please, you might find yourself unemployed but you wouldn't get packed off to the army.

Hollywood in the 1940s was full of German refugees. But Wisbar, like Douglas Sirk (who had helped make a star of Zarah Leander and had left Germany about the same time as Wisbar), was regarded with suspicion because he had been willing to work under the Nazis for several years. Wisbar later told Will Tremper that Jews in Hollywood referred to him as Kommißkopp (drill sergeant).

It's not certain what Wisbar was doing during his first few years in America. Much later, when people were actually interested in what he had to say because of his success on television, Wisbar told reporters those times were very lean. On December 16, 1953, he told the *San Mateo Times* that he arrived in the U.S. with only 60 cents in his pocket. He shared a room in Harlem with another immigrant and was starving. According to Wisbar, when Christmas came around (the article says it was 1939 though Wisbar would have been in America for Christmas of 1938),

> I received a huge box from a millionaire acquaintance in New York, delivered in style by a uniformed chauffeur and promising to end our food problem for many days to come. What was found however was a box of 24 bottles of French champagne. No one laughed as hysterically with empty stomachs.

I do not know how Wisbar earned his living during this time. His permanent resident status was not achieved until 1941. Eva did not ask for any support for their daughters Tania and Maria. Maria thought Wisbar and Vera von Langen were living on the sale of jewels that von Langen had managed to smuggle out of Germany. I've found no reference to Wisbar in the movie trade journals until September 1942 when it was announced that Jack Barry of Minoco Productions (operating in New York) had hired Wisbar to direct a series of films and Vera von Langen would star in some musical shorts; but nothing came of this.

Wisbar did make the news for other reasons. In November 1941, he testified before a U.S. Senate subcommittee holding hearings on a bill to promote the training of pilots and mechanics in the interest of national defense. The Senators were very intrigued by the glider hobby in Germany. After the First World War, Germany was forbidden to have a motorized air force so the military encouraged the interest in designing and flying gliders, which was the rage among young people. When the Luftwaffe was formed years later, they already had at their disposal thousands of people who knew the rudiments of flying planes. Wisbar presented himself as an expert witness on the subject (see the *Rivals of the Air* essay for details) and claimed he had even been offered the management of the main glider school at Rossitten in 1927. There is no doubt Wisbar was a glider pilot. At one point in the '30s, while Wisbar was secretly planning on leaving Germany, Göring asked him if he would be willing to do some aerial camerawork for the Luftwaffe. Wisbar managed to delay things until he was safely out of the country. Whether Wisbar was as important in the glider movement as he claimed has not been verified. At the subcommittee hearing, Wisbar did manage to work in a plug for his proposed movie about gliding but nothing further was heard of this project. For all we know, Wisbar might have invented it on the spot in the hopes of stirring up some publicity.

In 1943, Wisbar got his first American film credit with Monogram's anti–Nazi melodrama *Women in Bondage* which got more publicity than the usual low-budget epic. Wisbar wrote the original story and was listed as technical advisor. One source says that Wisbar was considered as a possible director for *Three Russian Girls*, an American remake of the 1941 Soviet film *The Girl from Leningrad*. The movie, which was originally intended as a vehicle for Greta Garbo, ended up being co-directed by Henry S. Kesler and Fedor Ozep.

Also in 1943, the Office of Strategic Services (a predecessor to the CIA) was working on producing a profile of Hitler; Wisbar was interviewed. Wisbar, described in their notes as "one of the most successful moving picture directors in Germany," claimed that Hitler frequently telephoned him about details of films in production and even about minor characters in the cast. Wisbar got the impression that Hitler devoted about an hour a day to politics and the rest of his time to movie details. Several times Hitler interfered in film productions, stopping and shelving films on the appeals of actresses.

Wisbar said that this happened so frequently that it was extremely difficult to manage the girls (who were so often guests at the Chancery) since they threatened to complain to Hitler if they did not get the part they wished or if the script wasn't changed to suit their fancies. Wisbar said that there were frequent meetings between Dr. Goebbels and different film directors in which they were urged to do Nazi films that "would give the people what they want." The films were to be "repetitious, simple, devoid of all subtlety and with no concern for the artistic element." This doesn't really sound like Goebbels. In any case, Wisbar claimed that Goebbels illustrated this by relating how, at a meeting on a cloudy day, he held off introducing Hitler while keeping one eye on the clouds. Goebbels made it a point not to announce Hitler until just when the sun broke through. The report also stated that Wisbar had directed Leni Riefenstahl, who told him that there was no abnormal sex in her relationship with Hitler. This was somewhat at odds with what others in the report said about Der Führer's sexual proclivities. (Riefenstahl later denied having a sexual relationship of any sort with Hitler.)

In the passage on Wisbar in *Es wird im Leben die mehr genommen als gegeben* (a lexicon of German and Austrian film people who emigrated between 1933 and 1945), it is stated that Wisbar was sent overseas by the U.S. War Department but I've found no evidence of that. Possibly, the authors are confusing Frank's history with Eva's. Because of her fluency in Russian, she was sent by the Pentagon in the summer of 1944 to interview Russian prisoners who had been held by the Nazis and to look over some captured documents. Eva also did some spying for the U.S. Air Force in the 1950s

When Eva did go abroad in 1944, daughters Maria and Tania were sent to live with their father and Vera von Langen for the summer. Maria found von Langen "beautiful and friendly and not at all like her terrible reputation." Frank still had not made any progress in Hollywood, so von Langen had to work as a sales clerk in the cosmetics section of a department store. No doubt she found this a dreary contrast to her glamorous life in Germany. She and Wisbar divorced in 1948.

The success of *Women in Bondage* did not significantly improve Wisbar's fortunes. Producer Herman Milawkowski, a fellow Lithuanian, bought Wisbar's original stories *Desert Comedy* and *Immortal Spring* but neither went before the cameras. Another Wisbar story, *Aquacade*, was purchased by Lindsley Parsons of Monogram and retitled *Water Amazons* (apparently, it was about a girls' swimming team). It didn't make it to the screen under either title. Wisbar's *The Fighting Madonna* did get filmed by Republic as *Madonna of the Desert* (1948), three years after Wisbar wrote the story.

From the March 18, 1944, issue of *Showmen's Trade Review*, we learn the following: "Henry Sokal, for 18 years an independent producer in Europe, has been assigned by Monogram to produce *Face of Marble*, horror story adapted for the screen by Frank Wisbar. Sokal specialized in horror films in Europe." And from the September 15, 1945, issue of the same publication: "*Face of Marble* with an original story by Thiele Hartman [sic] with screenplay outline by Frank Wisbar, has been purchased by Monogram for production for 45–46. Jeffery Bernerd will produce." *The Face of Marble* didn't petrify audiences until January 19, 1946, and Wisbar's name was nowhere in the writing credits.

In 1944, Monogram announced that it was going to do a Cinecolor adaptation of *Black Beauty* with Wisbar writing the screenplay. This proved to be yet another unrealized project. (Independent producer Edward L. Alperson did a screen version in 1946.) Wisbar's first chance to direct in America came from PRC, a company squatting even lower on the film totem pole than Monogram. In 1946, Wisbar was signed to do three films, the first of which was *Strangler of the Swamp* wherein Wisbar refashioned *Ferryman Maria* as a ghost story. The movie has achieved cult status over the course of time but contemporary reviewers found it to be just another horror cheapie. Wisbar's *Devil Bat's Daughter* overall got better reviews than *Strangler* though today's vintage horror fans collectively hold their noses. Wisbar also did *Lighthouse*, a drama with slightly noir-ish overtones, and he substituted for Lew Landers on *Secrets of a Sorority Girl*.

Wisbar then went on to Screen Guild, another Poverty Row outfit. He directed 1947's *The Prairie*, filmed entirely indoors on a rather peculiar set which brought the film a little more notice than the usual western fare. Wisbar also co-scripted *Rimfire*, a murder whodunit set in the Old West, and put together *The Mozart Story*, a re-edited, English-dubbed version of an older German film about the great composer with some new scenes added.

No doubt Wisbar would have continued to work on Poverty Row had it not been for the advent of television and his own canniness in getting in on the action. There may have been little prestige in grinding out quickies for PRC and Screen Guild but it was very good apprenticeship for television where keeping the traffic moving and staying within the budget were essential. *Fireside Theater*, an anthology show that began in 1949, attracted little attention until Wisbar took over as producer (and sometimes director and writer). It became one of the most popular TV shows of the early '50s and won several awards even though critics were often scornful of its low budget, second string actors and often trite or sentimental storylines. Wisbar was also prescient enough to realize that live television, then the norm, would be replaced by film and *Fireside Theater* became the first TV series to be done entirely on film.

Wisbar—whose public profile in America had seldom rated more than an occasional mention in the trade papers—now found his name and work in the *Los Angeles Times*, *Life* and the *New York Times*. He was asked for his opinion of current movies; he was disappointed with *The Red Badge of Courage* but liked *A Streetcar Named Desire*, *A Place in the Sun* and *Sunset Blvd.*, hardly controversial choices. He joined the board of the Motion Picture Charities Committee. He judged contests. He talked to the press about trends in television and technological innovations. He defended American viewers against charges that they were unsophisticated and without good taste. Of *course* they had good taste: They liked his show!

Perhaps *Fireside Theater* and Wisbar succeeded in part because they did indeed give people what they wanted: something predictable, undemanding, usually optimistic and very family-oriented, cathode ray comfort food. However, Wisbar's promotion of family values did not extend to his own family. Eva ultimately sued him for child support and he nearly went to jail over it. Eva had always taken care of Tania and Maria on her own but she suffered a heart attack in 1948. Though she recovered, she worried about the future of her girls and wanted to make sure they attended college. Frank's settlement with her guaranteed that. In the meantime, Wisbar married again: Dolores Carlock came from a rich and socially prominent family. Well-versed in the arts, she became a fixture on the *Fireside* set. In spite of this shared interest, the marriage didn't last.

Eventually, the ratings for *Fireside Theater* declined and in late 1954 Wisbar resigned over a "policy dispute" though the show quickly returned from the ashes as *Jane Wyman Presents Fireside Theater*. Wisbar dropped from the TV scene for almost a year but then returned promoting an experimental color series titled *Valley of the Blue Mountain*, with each story concerning different residents of the Blue Mountain. From the November 29, 1955, *New York Times*:

> Mr. Wisbar has built a complete ranch on 2000 acres in the valley where most of the photography will be done. While each story will feature a different actor in the leading role, a connecting thread will be provided by the character of a widowed ranch owner played by Bonita Granville. Mr. Wisbar said the series was prompted in part by the fact that "many good TV scenarios cannot be used on ordinary television programs because they call for considerable outdoor photography." By building a self-sustaining and permanent location site, the director feels he has the answer to the problem.

The series was not sold. Perhaps Wisbar was premature in promoting a color show before the idea of color television firmly took hold. Wisbar's *Valley of the Blue Mountain* pilot was broadcast in 1961 as part of the series *The Best of the Post*.

Wisbar became an American citizen in 1947 and later was quoted as saying, "There is only one country in the world for me—and that country is the United States of America." However, in December 1956, he returned to his native land and subsequently became a citizen of the Federal Republic. Wisbar had been to Germany for a visit in 1950 and later brought his 79-year-old father (a resident of the communist German Democratic Republic) to the U.S. for a vacation but we don't know why he decided to go back for good. The German film industry was slowly getting back on its feet in the mid– to late '50s so perhaps Wisbar felt it was an opportune time to get in on the action. Back in Deutschland, he met and married Annemarie, a secretary at Ufa. She gave him one son, Matthias, born in 1959.

Wisbar's first film back in Germany was *Sharks and little Fish*, a submarine war epic. He followed that with *Wet Asphalt*, an exposé of journalistic fraud scripted by Will Tremper, someone who certainly had an intimate knowledge of the subject. Wisbar then did other war films: *Dogs, Do You Want to Live Forever?* (*The Siege of Stalingrad*) and *Darkness Fell on Gotenhafen* (concerning the sinking of a refugee ship by the Russians at the end of the war). Wisbar preferred to call them anti-war films. They did very well and received good reviews but, as we shall see in the essays about them, they were very controversial in that they seemed to absolve the German military of responsibility for the horrors of the Third Reich. This is indeed what you might expect from someone who took pride in being a military man, but Wisbar was confident he could not be accused of being militaristic since he had been out of the action and in America during World War II. Given the Cold War and the rearmament of West Germany, championing the military was good politics. *The Officer Factory* was a thriller set in a military school during the last days of the war and the attempted assassination of Hitler was part of the plot. Only *Barbara* (1961), Wisbar's sole color film, with its island femme fatale and undertones of mysticism, seemed to hearken back to the Wisbar of the '30s. Wisbar also directed *Commando* (1962), a routine actioner which did have the (then) novelty of being set during the Algerian revolt against French rule. His last theatrical film, 1963's *Breakthrough Locomotive 234*, was about a family's escape from East Berlin.

When he made *Wet Asphalt*, Wisbar told Will Tremper of the importance of getting things absolutely correct in your films because future generations would be watching. But the director seemed to have a change of heart shortly after, at least according to an interview he gave to the newspaper *Kultur* on November 1, 1958, before the release of *Dogs, Do You Want to Live Forever?*:

> Film isn't meant to last. Film is modern, present, time-bound like a newspaper headline. I never experienced a film that stood the test of time. After 10 or 15 years, a film seems to come from Grandma's fashion mag, yellowed, dusty, and one doesn't understand why it caused a sensation back then. *The Cranes are Flying* has a big audience in Germany today. The film has lots of real and contemporary stuff, and it's wonderful to look at. Yet it would be blasphemy to call this film art. It will be forgotten after a couple of years. Who does know anything today about *Battleship Potemkin* and *Storm Over Asia*? No, young people today have heard of them. Just

back then these films were great and considerable, because they were contingent upon their time.... Film as art? No! Art possesses a criterion solely posterity can decide on. It's a permanent value, a value of eternity. Mozart is eternal. So are Rubens and Shakespeare.

These were very curious sentiments coming from someone who always expressed a near-religious reverence for film. He seems cynical and almost bitter. Was he reflecting on how his own best work from the '30s (*Ferryman Maria, The Unknown, Anna and Elisabeth*) was largely forgotten? He went on to say that film's single purpose is to entertain, not edify or enlighten, and it could hardly be otherwise given the collaborative and commercial nature of the medium:

> Assume that an important film comes into being. Perhaps you would call it art. I'd just call it a hand-crafted product. In the best cases, it may deal with an important subject but it just wouldn't occur to my mind that we technicians of the entertainment industry could create something that's permanent beyond our time.... A film isn't just the product of a single person who believes he had to tell the world something special. A film results from the efforts of many people who are putting the subject into an entertaining shape. Sometimes there is more than just one author. And one has to keep an eye on the interests of distributors and financiers, too. So, it's not a private matter. It's a loud marketplace. And it's grotesque to think that in this way art could arise or to be sought.... Yet one endeavors to create the best possible thing in the very frame of the conditions.... Here author, director, actors, technicians and a lot of money are assembled to present something to the audience that craves to be entertained and that can be digested by them. In this industry, there is no space for solitary experiments and fantasies.

Had Wisbar felt that way in the 1930s, he might have pleased Dr. Goebbels after all.

In the mid–1960s, Wisbar turned to German television. There was no German equivalent of *Fireside Theater,* but movies made for TV were popular and Wisbar was kept busy writing and directing. His choice of subjects was offbeat and included a version of Thomas Wolfe's rarely produced play *Welcome to My City* (retitled *Welcome to Altamont*), about a race riot in the '20s, and the satirical *Uncle Phil on TV*, an adaptation of a J.B. Priestley short story of a haunted television set. In January 1967 he directed his last teleplay, *Escape on the Baltic Sea*, which covered the same tragedy as his earlier *Darkness Falls on Gotenhafen* Two months later, early in the morning of March 17, Wisbar crossed over to the other shore for the last time. He had been suffering from arterial sclerosis and succumbed to it in the St. Vincent and Elisabeth Hospital in the town of Mainz. He was buried in the Ohlsdorf cemetery in Hamburg. His obituaries, both in Germany and America, were brief. His best films were tainted by the time in which they were made. Annemarie Wisbar was particularly sensitive to her late husband's reputation and in addition to getting Eva's book withdrawn, she sued the tabloid newspaper *Bild* for saying that Wisbar was cozy with the Nazis. Annemarie issued statements from the Federal Republic stating that her husband had been cleared of any association with the Nazis. *Bild* published a retraction.

Someone who knew Wisbar well said he was a man without a "moral compass." That may be but we will let the great film historian William K. Everson have the last word: "On the strength of *Anna and Elisabeth* and *Ferryman Maria*, he is certainly entitled to rank as one of the screen's most individual poets, and the word is not used lightly."

The Films and Television Programs

Im Bann des Eulenspiegels
(Under the Spell of the Owl Mirror)
Kollektiv-Film GmbH
Released on December 14, 1932
78 minutes

Cast: Franz Weber as Baron Altmann; Ursula Grabley as his daughter Elli; Oskar Karlweis as Menzel, prison supervisor; Till Klockow as Lissy the prison nurse; Karl Platten as Chefartz the prison physician; Theo Lingen as Rosnowsky the financial agent; Hugo-Fisher Köppe as the first prison escapee; Raimond Janitschek as the second prison escapee; Hedwig Wangel as Widow Schramm, owner of the Paradise Bar; Olly Gebauer as her niece Adelheid; Fritz Beckmann as Uncle Max; Emmy Wyda as Aunt Ida; Marion Taal as Marion; Ernst Wurmser as the doorman.

Credits: Director: Frank Wisbar (as Frank Wysbar); Assistant Director: Jules Meery; Screenplay: Ernst Länner, Wolfgang Wilhelm, John H. Kafka; Producer: Herbert Ephraim, Karl Wilhelm; Photography: Herbert Körner; Production Designers: Fritz Maurischat, Karl Machus; Costumes: Wilhelm Scholz, Margarete Scholz; Editor: Wolfgang Becker, Alice Ludwig; Sound: Hermann Dirkhofer; Music/Conductor: Herbert Lichtenstein; Lyrics: Gerd Karlick; Unit Production Manager: Gösta Nordhaus; Location Manager: Ernst Braun.

Trade papers in 1932 announced that Frank Wisbar and Kollektiv-Film would do a movie version of the 1929 Ilja Ilf-Jewgeni Petrow comic novel *The Twelve Chairs*. The book concerns the search for a fortune in jewels hidden in one of a dozen chairs during the Russian Revolution. However, Wisbar was not able to get the film rights (presumably because they were too expensive for a small independent movie company) so instead the basic premise was simply rewritten, with an ornate mirror being substituted for the chair and without the satire of the new Soviet society.

As mentioned elsewhere, Kollektiv-Film lived up to its name in that there was little of the hierarchy found in studios like Ufa, and cast and crewmembers were encouraged to contribute ideas. They were also expected to defer their salaries (or part of them) until the film was released and turned a profit. Wisbar's friend Dr. Herbert Ephraim was a big investor in the company.

Another thing that made *Under the Spell* out of the ordinary is that Wisbar planned to do the whole picture as a "paper film" which he felt would make scripts redundant and would save film companies a great deal of money. Fritz Maurischat, who had worked on *Mädchen in Uniform* with Wisbar, drew 296 sketches on paper which could then be shown on a rotating wheel. The impression was better than with a normal script. They could determine all things before start of filming in the studio so the shooting of useless material could be prevented. This was the idea, anyway. Every crewmember and actor got a minimized paper film roll and the whole film was on eight rolls. Each roll was 34 meters long and 34 centimeters wide. Due to less studio rent and less equipment, they hoped to save 30 percent on production costs. Paper film, according to composer Herbert Licht-

Im Bann des Eulenspiegel—"A funny search for money and love!" Pictured are Oskar Karlweiss and Ursula Grabley.

enstein, was also good for the composer for it would give him a better possibility to shape music for the film.

But on set, the actors, especially Theodor Lingen, made fun of it, carrying these big rolls of paper all over. The idea simply didn't work and Wisbar had to resort to a traditional script. However, the experiment did get some publicity and Wisbar demonstrated the paper machine to the press even though he had given up on using it. The idea of course survived as what became known as "storyboarding." But shot by shot storyboarding was a luxury for big studios and pricey movies, not at all a practical reality for independent filmmakers struggling with tight schedules and low budgets.

This synopsis of *Under the Spell* is taken from *Film-Kurier*:

Klemmke, a notorious thief, has hidden $10,000 in loot in an ornate mirror with an owl design. However, he has been arrested and sent to prison before he could get the money. In jail, while in the sickbay, he reveals all this to another inmate. However, Lissy, the nurse, and Menzel, an officer at the prison, overhear the conversation. Menzel decides to track the mirror down and he locates its owner, Baron von Altmann. The Baron's daughter, Elly, becomes attracted to Menzel. It turns out however that von Altmann has sold his villa—mirror and all—to a hotel corporation. He and Menzel agree to find the mirror and split the profits 50–50. However, they are in for a surprise: The hotel executives were so taken with the look of the mirror that they had ordered thousands of duplicates made and stored in a factory.

Menzel and von Altmann search the factory warehouse but can't locate the right mirror. They discover that the mirror they are looking for was probably sold to a widow named Schramm. She is holding a party which Menzel and the Baron crash in hopes of finding the mirror but no luck. In the midst of all this, Elli and Lissy both vie for the affections of Menzel and are more interested in him than the money.

Rosnowsky, a crooked friend of the Baron's, gets involved in the quest. The others begin to suspect that Menzel has actually found the money in one of the mirrors and is just holding out on his companions. Elli however believes Menzel. It turns out Max, a relative of Mrs. Schramm, has the mirror but it's part of a maze of mirrors in his funhouse. The characters all head for the carnival but now they are joined by Klemmke who has just escaped from prison with another convict. There's a frantic search through the hall of mirrors but it is Klemmke who finds the right one and destroys it, uncovering the money. Now everyone else knows that Menzel was telling the truth. Klemmke escapes with the loot but the police are following him and, realizing he's trapped, the crook throws the money into a confetti mill. Menzel doesn't have the fortune but he does have Elli and has managed to save his job as well.

It sounds like a wild ride. Alas, we have not been able to get a first-hand

The climax at the carnival in *Im Bann des Eulenspiegel*. Clockwise (from top left): Ursula Grabley, Franz Weber and unidentified actress, Theo Lingen and clown, Theo Lingen (on piano), Oskar Karlweis (seated), unidentified actor, Franz Weber.

look at the movie though it is still extant in the German film archives. Wisbar later commented that the movie was a commercial and critical flop: "A then famous critic wrote 'Either Wisbar is brilliant or a lunatic. We think he's a lunatic.'"

Im Bann des Eulenspiegels (1932)

The stolen loot ends up as confetti in *Im Bann des Eulenspiegel*. Top: Ursula Grabley, Oskar Karlweis, Franz Weber.

Oskar Karlweis (Menzel) was an Austrian singer and actor whose most famous movie was the musical comedy *Three from the Filling Station,* Germany's most successful film of 1930. Karlweis, who was Jewish, used some Yiddish shtick in his character but soon the actor would be fleeing Hitler's Third Reich back to his native Austria and then staying ahead of the Nazi juggernaut until finding safety in America. He struggled with English for a time (though his peculiar pronunciation could be used to comic effect) but mastered it and had a Broadway hit with *Jacobowksy and the Colonel* (1944) with Louis Calhern. He remained primarily a stage actor though he did the occasional movie, including a straight dramatic role in the excellent spy thriller *Five Fingers* (1952).

Ursula Grabley (Elli) started her film career at the end of the silent era with the circus drama *Katharina Knie* but she had already achieved success on the stage and as a dancer. She was a familiar face in light comic roles throughout the '30s and was famous for her bobbed hair look. She became a less familiar face after having some kind of run-in with Dr. Goebbels. Grabley was able to do some stage work during her forced hiatus from the film world. She returned to the screen in a minor film, *Zwielict* (*Twilight*) with Paul Wegener. Her last film, *Life Goes On*, was meant to be a major propaganda movie comparable to *Kolberg* but the fall of the Reich prevented its completion. After the war, Grabley found regular work in supporting roles on stage and screen as well as dubbing the voices of Lucille Ball, Paulette Goddard and others for German releases of their films.

Theo Lingen (Rosonowsky) had an extraordinarily long career in German and Austrian movies, chalking up over 200 films as well as numerous stage performances, most notably for Berthold Brecht and Gustav Gründgens. While he appeared in serious films like *M* and *Testament of Dr. Mabuse*, he was primarily famous for his comic roles, often playing obnoxious servants, annoying bureaucrats and fast-talking crooks. He had a very broad comic style that some have said bordered on the hysterical and he was often paired with another comic actor, Hans Moser. Lingen also wrote scripts and directed a number of films, including a series of shorts about the legendary medieval prankster Till Eulenspiegel. That subject had interested Frank Wisbar as well though he was never able to do a film about him.

Fritz Maurischat was an excellent set designer and art director who worked with Wisbar on numerous occasions. The paper film idea for *Under the Spell* no doubt originated with him. In the silent film era, he worked on Paul Leni's *Waxworks* and Gennaro Righelli's *Svengali* and did special effects as well, collaborating with Eugene Schüfftan to create the "Schüfftan process" which involved the use of mirrors to create special effects. Maurischat stayed in Germany during the Third Reich and worked on the ill-fated 1943 production *Titanic*. The film's director Herbert Selpin made the mistake of complaining about the Third Reich to his scenarist Walter Zerlett-Olfenius, who promptly ratted him out to the Gestapo and Dr. Goebbels. Selpin was arrested but Maurischat, at great risk to himself, went to Zerlett-Olfenius and begged him to withdraw the charge. A devout Nazi, the writer refused, and the unrepentant Selpin was found hanged in his cell. Maurischat also supervised the special effects involving the sinking of the *Titanic* and kept a detailed log about the filming. After the war, Maurischat's film career was fairly minor though he did some work for the stage and television. His last film *Darling of the Gods* (1960) was about another victim of the Nazis, Renate Müller.

In Austria, *Under the Spell of the Owl Mirror* was titled *Eine tolle Sache* (*An Awesome Affair*). The film did not prove to be awesome for Wisbar as it received little notice or critical interest. The one review we have been able to find was lukewarm:

> The premise is witty. Typical comedy technique. Shooting and editing well done. Cute music. Average acting. Lingen is not at his peak. The language uses North German slang and is understandable in the dialogue but the song lyrics are incomprehensible. The drunkenness scene could have been cut. The theme that money can't buy happiness enhances this modest comedy. Harmless entertainment (*Der Gute Film,* March 30, 1934).

Anna und Elisabeth (*Anna and Elisabeth*)

Kollective-Film GmbH
Released on March 9, 1933
76 minutes

Cast: Dorothea Wieck as Elisabeth; Hertha Thiele as Anna; Maria Wank as Elisabeth's sister Margarete; Mathias Wieman as the organist Mathias Testa; Dorothea Thiess as Anna's mother; Carl Wery as Anna's father; Carl Balhaus as Martin; Wilhelm Kaiser-Heyl as Pfarrer; Roma Bahn as Mary Lane; Margarete Kestra as Helena; Doris Thalmer as Nena; Sybil Smolowa as Schiefhals; Karl Platen as Dorfarzt; Robert Eckert as Gutsnachbar; S. Elfeld and José Maria Lepanto as the Bishop's advisors.

Credits: Director: Frank Wisbar (as Frank Wysbar); Screenplay: Gina Fink, Frank Wisbar Photography: Franz Weihmayr; Editor: Alice Ludwig; Music: Paul Dessau; Still Photographer: Eugen Klagemann; Production Designers: Fritz Maurischat, Heinrich Belsenherz, Hans Curjel; Costumes: Otto Sucrow, Hans Kothe; Sound: Herman Birkhofer; Producers: Frank Wisbar (Wysbar), Hermann Ephraim; Unit Production Manager: Max G. Hüske; Location Manager: Erich Frisch; Artistic Advisor: Dr. Hans Curiel; Commissioned by Terra-Film AG.

> When an unclean spirit goes out of a man it wanders through waterless country looking for a place to rest and not finding one it says: "I will go back to the home I came from." But on arrival, finding it swept and tidied it then goes off and brings seven other spirits more wicked than

itself and they go and set up house there, so that the man ends up being worse than he was before.

—Luke 11:24–26

When Frank Wisbar came to America and tried to get into the movies, he found that his slight claim to fame rested entirely on the 1931 *Mädchen in Uniform (Maidens in Uniform)*. Publicity sometimes claimed—mistakenly—that he had directed the film whereas he was really just a member of the production team. It was the only one of his German films that had any resonance with the American moviegoing public and reviewers: For a German-language film with subtitles, the film had done extraordinarily well in America and played in 1,000 theaters according to publicity. One wag claimed that the reason for the film's popularity was that viewers were hoping for a look at maidens out of uniform. Wisbar's other films played mostly in New York City and after the Hitler regime began persecuting the Jews, cinemas specializing in showing German films were boycotted; by the mid-'30s, most of them either changed fare or went under. In the end, this also affected films like Fritz Lang's *M* which was made before the Nazi takeover but was slow to get released in America (it did play in an English-dubbed version). *Maidens* was ulti-

Dorothea Wieck (left)and Hertha Thiele, the stars of *Mädchen in Uniform*, reunited one final time in *Anna und Elisabeth*.

mately withdrawn from theaters but critics had used every accolade in their dictionaries to praise it so its reputation remained strong even after it was no longer being shown.

Wisbar later claimed that he was responsible for the controversial film's initial bookings in Berlin. He had a hard time finding an exhibitor willing to show it but eventually it premiered in a small theater. When Wisbar went back the next day to see how it fared, he was astonished to find that it was doing smash business. It became an international hit.

Maidens in Uniform, based on the play *Yesterday and Today,* is set in a girls' school where the students are subject to Prussian discipline and the Spartan regime of the headmistress, who feels that letting the girls go hungry is good for their character. Fourteen-year-old Manuela (Hertha Thiele), who has lost her mother, has a hard time adjusting to this regimen. She develops a crush on the school's most popular teacher Miss Bernburg (Dorothea Wieck). At a party, Manuela gets tipsy from the spiked punch and declares her love for Miss Bernburg. The headmistress, furious, orders the other girls to ostracize Manuela and prepares to dismiss Miss Bernburg, whose liberal teaching methods do not meet with her approval. The distraught Manuela prepares to hurl herself from the top of a high staircase but the other girls prevent her just in time. The headmistress is taken aback but there's little reason to think she will abandon her ways. In the play, Manuela does jump (from a window, not a stairwell); the real-life girl who was the basis for her character ended up a cripple as a result.

The play certainly could be seen as having a lesbian undertone but that often depended on who played Bernburg. If the actress was middle-aged and plain, the relationship with Manuela could be seen in the mother-daughter vein. A younger, sexier actress playing the part could suggest a different subtext. However, the film mainly got into trouble for its condemnation of the Prussian education system. Critics worldwide failed to mention the lesbian aspect (though a *Folies Bergère* spoof of the film certainly didn't overlook it) even though Wieck's Bernburg was hardly matronly. It wasn't until decades later that the film was hailed as a milestone by feminist and gay commentators because of its positive portrayal of an erotic relationship between two women. Its status was cemented by it having an all-female cast and a woman director (Leontine Sagan, though Carl Froelich acted as co-director). The film made stars of Wieck and Hertha Thiele (who received a lot of fan mail from women, some of them love letters).

Wisbar's *Anna and Elisabeth* was an attempt to capitalize on Wieck and Thiele's newfound fame with ads for the film putting the names of the actresses over the title. Like *Maidens, Anna and Elisabeth* was financed on a collective basis; that is, cast and crew deferred part of their salaries which would be made up (and then some) when the movie was released and every-

Anna und Elisabeth—Top: Anna (Hertha Thiele) flees the scene of her brother's resurrection. Middle: Martin (Carl Balhaus) discusses the situation with Anna's mother (Dorothea Thiess). Bottom: Testa (Mathias Wieman) comforts Anna.

one could share in the profits. In an interview many years later, Thiele said she took 25 marks a day for *Maidens*, a fourth of her usual salary. The movie ended up making millions but someone in production—Thiele didn't know who—absconded with much of the money. Not about to let that happen

Anna und Elisabeth (1933)

again with *Anna and Elisabeth*, Thiele and Wieck insisted on being paid in advance.

However, the new production was a very different movie from *Maidens*; the playful eroticism of the first film gives way to obsession and perhaps madness. It is grim, ambiguous and nearly humorless. Nonetheless, it remains a fascinating study of the emotional underpinnings of spirituality.

This synopsis is based on a viewing of the film:

In a small coastal Italian village, the simple peasant girl Anna attends her dying brother. On a nearby island lives Elisabeth, a wealthy woman who has been confined to a wheelchair all her life. The doctors have examined her once again and have concluded her case is hopeless. Elisabeth is embittered and angry though her sister Margarete and her friend, the organist Mathias Testa do their best to comfort her and get her to accept her situation.

Anna's brother dies, and she goes to the doctor to get a death certificate. In a scene missing from current prints of the film, she encounters Testa who tries to console her: "You mustn't cry, Anna. Everyone must meet it once—sooner for one, later for another." A passerby, seeing them together, remarks: "If you look at him, you would not think how deathly he sick is." (We never learn exactly what Testa's illness is. The synopsis in *Film-Kurier* describes him as tubercular.)

Back at her home, Anna prays over her brother, begging God not to take him. Suddenly, his hand, which was clutching a crucifix, begins to move. Anna bolts from the room screaming. Soon the word is out: Anna has performed a miracle and brought her brother back to life. The villagers gather outside her home to pray. The only skeptic is the local priest who, while admitting the event is quite unusual, isn't convinced it's a miracle: "If everything that happens that you can't understand would be a miracle, then our dear God would have a lot to do."

Mathias tries to convince Elisabeth to accept her lot: "I am not unhappy that I am like this. I live outside of mankind. It has many advantages but you, Elisabeth—you are torturing yourself." Elisabeth rejects Mathias' fatalism and tells him she knows she will someday walk.

Anna tells her friend Martin that she's afraid to go home because of all the fuss and she can't understand what the villagers are expecting. Martin argues that she should not let people take advantage of her. A woman with a crooked neck—the object of mockery among the little children who torment her—approaches Anna and begs to be cured. Anna tells her she can't help her but rather she should put her faith in God. The frantic woman grabs Anna's hand and forces her to touch her neck. Shortly afterwards, the woman approaches the crowd singing hymns in front of Anna's house and reveals that she's completely cured: "She merely put her hand on me, then I felt a sort of shock." In spite of the priest's admonishment to the crowds to disperse, the villagers are more excited than ever. In the retelling of the story, it is said that a light appeared over Anna's head as she worked her miracle.

Anna doesn't know what to make of any of this but Martin, having apparently softened his attitude, speculates that people can be cured if they want it badly enough. And if faith could move mountains, why should it not straighten out a crooked neck? Testa tells Anna, "[These] people believe in you, they want to believe in you, and their belief helps them. You shouldn't rob them of it." But when Anna asks Testa if he believes in her, he replies that he's not sure and, in any case, he's not meant to be helped by her.

Not surprisingly, Elisabeth is enthralled by these stories of miracle cures and wants to see Anna, but Margarete rejects the idea: "You can't go sit in front of her house and wait for the miracle like all those crazy farmer women." Mathias agrees to fetch Anna and bring her to the island. He tells Anna that the meeting will be kept secret and no one else will be present and that just talking to Elisabeth may help her. Elisabeth tells Anna she believes in her power to heal but Anna responds, "I can't do it. I can't—one shouldn't try [to be] God." Anna becomes horrified at the woman's hysterical insistence and tries to leave the room but Elisabeth reaches out after her—and stands. Another miracle!

Elisabeth visits the shore to show the people what has happened and the whole village turns out. Elisabeth wants Anna to stay with her and prepare for a ministry of healing. Anna, no longer sure what she should do, agrees. Worried, the village priest warns Elisabeth, "[I]t would be wrong to lure this simple human creature upon a path which can only mean disaster." However, the bishop has gotten wind of the events and is sending his emissaries to investigate. Martin, indignant that Elisabeth is virtually holding Anna prisoner, comes to see his friend. She tells him that while she's not happy to be away from him and her family, she is beginning to wonder whether God may indeed be working through her.

The household servants complain that Elisabeth's temperament is worse than ever in spite of her cure. Elisabeth insists that Anna remain isolated and solitary to gather her strength. They are disturbed by the arrival of an obnoxious lady who introduces herself as "Mary Lane—New York Publicity Society." She tells Elisabeth that Anna's miracles must be properly publicized with photos and newspaper articles. Elisabeth tells her to leave but the persistent PR agent predicts she will change her mind.

The bishop's advisors want Anna to come to the rectory to submit to an investigation of her miracles. They acknowledge that God could be the origin but they must certain the source is not elsewhere. They agree to hold the meeting the following day in the prayer hall so all the villagers can attend. Anna and Elisabeth eagerly await the next morning.

Testa takes a turn for the worst so Elisabeth brings Anna to his sickroom in the hopes that she can heal him. Anna prays over him but he quietly expires. Disillusioned, Anna flees back to the village and seeks out Martin. Elisabeth follows her. The bishop's envoys have arrived and the prayer hall is full of people, some of them sick and in hope of a miracle.

Anna refuses to go to the meeting and insists she has no special power and the death of Mathias proves it. Elisabeth responds that Mathias lacked faith but Anna is adamant that she no longer believes. Elisabeth wanders out in a daze. Anna is suddenly afraid for her and frantically calls out her name just as Elisabeth throws herself into a quarry.

Dying, Elisabeth is brought back home and asks to be alone with Anna. "Anna, I've never been so free," she tells her. "I have reached my goal and you, Anna—you shall also be happy." Then she dies, leaving Anna free to resume her old life.

There are several different interpretations one could give to the strange events of the story. The miracles could be just that: divine interventions in the ordinary world. Anna's brother really was dead and his resurrection no different from that which happens at the climax of Dreyer's *Ordet*. This would not necessarily make Frank Wisbar a believer; it could just be a "what if?" scenario. If this is the case, then Elisabeth's mistake is perhaps in believing that Anna herself actually possesses the ability to heal rather than acting as a mere conduit to God's power. In the Gospel of Mark, a sick woman in a crowd pressing on Jesus touches his robe and is cured. Jesus is "immediately aware that power had gone out from him" (Mark 5:30). Elisabeth feels that Anna must have a similar force of energy residing within her but the priest tells Elisabeth that her cure is the work of God, not Anna. Elisabeth's own cure may be the last of this cycle of miracles but she incorrectly believes that Anna can make them go on and on. Elisabeth's obsession with her own illness, a fixation that has prevented her from seeking any positive outlook on life, has been transferred to Anna. Elisabeth has not sought out a new and loving direction but remains mired in her unhappy past rather than simply being grateful for her second chance. She's no happier than she was when she was crippled and, as her long-suffering staff notes, she may even be more impossible to deal with. She's still a cripple in spite of having been healed.

Anna's reluctance to play the prophetess in some ways prefigures the plot of Brian Moore's 1983 novel *Cold Heaven* wherein Marie, a lapsed Catholic, has a vision of the Virgin Mary pointing out a site to be used as a sanctuary. Marie refuses to acknowledge the vision and goes about her business. Marie is then hounded by odd and seemingly supernatural events (including the resurrection of her estranged husband, recently killed in an accident) until someone else sees the same vision and acts on it. The point is that Marie, far from being reassured that there *is* a God, wants no part of

Anna und Elisabeth (1933)

Anna und Elisabeth—Top: Elisabeth (Dorothea Wieck) frantically demands a cure from Anna (Hertha Thiele). Bottom: Dorothea Wieck, Hertha Thiele, Mathias Wieman, and Hertha Thiele again at right. Elisabeth does indeed walk but is not cured.

the world view faith would force her to accept. Likewise, Anna, while she has faith, doesn't want her simple life interrupted and diverted to another course. Ultimately, her failure to cure Mathias and the death of Elisabeth sets her free from a role she does not want.

A *Variety* review of the film claimed that the story was "based on the Konnersreuth miracles which created such a sensation a few years ago." Konnersreuth, a small Bavarian village, was the home of Therese Neumann, a peasant girl whose visions drew crowds of believers. In 1927, a commission made up of bishops and physicians examined some of Neumann's "miracles," notably the stigmata (the crucifixion wounds of Christ) that would appear on her hands and her ability to survive on only the Eucharist for nourishment. The church never recognized these claims and many think she was a self-deluded hysteric and fake. She was also anti–Hitler and one of her converts, journalist Fritz Gerlich, was an articulate and forceful critic of the Nazis (which eventually led to his murder). Though the Third Reich harassed and denounced Neumann and her family, they did not arrest her. No doubt Wisbar heard of these events though whether they inspired *Anna and Elisabeth* is impossible to know. It's interesting that he set the film in Italy rather than Germany; perhaps he purposely didn't want his film identified with the Neumann hoopla. However, Dr. Goebbels was not thrown off the scent by the change of locale: "Typical Jewish-intellectual kitsch, degenerate and made for confusing the senses of the people. There is no place for these ruminations indoors while our brown legions march outside." (Goebbels also frowned on the collectivist financing, thinking it reeked of the Soviets.) Hertha Thiele was quite convinced that the miracles are what the Nazis mainly disliked about the film.

A second way to interpret *Anna and Elisabeth* is to rationalize the miracles. In other words, Anna's brother was just in a coma, not really dead, and the woman with the crooked neck and Elisabeth were victims of psychological disorders, not physical ones, and responded to the power of suggestion. The gospel healings are sometimes explained away on this basis, especially as people in New Testament times believed sickness, especially what we now know as mental illness, was the work of demons who could be cast out. But Mathias was really dying and merely believing that he could be well could make it so. Some reviewers certainly took this line. However, against this interpretation is that healers from Jesus to Rasputin were charismatic figures who believed they could really heal the sick. Anna's lack of self-confidence makes her an unlikely candidate as a worker of miracles. While Elisabeth certainly fits the image of a hysteric who cannot walk for psychological reasons, the script notes that she has been in a wheelchair all her life and that the doctors are powerless to help her, indicating that her ailment is physical rather than mental.

Still one other way to look at the film's miracles is that they are simply inexplicable but not necessarily benign. In François Mauriac's *The Lamb*, the idealistic young seminarian hero has a disconcerting encounter with an older priest who seems to believe in a wholly rational religion. When the hero persists in his enthusiasm, the priest warns him that there may indeed be something out there but it may not wish us well. Instead of comforting, the miracles may be seen as disruptive, a mysterious violation of the natural order and not things to be sought out. Anna doesn't shout "Alleluia!" when her brother returns to life but runs screaming from the room as though he were a ghost, not an answer to her prayers. Interestingly enough, her brother disappears from the story and we learn no more of this modern-day Lazarus. Mathias doesn't want a miracle for himself though he appreciates the good effect such beliefs can have for others. He accepts his own end as part of the natural order of things. Perhaps Mathias is standing in for Wisbar, a sympathetic observer and outsider but not one to commit himself to that which is unknowable.

Some of Thiele's memories of *Anna and Elisabeth* seem a bit muddled. According to Thiele, it began shooting on January 5, 1933, in Melcesine on the eastern shore of Lake Garda near Verona and wrapped at the end of April. However, the film's censorship date was March 29, 1933, and it premiered on April 12. She also says that the movie was almost immediately banned by Dr. Goebbels; but in a 1933 interview with the *Los Angeles Times*, Dorothea Wieck stated that the new government had no problem with the film, and that it was released without a single cut. What's more, in the wake of the great critical success of *Ferryman Maria*, *Anna and Elisabeth* was reissued in 1936, certainly not a possibility if the film were banned.

The critic for the *Hamburger Nachrichten* (obviously, it wasn't banned in Hamburg) was quite taken with the movie. From that April 16, 1933, review:

> In this film one experiences a strange story that can be described as a legend, a kind of paraphrase of the ancient theme of wonders.... Yet it is contemporary because it portrays the unfolding of energy from person to person, soul to soul. The film gives no answer how to grasp these interrelations. Director Frank Wisbar is content with just displaying the "miracles." Wieck in her role portrays moments with deep and grasping expressions. Her death scene is a kind of transfiguration. But Thiele fades out in the role of the woman saint. She acts too intellectual, too cool. This lacks the touch of the supernatural.... Mathias Wieman, playing the role of an ill man, acts true to life.... The lush Italian landscape provides a contrast to the misery of the people.

When the film played in Hamburg again in March 1936, the critic was equally enthusiastic and felt that the film had not dated in the least and that Wisbar's direction was audacious, refreshing and brisk "Like *Ferryman Maria*, *Anna and Elisabeth* is timeless" (March 14, 1936).

Emile Veullemoz's review in *Le Temps* (December 8, 1933) echoed its German counterparts:

Hertha Thiele and Dorothea Wieck have exceptional cinematic virtues. Their modes of expression have admirable nobility and simplicity. They create something apart from words—a surprisingly eloquent and pathos-filled screen language that has a mysterious and ennobling quality.... The film bears little resemblance to the commercial productions with which we are inundated. What the writer-director considers is quite a disturbing problem where the facts themselves remain enshrouded in mystery. Do certain beings have the unfathomable power of vanquishing the automatism of natural law? Can an innocent young girl and a passionate believer create around themselves miraculous possibilities by only the radiance of their faith? The work is done in an absolutely remarkable cinematic style with grandeur and dignity. Frank Wisbar has rediscovered the beautiful, engulfing images that we so admired in those old Swedish films and whose secret seems to have been lost. This is a picture that shows it is perfectly possible to impose on the talking picture the highly artistic discipline of silent film that began to create an art of the screen so powerful and personal.

On September 12, 1933, François Vienneuil of *Action Francaise* expressed his disapproval in scornful language that often defies translation. But we have tried our best:

We hardly anticipated seeing some miracles on the screen this week. Not miracles of cinematic technology but real miracles! The screen ought to be able to craft a good relationship with the unbelievable, the amazing but the fantastic, the strange are in principle ideal subjects and are in fact the most dangerous. The authors of *Anna and Elisabeth* aren't ignorant of this. Having the courage of an unusual beginning, they then opted to develop average elements, which are the worst solutions in this case.... The scenario is due to touch those believing souls, while cautiously providing some scientific arguments. Evidently, we do not ask the cinema to take sides when the theologians themselves refuse to do so. But one might hope for a slightly less elusive and slippery scenario. No one should be shocked. There will be something for all tastes. The obvious uncertainty of the authors leads them to within two fingers of parody. Northing would be easier than a farcical summary of *Anna and Elisabeth* wherein one might comment on some of the protagonists' reactions.

Most of the performers in M. Wisbar's film, who should be acting skeptically or excitedly, are quite ill at ease in their roles. None of them believes in the scenario. What they can do, like most of the Germans, is feign great solemnity, sententiously hammering home their lines. The show is thus more pompous. The petite Hertha Thiele has several truly poignant expressions of a strong gamine troubled by the prodigious power thrust upon her.... The strange beauty of Mlle. Dorothea Wieck, much more aristocratic than Brigitte Helm, deserves a less awkward tribute.

As for the end product, the film is obviously well done. The photography regains a nuanced sensitivity almost entirely discarded over the past five years due to the improvement of lenses.... In every moment, there is evidence of this consciousness in the work that we are not entitled to dismiss. But to make the excitement of the people more credible, the scene is set in Italy, unfortunately there is an irritating contrast among the luminous landscapes, between some extras and the Germanic physiognomies of the actors, their delivery, an intolerable slowness more than in any other film, the studio decor that stifles one as did the old Expressionistic style.

The last criticism, if we're understanding it correctly, has some validity. The crowds demanding miracles are much too polite, well behaved and restrained. We would expect more emotion and expressiveness of God-intoxicated Italian villagers.

Across the pond, *Anna and Elisabeth* was found to be earnest but a bit dull. From the spring 1934 *Cinema Quarterly*:

> This is primarily an acting film and does not enlarge our experience of cinema. It is unfolded slowly and deliberately with great emphasis of detail but like so many German films it tends to meander before arriving at the point.... No matter how much the Germans leave their studios and get into the open air, they still retain their studio mind. This is the great fault of this picture. Frank Wisbar could learn a great deal from Duvivier.... Dorothea Wieck shows a considerable power of emotion, but is inclined to give way to mannerisms which become irritating. Hertha Thiele, on the other hand, plays less sensationally and more capably. In addition, Mathias Wieman's consumptive is a restrained and wholly admirable performance.

The *New York Times* (July 2, 1933) found merit in the film but had some reservations:

> This is the first piece of direction I have seen by Frank Wisbar, and there are many scenes in it which point to an exceptionally strong talent for the tragic and the pictorial. Wisbar has a sensitive hand for the more delicate shades of feeling and also knows how a dramatic climax is cut to a point. If only a large cannon cracker could be placed under his directorial chair. There are so many sequences where the interminable deliberateness of the tempo gives you the fidgets—but confusing ponderousness with depth has always been one of the Teutonic fallacies.

Variety, which had initially reported that *Anna and Elisabeth* was about the Joan of Arc legend(!), gave the film high marks for artistry but found it unappealing. From the May 2, 1933, review:

> It's almost painfully boring which however is not the director's fault but that of the theme selected, which is quite impossible pictorially.... The picture is carefully and conscientiously done if somewhat overacted in parts. It is very depressing however and most of the time almost painfully dragging. Anyway, young Wisbar, the director, along with some of his co-operators, has proved his mettle. It will be interesting to see him handle a real subject.

When the film played again in 1936, *Variety* was still bored though not entirely negative. From the July 1, 1937, review:

> Wisbar's direction loud pedals the solemnity of the opus and it proceeds with the pace of a funeral march.... Hints are plentifully given that the miracles are superhuman efforts of will on the part of the infirm, and the connection between the lady and the peasant girl continually skirts on the edge of infatuation on the part of the former. Skillful treatment accorded both these threads by story and direction.

The above critique is one of the few contemporary reviews noting that Anna may not have awakened feelings just in Elisabeth's legs. Today, gay and feminist critics often find a lesbian aspect to the relationship between Anna and Elisabeth but, whereas *Maidens in Uniform* is praised for being ahead of its time in giving a positive picture of homosexuality, *Anna and Elisabeth* is

Anna und Elisabeth—The villagers (top) believe that the strange events are miracles but Anna and Testa are not so sure. Clockwise from top: Hertha Thiele, Mathias Wieman, Dorothea Wieck.

sometimes seen as having an anti-gay agenda. Elisabeth's domination of Anna is like something out of *Dracula's Daughter*; she even looks like the vampiric Gloria Holden in some intense close-ups. It all suggests the exploitation of a younger woman by an older one. There is no scene comparable to the tender goodnight kiss between Manuela and Bernburg in *Maidens*. Elisabeth is using Anna for her own ends and there's also the class element of a poor girl being victimized by an aristocrat. "You don't really fit any more in the kitchen," Martin tells Anna when he comes to visit. Martin, whose lederhosen are always in a knot over Anna's absences, is her one chance for a normal, heterosexual life. After Mathias' death, Anna comes to Martin and pleads with him: "Help me, Martin. I won't do it any more—you must help me. I won't leave you any more—I will always stay with you. But help me!" Martin does everything but put up wolfbane when Elisabeth comes in pursuit. Anna's loss of faith in her power means that she no longer has any reason to stay with Elisabeth. Faced with the deprivation of her love object, Elisabeth imitates Manuela by throwing herself from a great height but, unlike the lovesick schoolgirl, she succeeds in her attempt at self-destruction. Her death prevents Anna from giving in to sexual temptation and Elisabeth sees her own end as liberation. It is sometimes thought that Mathias too is meant to be gay as old-fashioned thinking about homosexuality saw it as debilitating. Such an interpretation gives some extra meaning to his line about living apart from the world. For him too, death is the only solution. And to gild the lily, the silly PR agent comes off like a movie lesbian: unfeminine, belligerent and attired in men's clothes.

Did Wisbar intend any of this? That's hard to say but he was certainly astute enough to note the gay undertones between Manuela and Miss Bernburg in the wildly successful *Maidens in Uniform* and may have felt suggesting the same thing in this film wouldn't hurt its box office potential. The vivid close-ups of Elisabeth and Anna together certainly suggest a more-than-sisterly connection (though they remind me more of the characters in *Persona* rather than *Maidens in Uniform*). The night before the church hall meeting, there is a close shot of Anna hovering over Elisabeth as the latter says, "Tomorrow." The shot fades and then opens again to reveal Elisabeth standing over Anna and saying, "Today." Elisabeth is constantly repeating Anna's name, sometimes plaintively but often in a tone tinged with yearning. Anna only repeats Elisabeth's name (three times) after the latter throws herself into the quarry. Mystics sometimes describe their experience of the Divine in erotic terms and it may be Wisbar is hinting at something similar in Elisabeth's fascination with Anna. Elisabeth doesn't seem conventionally pious at all; God may be in His Heaven but on Earth, Anna represents Him.

The *New York Times* critic was very impressed with Wieck's portrayal of Elisabeth's first steps: "Miss Wieck shows a power and depth which I have never seen surpassed in a screen performance of this type. I have weighed my words carefully and they come with double force as I have never been an admirer of this actress." The Swiss-born Wieck was a descendant of Clara Schumann-Wieck, daughter of the great musician Robert Schumann and herself a famous pianist. Wieck's mother was also a musician and her father a painter. In her teenage years, Dorothea was encouraged by the German writer and poet Kabund to study drama, which she subsequently did under the supervision of Max Reinhardt in Vienna. Wieck subsequently worked on the stage in Munich and Frankfurt in a wide variety of roles and made 12 films in the 1920s. She was not well known in Berlin but supposedly Carl Froelich saw her picture in one of her father's photo albums and auditioned her for the part of Fraulein von Bernburg, a part with which she was identified for the rest of her career. (Or at least that's one version. Elsewhere, Wieck said it was director Leontine Sagan who wanted her after seeing her on the stage.)

After the success of *Maidens in Uniform*, there was some Hollywood interest in reuniting Wieck and Thiele for an American production. In the end, only Wieck ended up in Los Angeles where she was signed by Paramount in 1933. She was given the usual build-up with interviews, publicity articles and all the usual hoopla, but the studio didn't quite know what to do with her. In *Cradle Song*, she played a nun who becomes a surrogate mother to a little girl raised in the convent. It was a poignant story based on a classic play but the pubic wasn't interested. Wieck then was cast in the mediocre crime drama *Miss Fane's Baby Is Stolen*, a takeoff on the Lindbergh kidnapping (but with a happy ending) in which she played a rich lady whose baby is held for ransom by thugs. The actress found herself upstaged by the antics of Baby LeRoy in the title role. Unhappy with these parts, Wieck hoped to star in a film version of Balzac's *The Duchess of Langeais* (it had already been done as a Norma Talmadge silent, *The Eternal Flame*) but Paramount wasn't interested. There were complaints that she lacked sex appeal—though casting her as a nun or a mother would hardly boost her stock there. Her marriage to an outspoken Nazi did not increase her popularity in America. Also, the Reich was pressuring "Aryan" stars in Hollywood to return to Germany to participate in the "cultural rebirth" of the nation. Wieck went back to Deutschland in 1934.

Some time later, an account of her meeting with Hitler was published. Hitler was at a formal reception given to leaders of the automobile industry. From the April 7, 1935, *Washington Post*:

> The correspondent was chatting with Dorothea Wieck about her experiences in Hollywood.
> "I've never seen Der Führer," she said with the excitement of a schoolgirl. "Oh, I hope he comes this way too."

Hitler did. Walking with Dr. Goebbels and followed by his bodyguards, the reichsführer proceeded through two large halls, bowing or raising his hand in the Nazi salute.

He seemed impersonal, however, until he saw the famous actress. Then, a look of recognition came into his face.

"You are Dorothea Wieck, aren't you?" he asked. "I've admired you many a time on the screen."

The actress blushed at the compliment as Hitler passed on.

A few minutes later, one of his adjutants came to Dorothea. "The Führer asks you to come to his table," he said. Dorothea curtsied and departed for the Hitler table. Hitler's stern face relaxed into smiles.

From that point on, Wieck was labeled a "Hitler favorite" by the American press. However, if that was indeed the case, her subsequent films certainly don't reflect it as most of them were minor. She had a good part as the seductress Julia in the underrated third version of *The Student of Prague* but little notice was taken of the picture. Her subsequent roles were often in the supporting cast though she worked regularly. One source speculates that she was just the wrong "type" to reflect the Aryan image and another wonders if her sojourn in America caused her to be regarded with suspicion.

The American press reported that Wieck was killed during the bombing of Dresden. That proved not to be the case, though she was apparently injured. Her postwar career on film was inconsequential and usually consisted of small roles. She went back to the stage and one of her last parts was that of the stern headmistress from *Maidens in Uniform*, her antagonist in the original film.

Hertha Thiele would never be accused of being a Hitler favorite and stuck to her left wing political beliefs all her life (she later settled in communist East Germany). One of her earliest film roles was in *Kuhle Wampe, oder: Wem gehört die Welt?*, scripted by Bertolt Brecht. It told of the travails of a working-class family and how unemployment forces them to relocate to a tent city (the Kuhle Wampe of the title). The film has a documentary quality but seen today is more of historical interest than dramatic import. She also starred in *Little Man, What Now?* based on a book by Hans Fallada that was later banned. Thiele was a natural for the part of Manuela, having played it on the stage in Leipzig. While she thinks *Anna and Elisabeth* is her best work, few would agree.

Thiele's film career in Nazi Germany was, not surprisingly, very brief. In her last movie, the bizarre *Elisabeth und der Narr* (*Elisabeth and her Fool*). Thiele played a convent girl loved by three different men, including a dim-witted hunchback (Rudolph Klein-Rogge in the sort of drooling, wild-eyed role that would have been played by Dwight Frye if this were a Hollywood film). The Quasimodo-like madman ends up murdering her father and Elisabeth understandably chooses to become a nun. The film, directed by Thea von Harbou, ran into censorship trouble and ultimately flopped at the box office. Performance-wise, Thiele did not show much growth as an actress.

Thiele wrote to Dr. Goebbels asking about the possibility of doing a film version of Gottfried Keller's novella *Romeo and Juliet in the Village*—a project that also interested Frank Wisbar. She received the response that the book was in complete opposition to the policies of National Socialism. Her refusal to star in *Hans Westmar*, a propaganda film based on the life of Nazi "martyr" Horst Wessel, is sometimes seen as another nail in her coffin but given that film's checkered history, it seems a bit unlikely. In any case, Thiele was barred from the National Film Association; instrumental in her expulsion was her old boss, Carl Froelich. According to Eva Wisbar, Thiele, bereft of her many Jewish friends and despondent about her future, turned to alcohol and drugs. She found a more sensible solution and headed for Switzerland in 1937 where she did some theater but later trained to be a nurse. Some years later, she relocated to the Democratic German Republic where she did mostly TV. The rediscovery of *Maidens in Uniform* in the late 1970s led to interviews and acclaim. In 1983, Thiele was honored at a special program in West Berlin dedicated to actors who preferred exile to working in Germany. (The other honorees: Francis Lederer, Dolly Haas, Elisabeth Bergner, Curt Bois

Left to right: Dorothea Wieck, Hertha Thiele, Mathias Wieman in *Anna und Elisabeth*.

and Paul Andor.) Manuela remains her most memorable performance and has become a gay movie icon.

Mathias Wieman's gentle, world-weary performance as the doomed Testa has a subtlety that almost steals the show from Wieck's heavy breathing, nostril-flaring fanatic and Thiele's sad-eyed gamin. He had a long stage career of which his *Faust* (staged in 1940) was probably the highlight. He was quite content to interpret the role along the lines of Nazi thought and proclaimed that Nazi triumphs in Norway and Belgium gave the play additional relevance. Some of his films were also vehicles for Third Reich propaganda, notably the despicable plea for euthanasia *Ich Klag an* (*I Accuse*, 1941). In light of this, the contention that he was somehow on the outs with Nazi policy is very dubious. The writer Hans Fallada, in a mental institution in 1944, wrote in praise of Wieman, who had spoken favorably on the radio about one of Fallada's books that the Nazis didn't like and who sometimes visited the chronically troubled author. Fallada claimed that Wieman had become unemployable after completely falling out of favor with Goebbels over his performance in *On Higher Orders* which was severely criticized by Hitler, who supposedly said, "No Prussian officer conducts himself like that! I don't want to see this man in uniform again!" Fallada's account is muddled. The film he was referring to was actually *Untenmehmen Michael* aka *Operation Michael* (1937) where Wieman's performance was criticized not by Hitler but by Goebbels. Goebbels was also unhappy with Wieman's portrayal in *Cadets* (1939). These however were mere bumps in the road in the career of the man who had made Actor of the State and was appointed to the artistic advisory board at Ufa.

On a more positive note, Wieman starred in one of the most unusual films of the '30s, the Swiss *Die ewige Maske* (*The Eternal Mask*), a masterful psychological study—with Expressionistic touches—of a doctor's mental breakdown and his journey through his own troubled mind back to reality. After the war, once the Allies were willing to let him work again, Wieman did some films but was better known for his radio and recording work, most famously as the narrator for classical works like Prokofiev's *Peter and the Wolf* in 1950.

Carl Bauhaus, who has the thankless role of Martin, had done important work on the stage in the 1920s but only had bit parts in films like *Ramper der Tiermensch* (*Ramper the Beastman*, 1927) and *The Blue Angel* (1930). Brief, but perhaps more conspicuous, was his part in Fritz Lang's *M* wherein he puts the chalk mark on murderer Peter Lorre's jacket. Balhaus was a leftist so needless to say his opportunities in film and theater were very limited after Hitler came to power. However, he did not end up in a concentration camp but did serve in the army; apparently he was lucky enough not to see any serious action. After the war, he became well known as a movie director for DEFA in East Germany though most of his films had propagandistic aims (it's either noble Communists against the evil Fascists or noble Communists against the evil capitalists).

Though the locale for *Anna and Elisabeth* is sunny Italy, Franz Weihmayr's photography is dusky and low-key as though he's trying to drain the setting of any cheerfulness and suffuse it with an atmosphere of gloom. Whereas his work in *Ferryman Maria* suggests both magic and menace, here the effect is one of perpetual twilight, an uneasy fading of the sun with the characters caught somewhere between light and darkness. This is appropriate for a story about faith and doubt and one in which the heavens themselves seem to offer little comfort.

Paul Dessau's music matches the odd ambience of the film: When it's not downright eerie, it suggests exhaustion, a draining of emotion. The only time there's any uplift to it is in the moving and superbly edited sequence where Elisabeth shows the villagers she can walk. The scene ends with a shot of Elisabeth's now empty wheelchair and it is the only time in the film where Heaven seems to be smiling and the music matches up perfectly. Dessau also knows when not to use any music; e.g., the scene of Elisabeth's cure.

During Dessau's distinguished musical career, he worked with both Caruso and Puccini. In addition to being a musical director and conductor at various companies (including the Berlin Opera), he composed music himself. Much later he became identified with Bertolt Brecht, with whom he worked on *Mother Courage and Her Children, Man Is Man* and *The Good Woman of Szechuan* (as well as basing his opera *Puntila* on a Brecht comedy).

In the '20s, Dessau became fascinated with film and with the possibility of uplifting the musical tastes of the masses by doing operatic scores for silent movies. He did some musical experimental work as the talkies came in and wrote the music for several epics like Arnold Franck's mountain film *Der Weiße Rausch* (*White Ecstasy*, 1931) and *SOS Ice Berg* (1933). Dessau was Jewish and the triumph of Hitler meant flight first to France where he did more film scores (*Carrefour, Yoshiwara*) and then to the U.S. where he joined his pal Brecht in unhappy exile. Dessau did one serious piece, the Third Psalm for voice and three strings, but spent most of his time doing uncredited musical chores for films like *House of Frankenstein* and *The Naughty Nineties*. He did get credit for the PRC cheapie *The Wife of Monte Cristo* (1946) where he worked with fellow Germans Edgar G. Ulmer, Martin Kosleck, Fritz Kortner, Fritz Feld, Eugen Schüfftan and W.L. Bagier. One wonders if he ran into Frank Wisbar, who was under contract to PRC at the time. Dessau later settled in the German Democratic Republic where he continued to compose and write, notably the opera *The Trial of Lucullus* (another collaboration with Brecht) which the Communist authorities banned for its pacifism.

It would be unfair to compare *Anna and Elisabeth* with *Maidens in Uniform*; the latter is a straightforward drama based on a stage success while the former is elliptical in content and style. Hertha Thiele was once told she had a face out of Botticelli but one that suggested depravity. Wisbar might have done better to play on that quality a little more. Thiele's performance is very one-note, even allowing for the fact that Anna is meant to be a simple village girl. Things might have worked better had there been more of a suggestion of collusion between her and Elisabeth. As it is, even when Anna comes to think that perhaps she *can* heal, Thiele doesn't seem able to convey a sense of change or self-discovery. After the slow, deliberate pacing of the film, the wrap-up seems to come too quickly: Anna loses faith and Elisabeth (apparently) goes mad and kills herself. Elisabeth's dying words are a bit too mysterious; is death really what she's been after the whole time, the only way she can escape her personal demons? Yet for a film that is sometimes seems a bit cold, the emotional turmoil of the characters leaves a lingering, melancholy impression. In the end, Anna and Elisabeth's world seems more haunted than healed by the promise of miracles.

The October 10, 1949, *New York Times* announced a number of television episodes Wisbar was doing for his *Fireside Theater*, among them "'The Golden Ball,' a condensed version of Wisbar's German film *Anna and Elisabeth*." Other news items claimed the story would be set in Mexico and star Marya Marco and Kippee Valez. However, a few sources claim that "The Golden Ball" is an adaptation of the Agatha Christie story of the same title. At that point in *Fireside*'s run, it was heavily dependent on public domain titles so paying royalties to Christie would not be in keeping with their meager budgets. In the absence of the film itself, it's hard to be certain. Still, it's fun to speculate on how Wisbar would have condensed his little masterpiece to 12 minutes!

Rivalen der Luft
(Rivals of the Air)

Ufa
Released on January 19, 1934
98 minutes

Cast: Claus Clausen as flight instructor Willie Frahms; Wolfgang Liebeneiner as student pilot Karl Hofer; Hilde Gebühr as student pilot Christine Steeger; Sybille Schmitz as private pilot Lisa Holm; Walter Gross as Palmström; Guzzi Lantschner as Pippin from Bavaria; Werner Stock as Otto from Saxony; Franz Zimmerman as student pilot Corduan from Berlin; Volker von Collande as student pilot Hanne from Hamburg; Hans Henninger as student pilot Schnitt from East Prussia; Florian Zeise-Gött as student pilot Haberkorn from the Pfalz; Wolff von Wernsdorff as student pilot Ox from England; Paul Henckels as Ingolf Kuntze; Rittmeister A.D. Röhre as the leader of the flight school at Rossitten; Karl Zutavern and Dr. Lübbesmeyer as pilots; and with the participation of pilots Otto Arndt, M. Bohlan, Alfred Böhm, Hans Deutschmann, Edgar Ditmar, Heini Dittmar, Wolf Hirth, Franz Orthbandt, Hanna Reitsch, Franz Stamer, Obit Tomm (First Lieutenant Tomm).

Credits: Director: Frank Wisbar (as Frank Wysbar); Based on an Idea by Philip L Mayring; Screenplay: Walter Forster; Producer: Karl Ritter; Music: Herbert Windt; Photography: Hans Schneeberger; Editor: Willy Zeyn; Art Director: Erich Czerwonski; Production Manager: Fritz Koch; Sound: Joachim Thurban; Musical Director: Franz R. Friedl; Made under the protection of the President of the German Air Sports Association Bruno Loerzer.

For several days starting on September 30, 1941, a U.S. Senate subcommittee held hearings on a bill "to promote the national defense and preparedness through the creation of a vast reservoir of airplane pilots and mechanics." The committee was particularly interested in the glider hobby that was so popular in Germany during the '20s and '30s and how that may have contributed to the training of pilots for the Luftwaffe. One of the 11 witnesses the committee called was Frank Wisbar, who presented himself as someone who had actively participated in the military oversight of the glider movement. Wisbar told the committee he was a movie producer and director from Hollywood though at that point Wisbar had neither produced nor directed in LaLaLand. He addressed the committee in both Los Angeles and New York City.

American kids may have been rabid baseball fans but their German counterparts had long been obsessed with gliders: designing them, building them and flying them. In the 1920s, flying schools were established and attracted eager participants. Contests and competitions were held on fields at Wasserkuppe, Göttingen, Rossitten and Rhön and encouraged by a couple of different quasi-government research groups. The Treaty of Versailles had forbidden Germany to have a motorized air force or attempt to develop one but nothing had been said about gliders (or rockets, for that matter). By the time Hitler revived the Luftwaffe, as many as 50,000 German men and women were qualified glider pilots. Getting around the restrictions and flying gliders became a matter of national pride, long preceding Nazi involvement, and local communities often financed young pilots. The glider movement was far more sophisticated and technologically advanced in Germany than in England or the U.S. and was an invaluable resource for the study of aerodynamics as well as a training ground for pilots and mechanics.

At the aforementioned Senate hearing, the following exchange occurred between Senator Joseph Rosier of West Virginia and Wisbar:

Rivalen dur Luft (1934)

ROSIER: Our understanding here is that you were connected to the moving picture industry in Germany in past years and that you had experience there in the production of glider training films which were used effectively by the Nazis in their glider training program. We would like to have a detailed account of what you did in that connection in Germany.

WISBAR: In my capacity as a former officer of the German Army, I had a special assignment of observing and studying the development of all possibilities of glider flying. I myself organized two glider schools in East Prussia. In 1927, I left the army and became a movie producer and director. In this capacity, I produced the first full-length glider picture in movie history for the U.F.A., one of the largest companies in Germany. The title of this picture was *Rivals of the Air*. That was a great success, because for the first time the public got an insight into glider flying and the public recognized the importance of this new sport as a means of educating youth. If you are interested, Senator, here are some remarks by critics and newspaper clippings concerning this picture.

It's not likely that the august body of the Senate took time out to peruse Wisbar's clippings but if they had—and were able to speak German—they would have discovered that *Rivals of the Air* was not a glider training film but a somewhat insipid romantic triangle set against the backdrop of a gliding school at Rossitten and ending with the big competition at Wasserkuppe (and with actual footage from that event). The film no doubt had a propagandistic aim with its

Rivalen der Luft—love and gliders. Left to right: Klaus Clausen, Sybille Schmitz, Wolfgang Liebeneiner, Hilde Gebühr. Wisbar claimed to be a significant figure in Germany's glider hobby in the 1920s.

depiction of the camaraderie, courage and patriotism of the glider students. Wisbar claimed to have received thousands of fan letters about the movie and says he offered encouragement and financial support to would-be aviators who came to him for help.

A number of prominent pilots participated in the film, including Edgar and Heini Ditmar with their planes "Condor" and "Käpt'n." (Heini won numerous air competitions and became the first pilot to cross the Alps in a glider.) Germany's most famous aviatrix Hanna Reitsch did some of the stunt work. Reitsch, who won many awards for her flying and was described by Wisbar in his Senate testimony as "my good friend," became a diehard Nazi and, as the war turned against Germany, even suggested to Hitler a plan to form a kamikaze suicide squad. That was too crazy even for Der Führer but he greatly admired Reitsch, who visited him in his bunker toward the end of the war. (Diane Cliento plays her in the 1973 *Hitler: The Last Ten Days*.)

Most of *Rivals of the Air* was filmed at Rossitten and Wasserkupe. Shooting conditions were Spartan with male cast and crew sleeping in tents. Hilde Gebühr and Sybille Schmitz, the only female cast members, stayed at a nearby hostel. It's not likely that a typical American film would have gone to such lengths but *Rivals*' storyline is strictly Hollywood.

This synopsis is a synthesis of material from *Film-Kurier* and a look at the surviving footage:

Young Karl Hofer, a poor student, is gifted at glider construction. At school, he shows his fellow pupils his invention, a lightweight glider that needs no fuselage or empennage. Karl's teacher, exasperated at the boy's poor grades and classroom antics, threatens to send a letter to his father.

Karl impresses glider instructor Willie Frahms with his airplane design. Frahms tells him that it may well be possible to build such a glider at Rossitten. Karl wants to be Frahms' pupil and requests places for himself and his friend Christine at the gliding school. Frahms consents—but Karl's father tells Frahms that he wants his son to finish high school.

Karl shows up at the camp anyway and tells Frahms that his father changed his mind and allowed him to enroll and that a letter is coming that will confirm this. Frahms and Christine, the only girl at the school, soon have feelings for each other much, to Karl's chagrin. The other boys at the school also enjoy having an attractive woman around and they give her the nickname Krischan (actually the name of Rossitten's instructor Alfred Böhm's glider). The students greatly admire Frahms, who completes an 11-hour flight in his glider.

Pilot Lisa Holm, who has flown from Moscow to Berlin, has to make an emergency landing at the camp and remains there awhile. Christine's gliding practice gets off to a rocky start when she misses her test. Lisa asks Frahms to give her another chance, which he does, but Christine makes a mistake and her plane is slightly damaged on landing. Karl comes to her defense and argues with Frahms. Karl becomes increasingly jealous of Christine's relationship with Frahms. And Christine resents the attention Frahms pays to Lisa. Karl's feathers become even more ruffled when Lisa tells him that Frahms and Christine are surely in love.

Christine seems to be having second thoughts about the glider school but Karl encourages her. The day of the C exam to become an authorized glider pilot approaches. Karl has told Frahms that his father's letter giving him permission to take the test is on its way but Frahms discovers the boy is lying and that the police are looking for him because he has run away from home. Frahms refuses to give Karl the flying pin that indicates he is now a glider pilot and the two have a quarrel which ends with Frahms striking Karl. Christine suspects that Frahms disqualified Karl because he does not want his competition at the upcoming gliding contest at Rhön.

Just before the Rhön contest, Christine and Karl learn that Frahms has talked to Karl's father, who has given permission for his son to compete. Frahms has also arranged a scholarship for Karl. Naturally, both Christine and Karl change their attitude towards Frahms. One of the rookie pilots crashes the plane Frahms had intended to fly in the competition. Christine and the other students work feverishly to repair it. They succeed but in the interim, Lisa has purchased another plane for Frahms and he decides to go with that one for the competition.

During the competition, Christine flies the newly repaired plane but almost runs into a thundercloud. Frahms, flying the other glider, sees that she's in trouble and follows her as she crash-lands by a lake. He joins her there, forsaking the contest which is then won by Karl. Karl gets the 5000 Marks prize and Frahms gets Christine.

Wisbar told the Senate committee about how young men got into gliding by inventing a "typical" story of a peasant boy named John who joins his little village's glider club. The club is run by a local auto mechanic, Mr. Smith. As John develops his skills and shows great enthusiasm for gliding, Mr. Smith writes regular reports about his progress to the flying academy at Wasserkuppe. When not gliding, John works as a drugstore clerk. John is a born pilot and is invited along with Mr. Smith to the competition at Wasserkuppe. John, beaming with pride, travels 1000 miles to the Wasserkuppe. The academy asks John to stay and train as a pilot and he joyfully accepts, passes the course and becomes a full-fledged pilot. The Academy even gets him a good job in a pharmacy in Berlin so he'll have something to do in between becoming a national hero and teaching other peasant boys to fly. Nothing is said about his love life, nor do John and Mr. Smith fight over a girl.

The reviews of *Rivals of the Air* we consulted—presumably not the same ones Wisbar brought to the Senate—were fairly favorable but with reservations. According to the March 20, 1934, *Sport-Tagblatt*:

> Director Wisbar solved the problem of connecting the sheer sporting plot to a storyline in an unobtrusive way.... In the foreground, there is always the flight performance and the ambition of the keen youngsters for gliding, their lives, aspirations and work.... In addition to that, the film gives insight into the companionate life of the trainee pilots who are infused with glorious spirit. They put their youthful enthusiasm into service. Like soldiers in the trenches they accept all deprivations and troubles and follow the great maxim: All for one! The storyline has some fine psychological nuances that cast a light on today's mentality of young folks. There's a high school student with his own problems at school. His father doesn't want him to dedicate himself to gliding yet the boy's raging strength overcomes every resistance. There's a young defiant girl who emulates men's deeds without shyness. Nowadays young people don't reach for one's pistol when they have a mental crisis. If they are made of sterner stuff like these boys from the Rhön they go to the gliding school and win 5000 Marks awards. The female youth wears trousers and becomes a rival to the boys. Still the sports girl remains a true woman. This shows the character of Christine, performed by the skilled Hilde Gebühr.... Claus Clausen portrays a pleasant virile gliding teacher who is a bit like Hans Albers: A tall blond fellow with broad shoulders and the right guy for chaps who need a strong hand. Wolfgang Liebeneiner, Sibylle [*sic*] Schmitz and Gussy Lantschner put in very naturalistic performances. The film may be a little boring for those who do not like sports. The movie will not be a big hit for a broad audience. But it will thrill young viewers, and that alone justifies the effort in making this film.

Der gute Film (March 22, 1934) found the storyline insubstantial:

> The film offers a good and comprehensive portrayal of gliding sports. There is excellent footage. Still there are some minor inaccuracies and technical weak points regarding the presentation of the sport. The film also shows life at the gliding school, and the spirit of comradeship and Führertum which is the requirement for this sport. It's a pity we have a story about childish and primitive jealousies and whims. This interferes heavily with the good impression the film makes in general. Life is not like this. It would be essential to create a plot from the same spirit that is representative of the milieu the story comes from. That would become a really valuable and satisfying piece of film. Half measures are harmful.
>
> The portrayal of the young folks is good and pleasant though too much time is spent on Hilde Gebühr. The cameraman has created very beautiful images, but his technique is not always satisfying. Standard German language, and in parts with Northern dialect, is articulate enough.... The film could be taken as an ad for gliding but only with reservations because of the inadequate story.

Publicity for the film emphasized the authentic locations and the realism in depicting gliding. A puff piece, supposedly written by Hilde Gebühr, tells how the actress heard she got the part while relaxing on the beach of Hiddensee and, though she was sad to leave her friends, she looked forward to making new friends at the glider school. But other articles, in language that smacks of the ideology of the times, extolled the virtues and athleticism of the new German youth and how the heroic solidarity of the young pilots was a tribute to the new comradeship.

The only copy of *Rivals of the Air* we've been able to find is missing huge chunks of footage. The glider competition finale is reduced to just a few incoherent minutes. All too intact are the hijinks at the school with the students mooning over Christine, wrestling like puppies and playing silly pranks. The tissue of misunderstandings that hamper the romance seem contrived though the actors are game enough. Perhaps more interesting—from a historical point of view—is the scene where the fledging pilots are given their flying pins (three gulls). The ceremony is preceded by the arrival of an official who, after giving and receiving the Nazi salute, barks out a tribute to the young pilots:

> In Rossitten ten years ago, this badge was created. It has been hard-earned for you and for the Fatherland by Ferdinand Schulz [the founder of the school who died in an air crash]. The whole world has inherited the badge in recognition of superior efforts of Germany with gliding. You are the guardians of that what Germany has conquered in years of misery and hunger. Do wear the badge dutifully and in honor. You are Germany's future. Be worthy of your dead predecessors: Do preserve the sanctuary in your heart.

Not too surprisingly, the Allies banned *Rivals of the Air* after the war.

Given the general tone of the film, it is a little peculiar that an Englishman also receives the pin (his name in the credits is "Ox" … short for Oxford?). Frahms says a few congratulatory words to him in English and the man responds in German saying how happy he is to have been part of this important program. A few years later, such a favorable picture of a Brit would be unthinkable. The presence of women pilots competing with the men is also something that would soon be frowned upon as the Reich pressured women out of the professions and back into the kitchen.

Claus Clausen (Frahms) would have made a good villain. He has a lean and hungry look with gaunt features and occasionally a maniacal glint in his eyes. His film career was not particularly distinguished. He had a good role in the pacifist film *Westfront 1918* (1930) and played the boyfriend in the pro-abortion drama *Cyankali* (1930) before doing a political about-face and starring in the tribute to Nazi youth *Hitlerjunge Quex* (1933) as well as a number of other Third Reich propaganda films: *My Life for Ireland* (1941), *The Great King* (1942) and Dr. Goebbels' last stand *Kolberg* (1945).

Hilde Gebühr's main to claim is that she was the daughter of Otto Gebühr, a famous character actor many times cast as Frederick the Great. Hilde's career was very brief with *Rivals* being her last film. She was only 35 years old when she died.

Sybille Schmitz (Lisa) was probably cast so she could once again don the aviator's outfit in which she looked so fetching in *F.P.1 Doesn't Answer* (1932). *Rivals* was her first collaboration with Wisbar.

Wolfgang Liebeneiner brings the appropriate youthful vigor and impatience to the part of Karl though at 28 he's a bit old to be in high school. (This is true of all the actors playing the teenage pilots.) Liebeneiner had a long career as an actor and director on stage and screen. He became prominent in the Third Reich movie world but according to Klaus Kreimeier he was "a man who had garnered almost all of the available state honors but was still regarded as a quiet opponent of the National Socialist State." Liebeneiner made a number of propaganda films for the regime but also tried to protect fellow film people who had run afoul of the Gestapo.

As mentioned earlier, only a truncated copy of *Rivals* seems to be around so it's hard to judge cameraman Hans Schneeberger's photography with so much of the aerial footage missing. He had worked on a few of Arnold Franck's mountain epics, as well as more conventional dramas like *Asphalt* (1928) and *The Wonderful Lies of Nina Petrowna* (1929).

Karl Ritter, one of the Reich's chief directors of propaganda films and producer of *Rivals*, thought Wisbar was the wrong choice for director, which is strange if Wisbar was as important in the glider movement as he claimed. (I suppose Ritter could have talking about aesthetics rather than experience.) At the beginning of his Senate testimony, Wisbar said that in 1927, he was actually offered direction and management of the Rossitten flight school but he turned it down and left the army to go into the movies. Nothing is said about this in publicity for *Rivals* and elsewhere Wisbar said he was a driving instructor during his last days in the army (see the biography chapter). He also testified that the Weimar government showed no interest in the young gliding pilots whom they regarded as "sort of dead-end kids." (Interesting to imagine *Rivals* with Leo Gorcey and Huntz Hall.) However, other sources say the government spent millions on the program funneled through the Ministry of Transport.

At the end of his Senate testimony, Wisbar was asked how America could best promote youthful interest in gliding and he responded with the following:

> I think publicity is everything.... Well, we are going to produce a picture. For this picture, I wrote a very simple story of how two boys in North Carolina had come to make glider flights possible, how these boys over all difficulties and obstacles at last achieve their aim of arousing the interest of the whole nation. It is a picture in which I will show how a group of boys starts out from nothing and builds their own plane and builds their own high performance sail plane and at last finds ways and means to arouse the interest of the nation in glider flying matters.

Alas, neither Hollywood or the U.S. government showed interest in producing such a picture.

Hermine und die seiben Aufrechten
(Hermine and the Seven Upright Men)

Terra-Filmkunst
Premiered on January 14, 1935
106 minutes

Cast: Heinrich George as Zimmermeister Frymann; Karin Hardt as Hermine Frymann; Paul Henckels as Schneidermeister Hediger; Lotte Spira as Mrs. Hediger; Albert Lieven as Karl Hediger; Karel Stepanak as Ruckstahl; Hans Henninger as Spörri; Friedrich Ettel as Gastwirt Aklin; Maria Krahn as Mrs. Aklin; Max Holzboer as Schmied Syfrig; Annmarie Steinsieck as Mrs. Syfrig; Alfred Schlageter as Tischlermeister Bürgi; Käthe Haack as Mrs. Bürgi; Armin Schweizer as Silberschmied Kurser; Ilse Fürstenberg as Mrs. Kurser; Eduard Wenck as Krugwirt Erismann; Carsta Löck as Marta, the Frymanns' housekeeper; Horst Beck, Walter Bluhm, Hans Fetscherin, Wolf Harro, Albert Heine, August Liebman, Paul Mederow, Kai Möller, Herbert Quandt, Heinz Rippert, Alfred Stratmann, Walter Vollmann, Volker von Collande, Walter Werner, Georg A. Profé.
Credits: Director: Frank Wisbar (as Frank Wysbar); Script: Hans Fritz Köllner, Frank Wisbar (as Frank Wysbar), Hans Martin Cremer (uncredited), Hella Moja (uncredited); Based on the novella *The Banner of the Upright Seven* by Gottfried Keller, published in his 1856 collection *The People of Seldwyla*; Photography: Franz Weihmayr, Hans Schneeberger, Heinz von Jaworsky; Editor: Lena Neumann; Music: Herbert Windt, A. Hörler; Producer: Ralph Scotoni; Co-Producer: Max Ikle; Unit Production Manager: Harry Detmann; Location Managers: Eduard Probst, Karl Buchholz, Willi Laschinsky; Alternate title: *Das Fähnlein der sieben Aufrechten* (*Troop of the Upright Seven*).

In 1935, Germany submitted three official entries to the 3rd Annual Venice International Film Festival: Leni Riefenstahl's *Triumph of the Will*, Hans Steinhoff's *The Making of a King* and Frank Wisbar's *Hermine and the Seven Upright Men*. The first two were ultra-nationalist epics but *Hermine* was a humorous parable about the old and young generations. Patriotism—Swiss, in this case—is certainly extolled but politics is treated lightly as are the people who take it too seriously.

Originally Heinz Paul, famous for his World War I movies, was supposed to direct but he fell ill and Wisbar took his place. Wisbar's movie closely follows the original story by Gottfried Keller who pokes gentle fun at the foibles of his Swiss countrymen.

This synopsis is from a viewing of the film:

The seven upright men are friends who meet regularly to discuss politics and life. They are led by Frymann, a rich carpenter, and Hediger, a poor tailor. The city council of Zurich requests that they represent the city in the

Hermine und die seiben Aufrechten (1935)

upcoming shooting match at Aarau, a festive occasion that draws participants from all the cantons (districts). Frymann and company decline, saying that they are not public speakers and the match requires a speech from the main participants.

The above scene is not in the book and it's not really clear in the film if a reluctance to speak in public is the sole reason for the seven refusing to participate (especially since they later change their minds). Possibly, they feel their independence would be compromised by going as an official delegation. At least one German film critic felt their reasons should have been made clear.

At one of their later meetings, the seven decide that the sharpshooting match is worthy of their approval. They will go to Aarau but representing themselves, not the city. Their wives will create a banner with the slogan "Friendship in Freedom." The men sketch the banner and the very sight of it inspires a stirring image of the seven of them leading a charge during a battle (they are superimposed over footage from another movie). Presumably the seven fought in the Napoleonic wars and the brief Swiss civil war of 1847. They decide to donate a gift and there is debate over just what it should be. A few of the men suggest—for a price—items they already own (a cow, a bed, a plough, etc.). They finally decide upon a silver cup.

Frymann has a beautiful daughter named Hermine. Ruckstahl, a young businessman noted for sharp practice, asks Frymann for permission to court her, providing she has not set her sights elsewhere. Frymann insists she has not: "I would know it. In my house, nothing happens that I don't know."

That of course is not true. Hermine and Hediger's son Karl are in love and meeting secretly, each rowing their boats to the middle of the lake. Karl has a low-paying government job and he fears Herr Frymann will not approve of his suit for that reason. Ruckstahl is more acceptable to Frymann because the carpenter is looking for a shrewd business partner.

Frymann discovers that Hermine and Karl are meeting and goes to his old friend to discuss the situation. Frymann and Hediger, who does not have a great deal of confidence in his son, agree that being in-laws would spoil their friendship. "Friends—not relations," they decide, and they agree to forbid the romance. The next time Hermine goes to the lake, she finds that her boat is docked and being painted. As Karl prepares to row across, his father insists on joining him in the boat. The two lovers, in a very funny scene, try to communicate by yodeling, much to the annoyance of their grumpy dads.

Mrs. Heidger, as well as the other wives, all favor the match and try to smooth things over for the lovers. The men may bluster and pontificate but their women can easily outfox them to achieve their own ends. The strength of women seems to be something of a running theme in Wisbar's films.

Frymann invites Ruckstahl to Sunday dinner. Karl and Ruckstahl are both doing their military service locally and Karl contrives to get Ruckstahl drunk at headquarters. As a result, Ruckstahl gets three days in the guardhouse which means he can't make Sunday dinner. Karl shows up instead but when he tells Frymann of Ruckstahl's punishment, the carpenter, instead of being indignant, is amused, recalling his own wild youthful days.

As the shooting match approaches, Frymann gets the short straw which means he must speak at the event. He is terrified at the thought but still attempts to write a speech. Hermine reads it and points out that he uses "therefore" in every other sentence, and that he dwells too much on the past instead of the present moment and its possibilities. Frymann revises his speech but is not confident of his ability to deliver it.

The day of the match arrives and hundreds attend. At the festival, Frymann discovers that Ruckstahl is dishonest and has little moral character. Karl wins the laurel prize at the shooting match, much to the astonishment of his father. Frymann nearly collapses at the thought of delivering his speech, and Hermine suggests Karl takes his place. Karl speaks from the heart of the virtues of the seven and their patriotism (his speech is taken directly from Keller's story though it is shortened a bit): "The seven have seen many countries but their motto always stood: Honor each man's Fatherland but yours you must love." His words are well received by the crowd and Frymann and Hediger drop their objections to their children's romance.

On September 21, 1935, the *New York Times* reviewer summed up the film nicely: "There are so many delightful views and so much harmless good humor that the spectators are kept mildly amused most of the time.... Strange to say, there is not a sad moment in the hour and three-quarters that the film runs."

The delightful views are from the location shooting at Zurich and four other Swiss cities, Zug, Lachen, Rapperswil and Freiburg, and due to the shining photography of Hans Schneeberger, Heinz von Jaworsky and Franz Weihmayr (who also worked with Wisbar on *Anna and Elizabeth* and *Ferryman Maria,* two films that could not be more different than *Hermine*). The lakes, beautiful buildings and cobblestone streets of Zurich are so bright and inviting they seem almost a fairy tale world of festivity, exuberance and plenty. However, there were budget problems involving the currency exchange and cast and crew had to return to Berlin to complete the film.

On March 23, 1935, Carl Düsterdieck, the *Hamburger Nachrichten* critic, wrote:

> The novel has become an efficient cinematic contribution, vivid and folksy. One feels an artistic mastering of the plot with humor that comes from the heart. The novel is re-designed through the image but its essence has survived. Wisbar's shaping of the plot is carefully thought out and artistically crafted. His direction is clear

The seven upright men present their flag at the finale of *Hermine and the Seven Upright Men.*

and vivid but he sometimes gets bogged down in the details though he always manages to get back on track. The mood is gay but presented in a creative way.

Not everyone felt that *Hermine* was completely innocuous politically. Nineteen thirty-five was the year the Nazi government made military service mandatory. The movie demonstrates that young people in peace-loving Switzerland have no problem with compulsory military service so the film could be seen as propagandizing for the same thing in Germany. Whether audiences would really have absorbed such a message from a light-hearted comedy romance is debatable.

Much of the film's humor comes from the hulking Frymann (Heinrich George) and his slightly built friend Hediger (veteran character actor and sometimes director Paul Henckels). George's bulk is used to good comic advantage in scenes where he seems to be bursting out of the new suit Hediger is making for him, and when he finds his huge hands encased in his Mrs. Hediger's yarn, preventing him from stomping into the kitchen and catching the lovers. His nervousness at public speaking is played for laughs but there is a certain poignancy to a blunderbuss of a man who freezes in front of a crowd.

Shyness was never George's problem as he was one of Germany's finest classical stage and film actors. He began his movie career in silent days, often playing supporting roles as crooks or working class laborers. As the sound period commenced, he scored a triumph as Franz Biberkopf, the ex-convict fighting to stay out of trouble in *Berlin-Alexanderplatz*. George had Communist sympathies and at one point went into hiding to avoid Nazi thugs who had him labeled as an "undesirable." However, he later switched sides and became an ardent Nazi though it's hard to say whether he acted out of conviction or opportunism (like Emil Jannings who would have bowed before the Tooth Fairy to maintain his elegant lifestyle). In any case, the actor who had played Emile Zola in Richard Oswald's *Dreyfus* went on to star in the Nazi propaganda films *Hitlerjunge Quex*, *Jew Süß* and *Kolberg* (his last film), earning the frequent praise of Dr. Goebbels. George paid for his complicity at the end of the war when the Russians arrested him and sent him to the Oranienburg concentration camp, which the Nazis had used for political prisoners. The authorities said George died during an appendix operation but most likely he perished of starvation as did 3000 of the camp's 4200 prisoners. His body was put in a mass grave but many years later his family, using DNA evidence, was able to identify it and give him proper burial.

Hermine is typical of the light romantic roles that occupied Karin Hardt during the 1930s. She was, however, a fine serious actress as shown by her performance in *Via Mala* (1948) where she played the abused daughter of a true domestic tyrant, not like the comic type played by Heinrich George.

Hermine und die seiben Aufrechten (1935)

Hardt became a good character actress and focused on TV for the later part of her career.

Albert Lieven makes Karl likable and attractive; Lieven played many such agreeable romantic parts in the '30s. When the Nazis took over, he headed for England with his Jewish wife. There he did some stage work but once the war broke out he became a movie Nazi, like so many German exiles. He was still doing it in even in the '60s in the films *Conspiracy of Hearts*, *The Guns of Navarone* and *Foxhole in Cairo* (where he played the Desert Fox Erwin Rommel). He also appeared in a couple of Edgar Wallace films, *The Devil's Daffodil* (1961) and *Death Trap* (1962), plus scores of television shows, including Wisbar's *Welcome to Altamont*.

Lotte Spira's Mrs. Hediger was one of her larger film roles and she plays it with zest. Spira's husband was Jewish and she gave in to Nazi pressure to divorce him. He died in a concentration camp, a fate that might have befallen her daughter Camilla (also an actress) if Lotte hadn't taken a spurious oath claiming that Camilla's father was actually Lotte's Aryan lover. Such was the insanity of the times.

Karl Stepanek's Rukstahl is the closest thing the film has to a villain though it's hard to take him seriously since, in spite of supposedly being such a smooth operator, he's inept enough to be easily outwitted by Karl and the ladies. Stepanek also turns up in Wisbar's *The Unknown* playing the sleazy nightclub manager in an appropriately oily manner-and looking much older than he does in *Hermine*. Stepanek made numerous films under the Nazis before deciding to abscond to England where he denounced them on the radio. He had left during the filming of Ufa's first important color film, *Women Make Better Diplomats*, which had been plagued by numerous production problems to which Stepanek's defection added still one more: According to *The Ufa Story*, all his scenes had to be reshot with another actor at a cost of 500,000 marks. Stepanek played numerous villain roles in England, often as Nazis. He reunited with Albert Lieven in *Brainwashed* (1960).

In Germany, *Hermine* did not do well. According to Eva Wisbar, it was because it had been labeled "staatspolitisch und künstlerisch besonders wertvo": politically and culturally valuable. Eva wrote that some people would see that label on posters at the box office and turn around and leave, fearing that they were in for a dose of propaganda, not entertainment. However, at the Venice Film Festival, *Hermine* was nominated for the Mussolini Cup for Best Foreign Film. It lost to Clarence Brown's *Anna Karenina*. *Hermine* and Frank Wisbar received a special mention and Wisbar was presented with a gold medal by Il Duce. Years later, Wisbar was fond of telling how he was obliged to flee Germany without any funds so he pawned his gold medal. It turned out to be brass.

Die Werft zum Grauen Hecht
(The Grey Pikes Wharf)
Pallas-Film GmbH
Released on August 20, 1935
89 minutes

Cast: Marianne Hoppe as Käthe Liebenow; Hans Leibelt as her father, the shipyard owner; Hermann Speelmans as Otto Menzel; Johannes Bartel as Franz Boehm; Fita Benkhoff as Mila Schellhase; Oscar Sima as Bernhard Münchow; Karel Stepanek as Ladewig; Ruth Eweler as Lisabeth Schmidt; Rudolph Klicks as Lehrjunge; Maria Krahn as Frau Wehmeyer; Artur Malkowsky as trucker; Ernst Behmer, Karl Bischof, Erwin Hartung, Paul Rehkopf, Lucie Rhoden, Ewald Wenck.

Credits: Director: Frank Wisbar (as Frank Wysbar); Screenplay: Frank Wisbar (as Frank Wysbar); Based on the eponymous novel by Hans Joachim Freiherr von Reizenstein; Photography: Franz Weihmayr; Assistant Camera: Wilhelm Schmidt; Production Designer: Robert A. Dietrich; Props: Max Klar, Paul Gaeble; Costumes: Johannes Krämer, Frida Stahl; Makeup: Fritz Siebert, Adolf Doelle; Editor: Lena Neumann; Sound: Martin Müller; Music and Lyrics: Friedrich Wilhelm Rust; Unit Production Manager: Eberhard Schmidt; Location Managers: Horst Kryath, Karl Buchholz.

This very minor Wisbar film need not detain us for long. It's a harmless comedy romance with pleasant scenery and agreeable leads. The story goes from being flimsy to over-plotted and doesn't resonate at all with Wisbar's usual themes even though he wrote the script, which was based on a novel by Hans Joachim Freiherr von Reizenstein. Von Reizenstein, who died before *Grey Pikes* was released, was also the author of the thriller *Obserwachtmeister Schwenk*, which was filmed twice (1935 and 1955).

Grey Pikes is no thriller. Otto and Franz are good friends and fellow truckers (though, in spite of numerous road scenes, they never seem to arrive anywhere so we don't learn what they are supposed to be hauling). Otto had earlier promised to marry Mila but has changed his mind about her. Mila however has been persistent in her attentions and Otto desperately wants to get away from her. (We learn all this from a conversation between Otto and Franz in a tavern.) Franz suggests that Otto move to a small town on the Havel River some distance away. Franz's friend Bernhard owns a car repair shop there and would certainly have a job for a crack mechanic like Otto. Mila, very anxious to get married, would likely set her sights on someone else if Otto were out of the picture.

The very next scene finds Otto in the little town. Bernhard is something of a grump but is suitably impressed with Otto's skills in car repair to hire him on the spot. Otto wanders into a nearby shipyard, the Grey Pikes, and

Die Werft zum Grauen Hecht (1935)

meets Käthe, whose father owns the yard. Otto and Käthe quickly become taken with each other. Otto also runs into Laedwig, an old acquaintance who is also sweet on Käthe. Otto and Käthe's love grows though Laedwig tries to interfere (he has a stupid grin and wears a silly sailor's hat so he doesn't present much competition). Meanwhile Franz is having a kind of romance with a young woman who always waves to him as he passes on his route. However, he becomes indignant when he sees her kissing someone in her yard. He finally gets the courage to stop his truck and talk to her and finds that she's attracted to him as well.

Mila has been sending letters to the different truck stops in an effort to find Otto and finally succeeds. She embraces him enthusiastically, a hug that is witnessed by Käthe, who then breaks things off with Otto. Otto tells Mila he's simply not interested in her. She quickly switches her affections to Bernhard who has heard she has a hypothec worth 14,000 marks, which would finance his dream of expanding his business to a second location. However, in spite of his ulterior motives, he does fall sincerely in love with Mila.

Otto explains things to Käthe who quickly takes him back. Mila and Bernhard get married but then Bernhard discovers that the house attached to the hypothec is over-mortgaged and the pledge is worthless. Bernhard, Otto and Franz get drunk and Bernhard hatches a scheme to build the new gas station after all. He convinces Otto to write to his father to get 4000 marks advance on his inheritance and use that money to expand the business. Bernhard, in an effort to get some space from Mila, decides to borrow Franz's truck and hit the road. Franz and Otto proceed to hire workers and build the new station. However, Otto's father refuses to give him the money so now the two can't continue the project and may even be indicted for fraud. Using the truckers' grapevine, Käthe tracks Bernhard down. He ends up crashing the truck but isn't hurt. Luckily, the truck is heavily insured so Franz and Bernhard become partners to continue the car business. Bernhard and Mila are reconciled and Otto decides to take a job in the shipyard.

That none of this is believable doesn't matter much. Marianne Hoppe and Hermann Speelmans have an upbeat chemistry and their lack of conventional good looks make them particularly well suited to each other. Hoppe had rather angular features and an aquiline nose which give her a kind of androgynous appearance while Speelmans is moon-faced and a bit portly for a romantic lead. Hoppe was a major star of stage and screen in Germany during the '30s and '40s. Speelmans was more likely to be cast as the hero's buddy rather than the hero (his role in Paul Wegener's *A Man Wants to Get to Germany* was perhaps a standard part for him) but he sometimes played the lead as in *Sherlock Holmes, the Grey Lady* (1937). Fita Benkhoff is appropriately annoying as the ditzy Mila though perhaps it was typical of the comic roles she usually played. She also turns up in Wisbar's *Petermann Is Against It!*, playing a straight romantic lead.

In Austria, the film played under the title *Der Liebeshafen* (*The Love Port*). It received a lukewarm review from *Der gut film Wien* (August 30, 1935):

> This film places young people into the region around the Havel lakes and shows the small and big hardships in everyday life. The shooting is gorgeous and atmospheric but the story is fraught with psychological flaws. This weakens the credibility. Dialogue is poor and repetitive and this makes some love scenes unintentionally funny. Here the direction has failed. The actors give good performances. Perhaps some better editing would have helped a tempo that is too leisurely. Music underlines the action in a nice way. The film tries to be a new kind of a folk play. It's interesting, but dramaturgically it does not really satisfy.

On August 28, 1935, the *Hamburger Anzeiger* was likewise reserved:

> We're happy at the film's attempt to depict current life. This film follows the novel of Freiherr von Reizenstein who died recently. Director Frank Wisbar has written the script. Alas this didn't lead to either a deeper or a temperamentally correct understanding of the motifs of the action. The script just shifts it. In this film the conflicts arise from the foolishness of immature men who do not realize their chances and put them at risk. It's against the nature of a folks play to lead to three happy endings. It's not obvious that the vivid life of our days can fulfill every wish. So, we have a lightweight yet very humorous entertaining film that has an almost epic scope. The cast is chosen appropriately. Hermann Speelmans is the always laughing and good-natured mechanic. Marianne Hoppe plays with strong internalization and economy of expression. She is the type of girl for our days. Oskar Sima and Fita Benkhoff are superb types. Truly a witty couple! This film is a beginning, but not a fulfillment on the way to the genuine volksfilm we're waiting for.

The film didn't make it to America until 1938. On April 30, 1938, the *Motion Picture Herald* reviewer found the film too long but "fairly entertaining" and "capably performed" as well as pleasing to "an audience of Teutonic origin." He *was* a bit annoyed by the title: "[It] translates literally to 'The Dock of the Grey Hecht,' a species of fish but, freely, the English title was given as *The Dock on the Havel* (the Hazel is a river). The *New York Times* reviewer (April 18, 1938) considered it slight but modestly enjoyable:

> Enlisting the services of several excellent actors and of a highly competent cameraman, Frank Wisbar has turned out a fairly entertaining comedy romance. The audiences at the 86th St. Casino Theater follow with considerable interest the not very dramatic adventures of Hermann Speelmans as a wandering auto mechanic trying to get away from a former sweetheart only to fall seriously in love with the attractive though none too comely Marianne Hoppe. After some confusion involving property deals smacking of high finance, Oskar Sima is matched with Fita Benkhoff along the shore of the beautiful Havel and all is well. There are no villains in the piece and the

romance is held down to a minimum. But there are lots of laughs and many lovely bits of photography.

The lovely photography was the work of Franz Weihmayr, who would soon bring his considerable skills to Wisbar's masterpiece *Fährmann Maria*.

While German reviewers may not have been enthusiastic about *The Grey Pikes Wharf*, according to one source the movie was one of three German entries in the 1935 Brussels film festival.

Fährmann Maria
(Ferryman Maria)

Pallas-Film GmbH
Released on July 1, 1936
83 minutes

Cast: Sybille Schmitz as Maria; Aribert Mog as the Man from the Other Shore, Peter Voss as Death; Carl de Vogt as the Fiddler; Karl Platen as the Old Ferryman; Eduard Wenck as the Mayor; Gerherd Bienert as the Landowner; Ernst Stimmel as the School Teacher.

Credits: Director: Frank Wisbar (as Frank Wysbar); Story and Lyrics: Frank Wisbar; Screenplay: Hans Jürgen Nierentz, Frank Wisbar (as Frank Wysbar); Script Editor: Alf Teichs; Photography: Franz Weihmayr; Editor: Lena Neumann; Music: Herbert Windt; Production Designers: Bruno Lutz, Fritz Maurischat; Sound: Hans Grimm; Unit Production Manager: Eberhard Schmidt; Location Managers: Horst Kyrath, Karl Buchholz; Distribution: Terra Films.

> In the heath comes the fog,
> And the full moon is rising,
> The white birches stand mournfully
> In the middle of the black moor.
> In the heath, there are fairy tales,
> Marvelous and without number
> Without beginning, without end,
> This was "Once upon a time" ...

An Austrian film magazine announcing the line-up for Terra Film's 1934–35 season included a blurb for the upcoming *Der Werwolf*, to be directed by Frank Wisbar and starring Heinrich George, Hertha Thiele, Peter Voss and Theodor Loos with music by Herbert Windt. Contrary to what I once assumed, this was not a horror film but rather an adaptation of a novel about the plight of the peasantry during the Thirty Years' War. It was meant to be a large-scale epic with big battle scenes involving several thousand extras. A subsequent (March 24, 1935) article in *Die Altoner Nachrichten* stated that the production had run into problems. They were planning on shooting on the Lüneburg Heath around the town of Schneverdingen but an unusually hot summer there had drained the swamp so production had to be postponed until the spring. In the end, the whole project got cancelled but apparently, some background footage on the Lüneburg had been shot. Wisbar was impressed by the look of the heath: the long grass shimmering in the wind, the rows of stately poplar trees, and the dark stretches of swampland. All this suggested magic and mystery and was the perfect setting for the right type of supernatural tale.

Wisbar had once thought of filming the Flying Dutchman legend which tells of a captain cursed to sail the seas for eternity. In the end, the curse is lifted by the love of a woman who sacrifices her life for him. The legend and the Richard Wagner opera based on it very likely inspired Wisbar to create his own ballad about the supernatural and the self-sacrificing love of a woman. One can also see the influence of Fritz Lang's *Destiny*, Murnau's *Nosferatu* and Carl Dreyer's *Vampyr*. But *Ferryman Maria* remains a unique film full of mythic undertones and poetry.

Fährmann Maria—a macabre triangle: Death (Peter Voss, left), the Maiden (Sybille Schmitz) and the man from the other shore (Aribert Mog).

The movie's unconventional approach starts with the credits. Only Maria is given a name ("the maiden Maria") while the other characters are described with appellations like "the man from the other shore," "the fiddler," "the mayor" and, most ominously, "Death" (press materials usually call him "the Stranger"). Such an approach to the credits is typical both of Expressionist drama and early silent film. Indeed, *Ferryman Maria* plays very much like a silent movie as there is very little dialogue (one can imagine a few title cards filling the bill) while Herbert Windt's music is almost continuous.

The slightly foreboding opening theme gives way to the music of the fiddler, who sings about the sparrow's beating its wings through the clouds as comparable to the soul looking through the light for the way to God's Heaven. The fiddler is being ferried across the river to the little village where he has been a frequent visitor. The old man running the ferry good-naturedly chides the fiddler for being something of a layabout who will likely tarry in the village even after he has finished his musical engagement. And to the fiddler's sarcastic response about what the ferryman has to show for all his hard labor, the old man tells him that, as of this day, he has saved enough money to buy the ferry; in the future, he will be working for himself. But man proposes and God disposes.

That night the ferryman is alone in his modest hut counting his money. The bell in the village tolls ominously and then across the river comes the hollow clang of the gong that informs the ferryman that someone on the other side is waiting to cross. The old man is tired but he has to do his duty. Windt's music is replaced by the drone of the wind as the ferryman pulls his craft across the river to see a silhouette on the other side. (This shot, with the silhouette in the background as the ferry approaches in the foreground, is very striking.) As Windt's music starts up again on a very sinister note, the silhouette moves forward to reveal a white-haired, stern-visaged man, dressed entirely in black. He motions for the old man to take him to the other side. Windt's music mimics the straining of the rope that pulls the ferry across. The ferryman starts to collapse and is caught by the stranger, who gently lowers him to the floor. Then the man in black guides the ferry back to the shore he came from.

A sign outside the mayor's office advertises the need for a new ferryman. The message also indicates that the old ferryman died of natural causes and was not, as rumor has it, the victim of supernatural forces. The fiddler hasn't yet left the village, much to the amusement of the mayor who thinks the musician is using the ferry being down as an excuse to idle away the hours in drink.

We see young Maria wake up after having spent the night sleeping in a barn. She is drawn to the sound of schoolchildren singing and she cautiously approaches the classroom to listen. They are singing the song whose lyrics are quoted at the beginning of the essay. This music will be heard in different arrangements several more times in the film. Though the song is about imagination and fairy tales, the fiddler subsequently uses it to improvise a romantic tune. When Maria sees a policeman nearby, she cautiously withdraws. This is observed by the mayor. He speaks to her kindly and is not concerned that she has no papers. She tells him she's looking for work and he invites her into his office to offer her the job of ferryman. This scene takes a peculiar twist in that we hear the mayor describing the job from inside while the camera remains outside focused on the door. The film was shot in Hildesheim and takes place almost entirely outside, with the camera venturing indoors in only a few instances: the ferryman's hut, the classroom and the church (certainly a real church, not a

Sybille Schmitz strikes a wistful pose against the Lüneburg Heath in *Fährmann Maria*.

set). It's hard to imagine a perfectionist like Wisbar being unable to improvise a simple office set if he wasn't able to find a usable authentic one. Yet the brief scene is a bit clumsy and would seem to be the result of some sort of snafu rather than an artistic decision.

Maria finds the ferryman's hut is bordered on one side by dangerous mudflats. She cautiously makes her way through them and settles into her humble new abode, unpacking the knapsack which holds her few possessions. Nazi cultural watchdogs like the periodical *People and Race* were offended at the idea of a dark-haired, gypsy-like heroine and claimed it was a violation of racial hygiene norms. No papers indeed!

Maria's new life is a lonely one as she must remain by herself, always ready day and night to transport people across the river. The time frame for the story is purposely vague. It could be set in the previous century or it could be in the here and now but in a remote rural area where people still travel by horse rather than car and live the simple lives of their forebears. This gives the story a certain poetic timelessness as though it's all happened before and will happen again. The movie's dreamlike atmosphere is not unlike what you find in *Vampyr* and Franz Weihmayr's misty cinematography is similar to the Dreyer film. But while *Vampyr* is a nightmare, disorienting and disturbing, *Maria* is closer to a legend or ballad, something the fiddler might sing about.

Late one night, Maria responds to the sound of the gong across the river. She pilots the ferryboat there but at first sees no one. Then a man cries out to her for help. He can barely walk so she helps him onto the ferry. He begs her to hurry as he's being pursued. The young man is sometimes described as a soldier but he wears no uniform. He has a long coat and spurs which suggests he has lost his mount. He is unable to assist Maria as she pulls the rope to the village shore. They get there safely and Maria brings the man into her hut. He is feverish and she puts him in her own bed and tells him she will gather herbs to heal him. The man becomes terrified as the gong sounds again. Half a dozen mounted men dressed in black are on the other shore and want to cross. They are like sinister figures from another world. Maria ignores them and eventually they depart.

Maria leaves the young man to rest and goes to gather herbs. (A couple of times he is described as having been wounded but he seems to be suffering from exhaustion and fever, not a physical injury.) She runs right into the fiddler who is very drunk and wants to cross over. Maria tells him that the jetty on the other side is damaged and she can't fix it until morning. The fiddler asks her if she is gathering herbs under the light of the moon for a love potion and makes a pass at her, suggesting that they go to her hut. Maria tells him that her hut is too poor to entertain visitors but she will be right back. As Maria tends to the young man, the fiddler begins playing his own version of the tune the children sang earlier. He passes out while Maria watches over the handsome stranger.

As the phantoms of the night dissipate with the coming of dawn, there is a montage of flowers, shimmering waters, grassy fields and a flock of sheep. Maria's folk medicine has worked and the young man is awake and well. He describes to her his Heimat, his homeland, as a kind of heaven. But there's trouble in paradise and there are enemies who must be overcome and he must return soon to aid in the struggle. He is saddened to hear from Maria that she herself has no Heimat, no place like home. She leads the life of a wanderer—like her current job of going back and forth with the ferry—without ever finding a real sanctuary where she is no longer a stranger in a strange land. Maria and the young man quickly become enraptured with each other. Their reverie is interrupted by the arrival of a local landowner who invites

Fährmann Maria (1936)

Maria to go with him to the upcoming harvest festival in the village. Much to his chagrin, she refuses.

The man from the other shore finds that he has lost a spur and is about to throw the other one away when Maria intervenes and insists on hanging it up as a souvenir, to remind her of him until he returns as he has promised. She also changes from her tattered dress to a long frock (and earlier she has

Fährmann Maria—Clockwise from top: The ferry, Death. Maria—with her new look—comforts her stricken lover. Maria in her cabin.

put up her hair). The young man is suitably wowed though Maria's new look gives her an old-fashioned, severe and strangely asexual look. Perhaps Wisbar is gently mocking the elegant dresses and gowns most actresses sported in German films at the time.

Things begin to go awry when the man begins to doubt Maria will wait for him. "Who are you?" he asks. "You won't be here when I return." Maria assures him she will not leave. He apologizes and they kiss. As night falls, his fever returns. He becomes delirious and, to the sounds of approaching hoof-beats, we see the sinister horsemen again with a web-like net superimposed in the foreground. The young man launches into a battle song but he is near hysterical as Maria tries vainly to calm him.

The gong from across the shore sounds and Maria dutifully pulls the ferry across and finds her passenger is the stranger in black (the music from the earlier scene with the old ferryman is repeated). He initially remains silent as they cross back but then he demands to know if Maria has recently taken a wounded man across. She denies it but he is insistent and produces a spur he found under the gong. As they get to the other side, the stranger strides towards Maria's hut but she stops him, saying that now she does remember and the man in question has gone to the village. The stranger insists that Maria guide him there. Maria shudders with dread as she begins to realize that her companion is no mere mortal.

The festival is in full swing with the fiddler presiding over the band as the villagers dance. People instinctively draw away from the man in black as he approaches. The landowner is there and his jealousy makes him bold. He suggests to the stranger that they play dice for a dance with Maria. The stranger wins. Since there is a superstition that those without a soul always win games of chance, the villagers become even more frightened. The stranger wants to leave but Maria insists that he dance with her since he won the game. The music gets faster and faster and then weirdly discordant as the stranger whirls Maria around and around while the other dancers retreat in horror. It's a very macabre sequence and likely to remind horror buffs of the dance in *Carnival of Souls*. Some artistic representations of Death and the Maiden have an erotic undertone as though the maiden is embracing Death willingly. There is some suggestion of that in this sequence as Maria's near-swoon while Death twirls her about might be seen as succumbing reluctantly but helplessly to a demon lover. Adding to this impression is the fact that she is saved when the obnoxious landowner who lusts after her intervenes and proclaims that the stranger is really Maria's paramour.

Maria breaks away and runs to an empty church. She prays that she may die in place of the young man. The Stranger enters and tells her he cannot be defeated with a prayer. Maria runs to the belfry and desperately begins ringing the bell. But after a second, there is no sound. "There will be no bells ringing in the village tonight," the stranger announces. But if someone is going to die, shouldn't the bells be tolling?

As they head back to the ferry, Maria begs the stranger to take her life instead of her young man. The stranger refuses and tells her take the shortest path back since he must claim his victim before dawn. Instead, Maria leads the stranger right into the moors. As they proceed through the bog, Maria continually prays, offering her life for her lover's. Her step is sure and she walks safely to dry land. She does not make the mistake of Orpheus who, thinking Eurydice was past the boundary of the Underworld, looked back too soon and thus lost her forever. The stranger is caught in the mire and, with his arms raised imploringly, sinks into the bog. Only then does Maria look back and see that he is gone. Windt's music rises to a triumphant crescendo as Maria walks away and hears the young man, fully recovered, calling her name. Maria seems transfigured, almost holy, as she tells him, "Now the way across is safe for you." "No, Maria," he responds. "For us both." The next morning, they board the ferry and this time the man can help her pull the rope as they cross. The fiddler joins them as well. When they reach the other shore, the ferry is allowed to drift away. Maria and her lover walk through a beautiful pastoral scene as the man proclaims "My Heimat." The children's song is heard again and is especially joyful and uplifting. The screen fills with Maria's face as she smiles. At last, she belongs. It's a particularly moving moment, especially when one recalls Sybille Schmitz's own sad fate.

Of course, *People and Race* was more concerned with ideological matters and voiced an objection to this last scene and the notion that country was not strictly a matter of birth or race but could be adopted. Possibly they are right on the Reichsmark as Maria's triumph *could* be seen as a veiled criticism of National Socialist racial policies, especially as coming from a man married to a Jew. According to David Hull Stewart's *Film in the Third Reich*, some of Goebbels' advisors urged him to ban the film because it could be taken as a parable of the defeat of Nazi ideology. However, Hans Jürgen Nierentz, who is given co-author credit on the script with Wisbar, was a Nazi Party member who wrote songs and poems praising the Third Reich and later briefly became the Reichsfilmdramaturg (whose job it was to examine planned film productions). Nierentz has no other film credits and we don't know exactly what his contribution was to *Ferryman Maria* but he certainly would not have lent his name to a story critical of the Nazis.

Goebbels, though he reputedly hated the film because of its ambiguity, did not ban it; he actually awarded it a prize for being "artistically valuable." With that award went a cash subsidy for Wisbar to use on his next film. In his diary, Goebbels called the film "a failed experiment." Nineteen thirty-six was a terrible year for film in the Third Reich so perhaps Goebbels did not

Fährmann Maria—Clockwise from top left: Death and Maria enter the village. Death and Maria at the dance Middle: Maria and her lover enjoy a peaceful moment. Bottom right: The landowner (Gerhard Bienert) interrupts Maria's dance with the Stranger. Bienert had a long and distinguished stage career but in the movies usually had small parts, often as either a gangster or a policeman. He was a communist but kept his opinions to himself during the Nazi era and lived to settle in East Germany after the war. Far left: Aribert Mog.

want to cause a ruckus by banning a film that was lauded by the critics (who would soon be abolished) and one that at least had artistic pretentions. As mentioned in the Wisbar biography, Eva Wisbar thought Goebbels spared the movie because Hitler pronounced it a good film. That might seem questionable given the dictator's taste in movies, but in Eva Braun's diary we read the following: "Have also seen *Fährmann Maria*. Here one can see how a girl can achieve a lot. Goebbels didn't like it very much. But I liked it." Goebbels did not think highly of Braun's critical acumen and referred to her as "that flapper" and resented her occasional attempts to interfere with "my movies." Braun's fondness for the film could be the basis for Eva Wisbar thinking Der Führer liked it. David Hull Stewart goes on to say that Goebbels saw to it that the picture received only a limited distribution but that's not really accurate given the fact that Wisbar, Sybille Schmitz and Peter Voss, who played Death, went on a nine-city tour to promote it.

Oddly enough, a few modern critics think the film may conceal a pro-Third Reich message. After all, the emphasis on Heimat is certainly in keeping with Nazi philosophy. The young man stresses the need to fight the enemies that threaten his land and proclaims that everyone must do his part. Maria's willingness to sacrifice herself may mean no more than the need for women to support their soldiers fighting for the Fatherland. He's a soldier; he should live forever! But again, the young man isn't a soldier nor is he being pursued by soldiers. The call to arms he sounds is the ravings of his fevered mind, hardly an endorsement of militarism. He's certainly not a heroic figure; Maria even has to help him when he gets his foot stuck in the bog.

Annemarie Wisbar thought the Nazis' problem with the film was that it was suggesting immigration, an escape from the Third Reich. It's unlikely that viewers of the time would take it that way, but one can't help but speculate that Wisbar might be thinking of Eva's desperate attempts to find a new Heimat for all of them. Eva made it possible for Wisbar to cross over to the other side just as Maria does for her lover.

Except for the possibility that Maria "the gypsy" and her search for a homeland *may* be a dig at Nazi policy, I find no political meaning to the film. The pursuing phantoms and the stranger wear black because it is the color of night which is usually associated with the supernatural, not because it was the fashion choice for the SS. Neither the young man's homeland—directly across the river no less and no different in appearance than from Maria's domain—nor the heath and village seem like real places located in time and space. The stranger isn't a Gestapo man in pursuit of a political enemy but an inexorable dark force come to separate the lovers. The young man's lapses into fever are like a spell cast by a wizard. Maria's magic ends up saving him twice, and she breaks the spell for good by outwitting the wizard. This is the domain of fairy tales, not realpolitik.

The real ambiguity of the film lies in the ending. Maria is a bit like Charon the ferryman of Greek mythology who pilots the living into the land of the dead (and receives a coin from his passengers for that service). But which side of the shore is the Underworld? Except for the treacherous swamp, the village side of the river is as pleasant and pastoral as the other shore;

there's certainly no indication that it represents the Underworld though that might be logical in that Maria leaves it for life on the other side. In this way, the ending would be somewhat similar to that of *Vampyr* wherein the hero and heroine depart the land of shadows by water. Their destination, however unknown, is presumably not inhabited by vampires and vengeful spirits.

However, in *Maria* the couple seems not to be entering into just another country but the final Heimat, Heaven. In the last scene of Fritz Lang's *Destiny*, the heroine, having failed to outmaneuver Death, leaves with him and her lover to the place beyond the wall, the abode of the departed. We don't know what's there and it's as somber a scene as the "Dance of Death" at the end of Ingmar Bergman's *The Seventh Seal*. In Wagner's opera *The Flying Dutchman*, the title character and the girl, having sacrificed her life, ascend to Heaven together. In *Nosferatu*, Ellen saves her husband and her community by dying for them and thus defeating Count Orlock. The way *Ferryman Maria* unfolds and with the influence of these other sources, you would expect that Maria would indeed give her life and that her reward would be to enter paradise together with her lover; instead it seems her *willingness* to die is sufficient. (In *Strangler of the Swamp*, Wisbar's "remake" of *Maria*, Wisbar had no choice but to provide a happy ending.)

Perhaps William K. Everson's notes on the film sum up the issue: "It cannot really be explained in logical terms. Death is presented as stern and unrelenting, but not without a certain humanity. Yet Death is defeated which is hardly possible." Unlike *Death Takes a Holiday* and *On Borrowed Time* where Death's work is temporarily suspended, his discomfiture in *Ferryman Maria* is simply on a limited and personal level. Perhaps this is a bit like *The Seventh Seal* wherein the Knight distracts Death just long enough for the family to escape.

In *Destiny*, Death is not an unsympathetic figure and says that it's unfair that people fear him since he is just doing the work of the Almighty. Death seems more menacing in *Maria*, a ruthless fanatic unwavering in his duty and not to be bargained with. As usual in a Wisbar film, God's role is acknowledged but His presence left vague. Maria runs into the empty church and prostrates herself in prayer. She is under the shadow of the cross but when she looks up she sees the stranger glaring down at her, as unyielding and remorseless as ever. He won't spare her lover so as they cross the swamp, Maria appeals again to God, who apparently answers her prayer. Sometimes one gets the impression that in Wisbar's universe, God is there but not necessarily omnipotent and is perhaps just one force among others. Here, He may be no different than a benign fairy godmother who intercedes on behalf of the heroine.

In December 1935 there was a special preview of the film in Hamburg's Lessing Theater. It was attended by Wisbar and "some friends" from Terra

Fährmann Maria (1936)

Sybille Schmitz and Peter Voss (barely visible on the far left) on the Lüneburg Heath behind the scenes of *Fährmann Maria*.

and Ufa. A critic who was there wrote that comments should be withheld until the movie's official premiere but proceeded to give a preview of what to expect. From the *Hamburger Nachrichten*, December 21 and 22, 1935:

> It's not a common film. It's more a film poem, a ballad, a cinematic composition. The film artist has achieved a symphonic overall impression by a dreamlike mood. This is cinematic poetry, the scenic shaping of the image combined with the dark tone of words and music, achieving the purest of aims…. Everything is music, story, image, word and the unspoken. This film takes place on the landscape of our heathen moor. But the image is oddly modified. It isn't the moor of our days. Wisbar looks back through time. This is the Werwolf heath. It's the gloomy landscape of old English ballads. For the first time a film captures the heath in its dark romance and demonic undertones. Somewhere near Soltau, Wisbar has found this landscape by a lonely sea. He made his film with artists who shared his vision. Sybille Schmitz, wisely guided by Wisbar, as "Ferryman Maria" experiences love for a strange wounded rider in an atmosphere of mystical events. She strides with trembling lips over the moor that sparkles in the moonlight, dry-shod like a saint while her enemy sinks with a wordless gesture. Here everything happens between dream and reality, in blue twilight of a revived romanticism.

Fährmann Maria (1936)

When *Ferryman Maria* officially premiered in Hamburg, critic Carl Düsterdieck recalled Wisbar's earlier appearance there and described him as "a youthful man with bright eyes and enthusiasm and a director obsessed with film as art." He goes on (and on) to extol Wisbar as "a poet who tries to capture the very essence of the German soul." He relates the film to "blood and soil," the notion that the heart of Germany is to be found in the countryside where village life perpetuates the values that are the most important. (The Nazis coopted this romantic movement for their own purposes.) The reviewer further praises Wisbar for achieving "a perfect blending of image and sound where the real and unreal co-exist [and where] the characters have a symbolic meaning that visualizes the nature of the German people" (*Hamburger Nachrichten*, March 7, 1936).

Licht-Bild-Bühne (January 8, 1936) was a little less flowery but still full of praise:

> This is a work that stands outside all genres of film hitherto known to us; this is legend on film.... The lighting of the peasant festival is reminiscent of Rembrandt; the fear visible in Maria's eyes recalls Kubin and Breughel. Sixty percent of the film was shot at night with marvelous results. In a dreamlike world of visions, symbols and legends, Sybille Schmitz gives the sincerest performance of her career.... A success that reaffirms the maturity of the German public.

When the movie premiered at Hildesheim where it was shot, *Film-Kurier* was there. On January 8, 1936, it reported:

> The representatives of the Berlin press came to Hildesheim to immerse themselves in this legend of the swamp. Sixty percent of the film is accompanied by a musical score. There is a spoken dialogue in 15 percent, which shows that from time to time it was necessary to counterbalance the sometimes untenable irrationality of the story. The cameraman's bravura technique is everywhere evident here. As a smile lights up Sybille Schmitz's face, rays of sunlight illuminate the moor that surrounds her.

When the film played in New York City, the *New York Times* critic was far less effusive. From his December 24, 1938, review:

> Turned out as a cooperative exercise by a first-rate group of Teuton film players under the direction of Frank Wisbar, *Ferryman Maria* is symbolical of the (sometimes) triumph of faith over desperation. Naturally, love helps a lot.... The brunette Sybille Schmitz of Vienna manages to put considerable conviction into the difficult character of Maria, despite her predilection for more sophisticated roles.... Based on an ancient legend, the simple story is developed so deliberately that it seems to drag occasionally, but spectators should not expect Hollywood tempo in screen efforts of this nature.

The critic praised the other actors as well but mixed up the parts played by Aribert Mog (the young man) and Peter Voss (Death).

A more serious and perceptive review of the film came from James Card in the June 1936 issue of the *National Board of Review Magazine*:

> The film, advertised as being symbolic and artistic, was very beautiful and at times moving. Photographed dimly, the moon-washed heaths, the ghostly poplars of the moors, made an effective background for Maria to gather her mystic herbs at midnight under the light of the new moon. And sensitive arrangements of traditional weird songs of the heath carried along the atmosphere consistently. Without the work of Sybille Schmitz as the strange girl Maria and the frozen faced menace of Peter Vosz [sic] as Death, the film would have remained nothing more than an exhibition of fine photography. Sybille Schmitz is one of the interesting personalities before German cameras.... With a magic, as mystical as the power of the herbs that as Maria she gathered in the moonlight, her polish, her suavity fell away; she became a young, mysterious girl of the heath whose love was convincingly stronger than death. She, together with Weihmayr on camera and Herbert Windt composing the music, made a film. Had the deportment of Death been as convincing, the film would have been great rather than simply exceptional. A speaking Death is not as terrible as he looks when he is silent. And his horsemen, bare-headed, mounted in the dusk on white horses, somehow convinced me beyond doubt that they wore business suits under their capes.

After mentioning that Schmitz was often typed as a villainess, Card added, "Someone realizing she was an actress, cast her as Maria." That someone was of courses Frank Wisbar, who gets mentioned only in passing in Card's review. Wisbar was Schmitz's favorite director and they had a strong rapport. According to Annemarie Wisbar, Frank's knowledge of psychology helped him to understand the insecure actress who was "walking a tightrope." Whatever the precise relationship of actress and director, Wisbar was fascinated by Sybille's face and in both *Ferryman Maria* and *The Unknown*, he includes numerous close-ups of her which capture both her arresting features and her mystery.

Schmitz was born in Düren, a small village near Cologne, to a conservative Catholic family. She was sent to a Franciscan convent school but later left to enroll in the Cologne Drama School over the objections of her parents who did not want her to become an actress. Soon after, Schmitz left for Berlin and was cast in small roles in the famous Deutsches Theater. However, hers was a face meant for close-ups, not the proscenium arch, and she quickly switched to the movies. She was cast in a couple of small but conspicuous tragic parts: In the leftist *Freihe Fahrt* (*Full Speed Ahead*) she plays a downtrodden and pregnant young woman who loses both her baby and her life due to overwork (a harrowing sequence) while in the famous *Diary of a Lost Girl* she portrays the maid who drowns herself after being raped. At the same time, she was enjoying some success on the stage with a good role in *The Criminals* with Gustav Gründgens.

As the silent era came to an end, Schmitz played a prostitute in the experimental *Überfall*. The role that brought the most attention was Léone in Carl Dreyer's *Vampyr* in 1931. Léone, the victim of a vampire, starts to transform into one herself. As her sister looks down on her sickbed, Schmitz glowers up at her with a horrible grin and a hungry look in her eyes. Schmitz's wolfish countenance ranks with the last close-up of Tony Perkins in *Psycho* as one of the most terrifying facial expressions in horror history.

Vampyr failed at the box office but producers took note of Schmitz and cast her in the hit sci fi-action film *F.P. 1 Doesn't Answer* (1931). She now began working steadily in noteworthy productions. Schmitz also enjoyed the wild social life of Berlin, had numerous affairs with both sexes, and indulged in drugs and excessive drinking. She continued her wicked, wicked ways even after the Nazis came to power but by the mid–30s, her career seems to have peaked and she was cast in fewer and lesser movies. Years later, she insisted it was because she had rejected advances from Dr. Goebbels. Goebbels' casting couch was infamous but there is skepticism today about Schmitz's claim. Schmitz's dark look did not fit Dr. Goebbels' vision of the perfect German actress as a blond, blue-eyed Aryan goddess. What's more, her instability became more and more evident. On one occasion, after a rowdy party, Schmitz sent a telegram to the head of the Winter Relief Program (the main Nazi charity) suggesting that, as part of his duties, he "should take freezing women to bed." Schmitz sobered up in a hurry when she got a visit from the Gestapo, an organization not famous for its sense of humor. The other partygoers, including Wisbar, were also interrogated. Nothing came of it but it was not the sort of thing that would endear her to a dour fanatic like Goebbels.

In 1938, Gustav Gründgens had to fight for Schmitz to star in his bizarre *Dance on the Volcano* but by 1943 Goebbels let her to be cast in an important role in *Titanic*, a major epic intended as anti–British propaganda. The film ran into countless difficulties, went way over-budget and was subject to frequent delays. During one such languid hiatus, the cast and crew indulged in heavy partying and Schmitz had to be carried to her cabin. In the end, Goebbels decided that the film, even though technically very well done, was a terrible mistake: At that time, Allied bombing of German cities was constant and a film showing mass panic on a sinking ship was hardly a morale builder. The movie was banned in Germany but was allowed to be shown in German-occupied territories where it proved to be a hit. While Schmitz was saddled with an unbecoming wig, her performance in the film was one of her very best.

In 1940, Schmitz married screenwriter Harald Petersson (who later specialized in adaptations of Edgar Wallace) and they spent much of their time in Austria, near the Italian border. Petersson reputedly had some ties with the Resistance and Schmitz later claimed that they had correspondence with some of the conspirators who tried to kill Hitler in 1944.

Schmitz's postwar career was not a success. Her drinking made her unreliable and audiences of the '50s preferred younger stars like Hildegard Knef (who played with Schmitz in 1951's *Illusion in Moll*). Schmitz and Petersson separated and for a time Schmitz took up with actress–stage producer Beate von Molo. Schmitz became increasingly depressed over her lack of work and fell under the influence of a corrupt doctor who, while treating her for neuralgia, got her addicted to painkillers. When Schmitz ran out of money to pay for the pills, the doctor may have suggested she vacate her clinic by killing herself. This Schmitz did, on Easter weekend 1955. The grim circumstances of her end brought her name to public attention once again. Werner Fassbinder's 1982 film *Veronika Voss* was based on her sad final years.

Aribert Mog is winning and handsome as the man from the other shore but he doesn't have a whole lot to do and spends half of his screen time either exhausted or delirious. However, the way he calls out Maria's name at the climax is full of power and poignancy and then when he speaks softly to her afterwards, it's almost like a prayer. More about Mog, whose career was cut short by World War II, can be found on the essay on *The Unknown*.

Peter Voss makes for a formidable Death though not as cadaverous as Bernhard Goetzke in *Destiny*. Wisbar makes him look particularly imposing and menacing by frequently shooting him from below. Voss turned up frequently in the '30s but usually in supporting roles. A year after *Ferryman Maria*, he was back on the moors but this time as the hunted rather than the hunter playing Lord Henry in *The Hound of the Baskervilles*.

Carl de Vogt's Fiddler is an amusing rogue and he and his music are a kind of Greek chorus to the action. De Vogt does his own singing in the film, which is not surprising since he often performed at cabarets, made numerous recordings (his fox trots were especially popular) and entertained the troops during the war. While no one considered him a great actor, he was an important star during the silent era, often working for Fritz Lang and appearing in many big-budget films, some of them epics like Manfred Noa's *Helen of Troy* where he played Hector. He retained his saturnine good looks but by the '30s he was mainly seen in supporting roles; the Fiddler was one of his most conspicuous parts in the sound era. De Vogt was also an ardent Nazi and Brown Shirt. However, he had a son named Karl Franz (born in 1917) and in the '30s people wrongly assumed his mother was de Vogt's wife, actress Clare Lotto. According to some sources, de Vogt had been married before and to a Jewish girl so that made Karl *mischling*, not a safe status to have during the Third Reich. But de Vogt was able to protect his half Jewish son. After the war, the Allies banned de Vogt from working in Berlin but Karl Franz had become a film producer and was able to throw some work his father's way.

Frank Wisbar directs Sybille Schmitz on the set of *Fährmann Maria*.

Master cinematographer Franz Weihmayr teamed with Wisbar on a number of occasions but is probably best remembered for his work with Zarah Leander, the Reich's answer to Garbo, in *La Habanera*, *The Blue Fox* and her other eight movies for Ufa. Weihmayr's postwar movies were largely undistinguished.

David Hull Stewart called Herbert Windt "unquestionably the greatest composer of film music in the history of the medium." Some would disagree but his scores for Leni Riefenstahl's *Olympia* and *Triumph of the Will* are considered masterworks. Windt, a Nazi party member, also scored less distinguished propaganda films like *Campaign in Poland* and *Victory in the West*. After the war, the Allies temporarily banned him but he was eventually allowed to return. His final score was for Wisbar's *Dogs, Do You Want to Live Forever?*

Many people in the *filmwelt* fancied themselves apolitical and relatively few were Party members. Oddly enough, four of *Maria*'s participants—Nierentz, Windt, de Vogt and Mog—were card-carrying Nazis. Wisbar must have felt a bit isolated.

Goebbels had no use for movies about the supernatural or the macabre and associated them with the "decadent" Weimar Republic, so there would be nothing else like *Ferryman Maria* during his watch. *Maria* subsequently had little influence. Some see a reflection of *Maria* in the 1972 German horror film *Nightshade*.

Rosen blühen auf dem Heidgrae (*Roses Bloom on the Grave in the Meadow*), a 1952 film, has many similarities to *Ferryman Maria*. It is set on the heath and much is made of the culture of simple agrarian life. The burly, bearded villain is stalking the beautiful country lass Dorothee, who much prefers her childhood sweetheart, recently returned to the village. Dorothee is obsessed with an old legend that tells how, during the Thirty Years' War (shades of *Der Werwolf!*), a cavalier raped a young woman who then lured him into the bog where both perished. There are some moody moments enhanced by occasional low-key photography as the old story seems to happen again. The villain rapes Dorothee who, like the girl in the legend, then entices him into the bog. Both are caught in the mire, but they are rescued in time. Dorothee is reunited with her lover while her rapist goes unpunished and even reconciles with his girlfriend (though why anyone would want this lecherous slob in the first place is hard to fathom). The film is interesting enough in its own right but, as far as acting, photography, music and direction go, it's hardly in the same league as Wisbar's film.

Ferryman Maria is the finest hour for both Wisbar and Sybille Schmitz. In a world gone mad with violence and cruelty, the morally flawed director and his tormented star are able, for one brief moment at least, to make you believe that love really can overcome death.

Die Unbekannte *(The Unknown)*
HP Producktion/Terra-Filmkunst
Released on November 12, 1936
92 minutes

Cast: Sybille Schmitz as Madeleine; Jean Galland as Thomas Bentick; Ilse Abel as Evelyn; Edwin Jürgensen as Minister Van Altendorf; Franz W. Schröder-Schrom as the industrialist Gieseking; Aribert Mog as Gerhard; Lotte Spira as Bentick's housemaid; Karl Platen as the servant in Platen; Karl Stepanek as the manager of "The Regina"; Karin Lüsebrink as the dancer; Herbert Spalke as the reporter; Charlie Cracker as the thief; Günther Polensen as the police officer; Hellmuth Passarge as Wachthabender; Curd Jürgens as Hans Wellenkamp; Lucy Millowitsch as a singer; Horst Breitkopf as a gentleman; Peter Kiwitt as a guest; Dodo Delissen as a singer.

Credits: Director: Frank Wisbar (as Frank Wysbar); Screenplay: Frank Wisbar (as Frank Wysbar), Reinhold Conrad Muschler, Adolf Lantz (uncredited);

Die Unbekannte (1936)

Based on the eponymous novella by Reinhold Conrad Muschler; Photography: Werner Bohne and Alexander von Lagorio; Production Designers: Benno von Arent and Artur Günther; Editor: Lena Neumann; Music: Hans-Otto Borgmann, the Philharmonic Orchestra, the Leipzig Gewandhaus Orchestra; Sound: Tobis-Klangfilm. A Wysbar-Schmitz Film.

Sometime in the early 1880s, the body of a young girl was found floating in the Seine. There were no signs of violence, leading authorities to conclude that she was likely a suicide. She had no identification so her corpse was displayed at the Paris Morgue in the hope that someone would recognize her. No one did, but a medical student was so captivated by her face that he made a death mask of it.

Or so the story goes. What is definitely true is that copies of the mask became immensely popular in artistic and literary circles in the early 1900s. Having a replica of a famous person's death mask as a household *objet d'art* was not uncommon (Beethoven's was especially chic) but here the girl was an unknown. Writers and artists were fascinated by her expression, especially the way her lips were pulled back in a smile. Is she embracing the peacefulness of death or just naively failing to realize its finality? There may be a suggestion of eroticism as well. Her smile was not as famous as that of the Mona Lisa but it was no less ambiguous. Stories and poems were written about "L'Inconnue de la Seine," many of them reflecting an embrace of death both romantic and morbid. She

Die Unbekannte—The unknown woman (Sybille Schmitz) finds peaceful repose in the final sleep. The pose is strikingly like the "real" death mask of L'Inconnue, a story forgotten today but well known in the '20s and '30s. Her tale is probably an urban legend.

attracted the attentions of Vladimir Nabokov, Louis-Ferdinand Celine, Richard La Galliene, Anais Nin and Rainer Maria Rilke.

By the 1920s and '30s, L'Inconnue had become something of a cult figure in both France and Germany with the Goth girls of their day imitating her mysterious appearance (though not usually her fate). She also may have been an influence on the look of actresses like Elisabeth Bergner and Greta Garbo. Was there ever a more cryptic mask than Garbo's expression at the end of *Queen Christina*?

Occasionally, attempts were made at demythologizing her cult. Some were skeptical that her placid expression could be that of a drowned person since being immersed in water would tend to bloat and disfigure the victim rather than transforming her into Sleeping Beauty. Efforts to trace the factual origins of the story got nowhere, though one amateur detective claimed that he had tracked down the mysterious model and that she was alive and well and the daughter of a German manufacturer of the masks. A variation on that story, wanting to have it both ways, claimed the teenage girl was alive when the mask was made but jumped into the Seine later! L'Inconnue's story was never verified but in the immortal words of Criswell, "Can you prove that it *didn't* happen?"

In 1934, L'Inconnue's fame got a major boost with the publication of Reinhold Conrad Muschler's *Die Unbekannte*, which featured the unlucky lady's death mask on the cover. In Muschler's novella, the waterlogged maiden is Madeleine, a teenage virgin and orphan who leaves her country home after her aunt dies. Madeleine heads for Paris and falls in love with Lord Thomas Vernon Bentick, a sophisticated and wealthy nobleman. They travel together and enjoy an idyll in the City of Lights but the affair remains chaste. Ultimately, Bentick decides to return to his American fiancée and leaves for Egypt to join her. Madeleine keeps her date with anonymous immortality in the waters of the Seine, making sure that no one will ever trace her to her beloved and sully his reputation. "Yes Tom," she exclaims as she goes under. "It's me. I'm coming." The last lines of the book: "Her face had a transfigured smile when she was found."

In spite of critical scorn, the book sold hundreds of thousands of copies internationally. Even though Muschler, a noted botanist, had sat out the Great War studying the flora and fauna of Egypt, he later became an ardent nationalist and supporter of Hitler, willingly divorcing his Jewish wife to prove his loyalty. The success of the book at just that period in Germany was no accident according to Ann-Gaelle Saliot's study of the history of L'Inconnue, *The Drowned Muse*:

> The advances of political democracy in Germany had brought suffrage and constitutional equality for women. In this context, the "shock of modernity" was very often experienced as a crisis of traditional male identity and authority. Male anxiety

emerged in complex formulations within the mass culture forms of popular literature and film. The figure of Madeline contrasts sharply with the liberated icons of *Neue Sachlichkeit*, embodying as she does a stereotyped and reactionary discourse on women. The story elaborated by Muschler, formulated to give life and substance to the Inconnue legend, in fact transforms the cast into a reactionary icon.

Die Unbekannte would seem to be an unlikely vehicle for Sybille Schmitz, who was no teenager in 1936. Nevertheless, the book attracted the attention of both her and Frank Wisbar, both of whom were riding the wave of the great popular and critical success of *Ferryman Maria* which had been awarded 150,000 Reichsmarks from the government as an incentive for more quality moviemaking. Terra Film gave the director and star their own unit to produce artistic films together. Schmitz felt that she was not reaching her potential as an actress and that she was too often being given routine roles (in 1935's *Der Herr der Welt* aka *Master of the World*, she had little to do except run away from a giant robot). She saw *Ferryman Maria* as her breakout film and hoped, with Wisbar at the helm, she had a future as a serious actress.

Wisbar started on the script with Muschler (the working title was *Madeleine*) but the results weren't satisfactory and the project stalled. Muschler's book was, after all, less than a hundred pages and did not have a great deal of plot. In June 1936, Wisbar and Schmitz went to London to enlist the aid of Wisbar's friend Adolf Lantz, who had written films for Brigitte Helm (G.W. Pabst's *Abwege*) and Anna May Wong (*Großstadtschmetterling* aka *Golden Butterfly*) and had even worked with Luigi Pirandello on a film adaptation of the playwright's *Six Characters in Search of an Author* (which didn't pan out). Lantz was Jewish and had fled Germany; but one of his last films before leaving for London was *Ray of Sunshine* which, interestingly enough, begins with a woman throwing herself into the Danube. Lantz and Wisbar hammered out a script for *The Unknown* and then Wisbar and Schmitz returned to Germany and started to film in July. No doubt they did not mention to Muschler that his little masterpiece had been reworked by a Jew. Indeed, what ended up on the screen was considerably different from Muschler's novella with Madeleine being transformed from naïve virgin to a woman of the world and the setting changed from France to Germany.

The film begins on an appropriately somber note with a shot of the exterior of a police station on a rainy night (the lighting is low-key and sets an atmosphere of gloom). The commandant enters and is told that an unknown woman has been found in the lake. He and a companion enter a dark adjoining room and the commandant shines a lantern on the body on a table. He pulls back the sheet and we behold the woman we will come to know as Madeleine. It is Sybille Schmitz strikingly replicating the expression of L'Inconnue. The two men are moved by the sight. "What could have brought her to this end?" muses the commandant. The shot of Madeleine being uncovered is rather similar to one in *Diary of a Lost Girl* wherein Louise Brooks pulls back the sheet from the face of the maid (Schmitz) who has drowned herself.

After another close-up of Madeleine, the flashback begins as if the whole tale is being told by her. One is reminded a bit of the opening scenes of the classic *Sunset Blvd.* and the not so classic *Scared to Death*; in both cases the corpse narrates its own story. The scene shifts to a nightclub called the Regina where Madeleine is a singer (she's elsewhere described as a dancer but the only dancing we see her do is with the customers). The nightclub seems to be a hangout mainly for her ex-lovers and would-be-lovers. Hans, a young man who has been rebuffed by Madeleine, tells a companion that he intends to marry her. "After all," he says, "Madeleine came from a good home." "Yes," snickers his companion, "but what happened after she left home?" His companion also warns Hans that it's dangerous to love Madeline and she has been the ruin of many a man who tried to reform her.

Madeleine sings a song that sums up her attitude towards romance:

> True love is a beautiful fairy tale
> I do not believe it, not today, not ever
> In my heart, the doors are not open to anyone, not even you.

We will hear this song more than once.

Madeleine journeys to Dinkelsbühl where she has another nightclub engagement. At the train station, scientist and explorer Thomas Bentick is being interviewed by a radio reporter. Bentick is soon to leave on a five-year expedition but his fiancée Evelyn is to immediately precede him to Cairo while Bentick attends to some last-minute business in Berlin. Madeleine sees someone steal Evelyn's purse and angrily confronts the thief. Evelyn is relieved to have the purse returned because it contained documents needed for their trip. She and Bentick thank Madeleine profusely. Perhaps as a concession to the setting of the book, Bentick is French though he has made his home in Germany (Madeleine later compliments him on his German).

Madeleine bumps into Bentick later that day and, learning that she is new to the city, he suggests that she stay at his hotel. At the hotel, Madeleine hesitates a bit at the hotel register when she is obliged to put in her occupation but she finally writes "fashion designer." Bentick invites her to dinner and she accepts. She calls the nightclub and tells the manager she will come the next day rather than that night. He tells her not to bother at all if she can't make her original engagement.

At dinner that night, Madeleine and Bentick are immediately taken with each other. He confesses that he peeked at her entry in the register and suggests she come with him to Berlin since she's more likely to find a job as a designer there. She consents and the two spend an enchanted evening together, marred only by the appearance of a singer who belts out Madeleine's "True Love Is a Fairy Tale" song, bringing Madeleine momentarily back to reality.

Why does the cynical Madeleine suddenly become infatuated with the charming scientist? In the book, it would make sense that an inexperienced country girl would immediately fall for a sophisticated man of the world but Madeleine has encountered other polished and wealthy gentlemen so her abandonment of her unromantic attitude seems arbitrary and contrived. Nothing has led up to it; it's just a given in the script. It doesn't help that Schmitz and Jean Galland (Bentick) don't have much chemistry together. Candlelight and good wine notwithstanding, Bentick comes off as slightly stodgy, hardly the sort of man to abandon all caution for love.

The couple travels to Stuttgart and arrives on a foggy night. The next morning, Bentick shows Madeleine the local church, empty except for one pious old woman deep in prayer. Bentick convinces the priest to let him play the organ (Bentick is truly a Renaissance Man). As Schubert's 8th Symphony reverberates throughout the building, Madeleine kneels and tries to pray but finds herself disoriented by the music and the somewhat unsettling atmosphere of the church. She is drawn to a statue of Madonna and Child with Wisbar alternating between close-ups of Madeleine and the statue. Madeleine ends up fainting. The meaning of all this is a bit obscure. Does Madeleine feel she's being judged for the sort of life she has led? Is she going from sinner to saint, Mary Magdalene–style? Schmitz was raised Catholic and no doubt often saw her mother pray in front of the Black Madonna in Cologne. Sybille abandoned her faith for the flesh pots of Berlin and may well be bringing something of her history to this scene. However, there doesn't seem to be anything pivotal about this moment and it doesn't come up again. As in *Anna and Elizabeth*, Wisbar seems to be looking at the transcendent as unnatural and frightening rather than a source of peace and inspiration. Better to leave the Burning Bush alone and go about your business.

Wisbar had some problems with the church sequence. When the local bishop refused to let him film in the church, the SA threatened a demonstration. Although the Night of the Long Knives had decimated their ranks and the SS had become predominant, the Brown Shirts were still around and ready and willing to cause trouble. They were keeping tabs on Wisbar but perhaps felt an anti–Catholic gesture could suit their purposes. Wisbar was appalled but fortunately was somehow able to convince the church beadle to let his crew in to film even without permission from his Excellency. The SA then called off their protest.

After Bentick and Madeleine arrive in Berlin, Bentick invites her to stay at his villa while she looks for work as a fashion designer. Madeleine has a

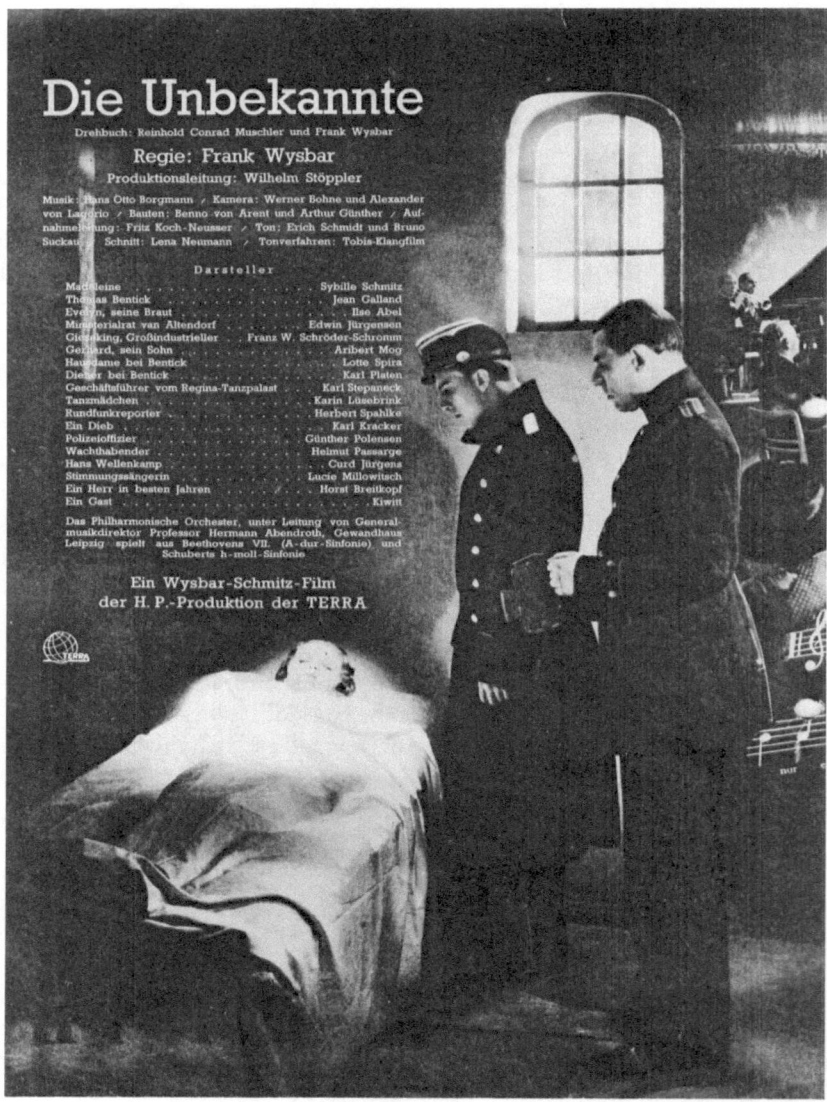

The police are mystified as to why such a woman would take her own life in *Die Unbekannte*.

disturbing dream: First she sees the map of the route to Egypt that she had noticed earlier in Bentick's drawing room, and then Evelyn, traveling by boat to Cairo. Evelyn looks fondly at a picture of Bentick but then Madeleine's countenance is superimposed over both images. Madeleine awakens reaching out for the image of Bentick but then becomes frightened. Hans-Otto Borgman's music becomes very dramatic at this point but nothing happens other than Madeleine getting up and going to the window.

The next day, while Madeleine strolls around, Bentick meets with the government minister van Altendorf who tells him that he must leave immediately for Cairo on a special mission (we never learn what or why it's so urgent; it's merely a sloppy device to keep things moving). Madeleine arrives at the café where she was to meet Bentick at the appointed time and runs into the sleazy character who managed her old club, the Regina. He offers her a job but she refuses and leaves in a hurry, fearful that Bentick will soon be there. Her cab leaves just as Bentick's car pulls up. Later she tells him, via phone, that she got confused and couldn't find the café. She overhears the servant repeatedly saying "yes" on the phone in response to Bentick and she sarcastically imitates his servile manner, saying "yes" again and again as she goes up to her room.

Bentick tells Madeleine the bad news that they have only one more day together but he has planned a boating excursion and a night at the Symphony. Madeleine would have preferred to have spent time together alone but Bentick wants her to meet his friends so they will look out for her once he's gone. On the yacht, Madeleine meets Bentick's friends, among them van Altendorf. She looks vaguely familiar to him but Madeleine remembers him all too well. Someone brings out a record player and the tune being played is none other than Madeleine's "Love Is a Fairy Tale" (it must be on Deutschland's Top Ten). Madeleine nearly swoons.

That night they go to the concert and hear Beethoven's 7th Symphony. During intermission, van Altendorf corners Madeleine alone and tells her he now remembers who she is. She was responsible for the corruption and suicide of a young student. Van Altendorf begs her not to bring Bentick to the same end. Madeleine promises him that no harm will come to Bentick because of her. They go back to the concert but Madeleine becomes distraught and they have to leave. At this point Bentick might well be assuming she just doesn't like music very much.

Back at Bentick's villa, Madeleine insists on going down to the wine cellar to pick out the wine herself. As the background music rises in intensity, Madeleine seems to be struggling with an inner conflict but finally gets herself together and joins Bentick upstairs. He has lit some candles for a little romantic atmosphere and only half-hears her comment "Now they remind me of funerals." Undeterred, Bentick declares his love for Madeleine but she tells him he knows nothing of her background. He insists that it doesn't matter. "I'm an unknown from an unknown world," she responds, and says that while she doesn't love him, she did enjoy their time together. She adds that she doesn't believe in true love. "Such an attitude must be hard on those who love you" is the dejected Bentick's response. They embrace as friends but Madeleine tells him she will not be going with him to the airport.

The next morning it is raining and Madeleine watches from the bedroom window as Bentick prepares to get in his car. There's a beautifully lit and framed close-up of Madeleine's face against the rainswept window. She closes the curtain so Bentick won't see her but after the car is gone she spends a long time looking at the spot where it was parked. Then she faints, even without the benefit of the Unfinished Symphony.

When she awakens, she begins a monologue in which she declares again and again that she does love Bentick. "He's not in Egypt, he's here with me," she says, perhaps echoing the last thoughts of the book's Madeleine as she goes down for the third time. Madeleine also reminds herself of her promise to van Altendorf that she would keep Bentick safe. In an exquisitely photographed final sequence, she walks into the lake at night. One close-up of Schmitz in this scene is photographed and lit in a way that is so much like similar close-ups in *Ferryman Maria* that it could pass as an outtake from that movie. The film ends with a close-up of Schmitz as l'Inconnue, the smile suggesting she has died content now that she has experienced true love. The moment has a special poignancy as one recalls Schmitz's own suicide about which there was nothing romantic. Schmitz's actual death mask is strikingly like her pose as L'Inconnue.

Wisbar described *The Unknown* as an attempt to "visualize optically the landscape of the soul." This sounds something like Carl Dreyer's *The Passion of Joan of Arc* but Dreyer had a saint, religious ecstasy and martyrdom as the foundation for his experiment whereas Wisbar's basic material is much more ordinary and less profound. Joan's suffering and death are her salvation; are Madeline's tribulations really on that level? She dies for Bentick, not Jesus, but her sacrifice scarcely seems necessary.

As a follow-up to *Ferryman Maria*, the film is a decided disappointment. It tries, unsuccessfully, to suggest the mysticism of the earlier film but Madeleine lacks the mythic and mysterious qualities of Maria, despite of Schmitz's plaintive and compelling performance. The film seems to suggest that she's something more than just a cabaret singer who sleeps around; it drops hints that men who love her are doomed, that she's a kind of Circe. This is a bit reminiscent of the 1930 version of *Alraune* wherein Brigitte Helm, as the eponymous heroine, plays a soulless destroyer of men, her birth the result of an evil experiment mating a murderer with a prostitute. Knowing that the man she has come to love will inevitably end up on her list of victims, Alraune drowns herself to prevent that. *The Unknown* suggests that's the reason for Madeleine's suicide even though Bentick is safely away in Egypt.

But there's nothing really sinister about Madeleine's character; she's not a whole lot different than Marlene Dietrich's Lola in *The Blue Angel* and the attempt to make her into the "woman no man can resist" doesn't work. If this were an American film, Madeleine would be played by Nancy Carroll and her beloved would be a naïve young man, the male equivalent of the book's Madeleine. The heartless siren would eventually cast aside her cynicism and, against all logic, fall deeply in love with the sort of "good" man she might have been expected to laugh at. Here Bentick is not naïve but the hackneyed situation is much the same.

Hans-Otto Borgmann's music doesn't help. It's overly emphatic and gives some mundane scenes an air of pretentiousness as though something of great import is happening. Beethoven and Schubert are added to the mix to provide a little more class but they seem extraneous too.

Wisbar called his film "uncompromising, without a happy ending." Of course, it couldn't very well be the story of l'Inconnue and have a happy ending. Muschler's original story perhaps appealed to shop girls who dreamed of being swept away by a sophisticated older man while male readers would have fantasized about having a fling with a submissive teenager before getting back to their bourgeois respectability. Changing the setting from Paris, the city of romance, to the more business-like world of Berlin, was another mistake and a local lake can hardly be a substitute for the dark mystery of the Seine. Whatever the reason for the book's great appeal, some felt it was a questionable choice as a vehicle for Sybille Schmitz.

Wisbar visited Hamburg just prior to *The Unknown*'s release to give a talk on his film technique. A writer for the *Hamburger Anzeiger* gave his impressions of the director:

> When Wisbar speaks he often talks with his hands, his gestures underlining the points he's trying to make. He has nervous fingers and fanatically burning eyes. He is one of the most peculiar men in the film world. When he talks, you realize that he is single-minded when it comes to his purpose, to solving whatever problem arises. He never takes the easy way out. His work is like a vocation. One might dislike his movies and his way of doing things but one has to concede that he's not afraid to try something different, to go against the conventional even if it is unpopular. He is someone totally dedicated to film as an art form and to exploring the possibilities of the camera. He wants to visualize what lies behind things. His films stir up discussion and this is positive.

When the film premiered at the Lessing Theater in Hamburg, reviews were favorable but not uncritical. "Zi" of the *Hamburger Anzeiger* (November 19, 1936) thought Wisbar should have dispensed with the Muschler book altogether and come up with an original interpretation of L'Inconnue's life and death. Still the writer felt that Wisbar, whom he describes as a "romantic poet of silence," captured "music of souls" and the imagery and sequences with little or no dialogue testified to the notion that "great love lacks words." "Zi" also praised Schmitz's sensitive portrayal though she had to cope with an inconsistent character. Jean Galland's low-key performance was also favorably noted. The critic pointed out that the first night audience applauded at the film's conclusion.

Critic Friedrich-Carl Kobbe of the *Hamburger Nachtrichten* noted in his November 28 review the rumor that the model for L'Inconnue was still alive and in her fifties but, whatever the truth of her story, her mask still had power as a picture of "injured innocence," a "childish face without guile." Schmitz's portrayal certainly lacked this "gentle girlishness" but was a valid reinterpretation in its own right even though the role was a dubious one for her. Kobbe was fascinated by Schmitz's unconventional looks which were not beautiful in the usual sense, but mask like, mysterious and fascinating. Kobbe compared her to Garbo, Annabella, Simone Simon and Anna May Wong and exclaimed that she was "unique among German actresses." He wrote that Wisbar's direction had its roots in French surrealism: "He doesn't contend with the foreground of the image. He's searching for the over-natural that is found in the background of things."

The one critic who mattered, Dr. Goebbels, was scornful and dismissed the film as "artificially constructed and sometimes foolish."

Many years later, David Hull Stewart, who had greatly admired *Ferryman Maria*, was equally unimpressed, writing in his *Film in the Third Reich*, "Unfortunately, everything right with the earlier picture went wrong here. For it would seem that the director was far less at home in the drawing rooms of Paris [*sic*] than in his Northern swamps."

Variety (December 16, 1936) was much more positive: "Gripping meller, slowly paced but outstanding through brilliant acting and superb photography. Great entertainment fodder for sentimentalists.... Chiller is bound to attract, if only for the unusual direction and Sybille Schmitz's work." The reviewer did not think too highly of Jean Galland:

> Frank Wisbar ... would have done better to select another partner for her. Jean Galland, French actor, as Thomas Bentick, is a heroic looking and elegant explorer, but hardly the type of passionate lover; moreover, he is handicapped by not speaking German fluently.

The Unknown wasn't the only time Galland didn't get the girl. In *Remous* aka *Whirlpool* (1935), he's crippled in an accident and commits suicide so his wife may be free; in the aptly titled *Amok* (1934), his unfaithful wife dies from a botched abortion; and in *Le Serment aka The Pledge* (1934), his bride prefers his brother to him. Galland occasionally played a villain (the title role in 1932's *Fantomas*, a German officer in 1937's *Marthe Richard*) but mainly took supporting roles from the '40s onward.

Aribert Mog was the male lead in *Ferryman Maria* but here he has barely a walk-on as one of Bentick's friends. Mog's main claim to film fame is his role as Hedy Lamarr's lover in *Ecstasy* (1933). They were an item off-screen as well, which gives an added dimension to the famous lovemaking scene wherein Hedy's close-up expression is meant to indicate orgasm. However, it wasn't Mog's prowess as actor or lover that produced just the right look but rather the director jabbing Lamarr repeatedly in the bottom with a pin! In real life, Mog was not as congenial as the heroes he portrayed on the screen but rather was a devout Nazi. He narrated Third Reich newsreels and played in two semi-documentaries funded by the government, *Ewiger Wald* aka *Enchanted Forest* (1936) and *Das Stahltier* aka *The Steel Animal* (1935). Mog got to die for his Führer on the Eastern Front in 1941.

Curd Jürgens—better known to English-speaking audiences as Curt Jurgens—has a brief but conspicuous role as the infatuated Hans. He had happy memories of the film and of Wisbar, whom he described as "der spökenkiekerische Metaphysiker," an obscure phrase indicting that the director was insightful and out of the ordinary. Jürgens also noted that Wisbar was way ahead of his time and used techniques that were later made common by Roberto Rossellini and neo-realist film. In his autobiography, Jürgens mentioned that Wisbar encouraged him and Schmitz (whom Jürgens found fascinating) to improvise the dialogue and business for their scene. The actor also lamented the fact that though the movie had "ravishing photography and unusual atmosphere," it was unsuccessful at the box office. Jürgens had a long stage and film career, often playing villains later in life. Unlike Mog, he was anti–Nazi and as a result did some time in a concentration camp towards the end of the war.

The public, unmoved by *The Unknown*'s gloomy romance, stayed away. It was the first and last film to bear the label of a Wisbar-Schmitz Production.

L'Inconnue's cult faded by the '40s although the lady would make occasional appearances in literature. She enjoyed a revival of sorts thanks to Rescue Annie, the cardiopulmonary mannequin. The mannequin was created in 1955 by toymaker Asmund Laerdal, who had saved his own son from drowning by using CPR and subsequently made the mannequin as a teaching device in first aid classes. He recalled that his grandparents had the mask of L'Inconnue on their wall and decided that would be a good face to use for the dummy. Thus, L'Inconnue became the "most kissed face in history" and helped saved thousands of lives in spite of her own tragic story.

Ball im Metropol
(Ball in Metropol)

Neucophon Tonfilm-Production/Terra
Censored on January 23, 1937
Premiered on January 26, 1937
84 minutes

Cast: Heinrich George as Rudolf von Waltzien; Heinz von Cleve as Eberhard von Waltzien; Hilde Weissner as Margit Steltendorff; Viktoria von Ballasko as Gertrud Selle; Elsa Wagner as Frau Selle; Ursula Weißbach as Lotte Schultze; Katja Specht as Eva Kresst; Franz Schafheitlin as Steltendorff; Fred Goebel as Studerke; Leopold von Ledebur as Count Kraßt; Heinz Klockow as von Restrow; Bob Bauer as von Puttkamer; Frau Finkelnberg as Baroness Malchin; Margitta Zonewa as female singer; Achim von Biel as the envoy; Fanny Cotta as the directress of the fashion house; Fred Köster as a guest at the ball; William Hutch as von Waltzien's elderly servant; Karl Platen as Werner, Eberhard's servant; Sascha Schöning.
Credits: Director: Frank Wisbar (as Frank Wysbar); Script: Wolf Neumeister, Ilse Maria Spath, Frank Wisbar; Based on the novel *Irrungen, Wirrungen* (*Trials and Tribulations*) by Theodor Fontane; Photography: Erich Claunigk; Editor: Lena Neumann; Art Directors: Fritz Maurischat, Anton Weber; Music: Walter Kollo; Conductor: Siegfried Schulz; Sound: Bruno Suckau; Costumes: Elisabeth Massary; Makeup: Alfred Lehmann, Luise Lehmann.

> As all my films, *Ball* is a part of me, it grew dear to my heart. Yet still, I'm not satisfied with any of them. And perhaps this isn't possible in the first place. But one has to fight for one's ideal. The audience is watching a completed movie. They can reject it or accept, show enthusiasm for it or be indifferent. They also might have some thoughts about the actors. But they have no idea about what has happened before the film was screened. And it's just as well. But one thing deserves to be known. I can tell you from my experience that a film emerges four times: first the exposé-idea, then the script, then the shooting, and then the editing. The film is changing four times, sometimes it changes bones at all [sic]. And sometimes in the end its own "father," the writer of the exposé, doesn't recognize it any more.
> —Frank Wisbar, after the premiere of *Ball in Metropol*

Frank Wisbar's second-to-last film under Nazi auspices was an inconsequential costume romance with a flimsy storyline. It was based, probably very loosely, on a Theodor Fontane novel which dealt with the summertime fling of an aristocratic officer with a poor girl. Fontane's books were popular with literary critics who praised them for their "poetic realism." But there's little poetry and even less realism in *Ball im Metropol*.

Ball im Metropol (1937)

The film opens with an oddly theatrical device uncharacteristic of Wisbar: After the credits, a giant curtain parts, revealing the action. This might be a reference to the characters having to adhere to their class roles as rigorously as stage actors stick to their scripts. We see Baron von Waltzien motoring over the grounds of his estate in the company of his nephew Eberhard. Eberhard has just returned from abroad and his uncle is encouraging him to go into politics to represent the conservative upper class. ("Berlin stinks of gasoline and Social Democrats," the baron later grouses.) Eberhard seems to regard his destiny with ruefulness; he is dutiful about it though unenthusiastic. The car stops at the baron's estate house and, even though there is no indication that the two have been out hunting, there is a close-up of a dead wild hog in the back of the car. Symbolism? Or road kill?

Baron von Waltzien is played by Heinrich George, a powerhouse of the German stage and screen, but sometimes cast like a Teutonic Lionel Barrymore playing crusty old curmudgeons with a bark worse than their bite, gruff but warm-hearted. That's pretty much what George is stuck with here.

We are now introduced to the baron's beautiful and elegant niece Margrit, who is married to the councilor Steltendorff. The latter is a cold and correct bureaucrat but his mask of rectitude disguises a jealous nature. A generous husband, he buys Margit a coat with a fur neckline for her to wear to the upcoming grand ball at the Hotel Metropol. She and Steltendorff quarrel after he is obliged to cancel going to the ball to deal with some foreign visitors. Annoyed, Margit goes to the ball on her own. There she meets Eberhard and we learn that they were childhood sweethearts though there is nothing between them any more but friendship.

After the first waltz of the evening, the guests retire to watch can-can dancers perform. (It's certainly an eclectic program that is being presented.) As is typical in a Wisbar film, there is a recurring song that comments on the action: "A whole day with you must be like a wonderful spring." Margit and Eberhard watch the show from a private box in the vast ballroom. Directly across from them, Steltendorff arrives with his foreign guests. Using binoculars, he sees Eberhard kiss Margit's hand (her back is turned but Steltendorff recognizes the very distinctive coat). Using *her* binoculars, Margit spots her husband and panics. She hastily takes her leave of Eberhard and runs into Trude, the sweet young thing who waited on her at the dress shop. Trude has come to the ball to repair one of the dancer's costumes but Margit prevails upon her to wear the fancy coat, hoping that Steltendorff will glimpse it and assume he's mistaken about seeing his wife at the ball. At Margit's request, Trude joins the surprised Eberhard in his box. The two immediately hit it off and Trude agrees to meet Eberhard later.

Finally free of his foreign guests, Steltendorff rushes to the box where he saw his wife. By now, only Eberhard is there (Steltendorff does not know him by sight). Trude and Eberhard meet later and, though Trude protests she is just a simple girl, they quickly fall in love Hollywood-style. Later that night, Margit tells Steltendorff that she had a headache and did not go to the ball after all. When he mentions the coat, she says that she earlier returned it to the shop for alterations. Her husband is not entirely convinced that he saw another coat at the ball.

Steltendorff goes to the dress shop to talk to Trude who confirms Margit's story that the dress needed some work done. Still skeptical, the councilor questions Trude sharply and the girl then says she borrowed the coat herself to wear to the ball. Steltendorff accepts this Cinderella story. Steltendorff is later introduced to Eberhard by the baron. He knows of Eberhard's earlier relationship with Margit and is disconcerted to see that he is both back in Germany and is the man he saw earlier at the ballroom.

The baron, Eberhard, Steltendorff and Margit attend a society riding show. The baron hopes Eberhard will take to one of the blue-blooded young equestrians but his monocle pops out when his nephew tells him he is in love with Trude. The baron does not approve and pays Trude a visit to urge her to give Eberhard up. He tells her that his nephew's career will likely be ruined if he marries out of his class. Trude agrees to break things off. When Eberhard comes to see her, she tells him that their match will never win society's approval. Eberhard responds that he doesn't care about rank or status and suggests that they go off to one of the colonies together. Trude rejects that notion and Eberhard leaves in a huff, convinced that Trude doesn't love him after all.

Steltendorff learns from one of Margit's friends that she was indeed at the ball. Steltendorff again confronts Trude, who this time tells him the truth. Tired of all the drama, Trude's boss fires her. Steltendorff challenges Eberhard to a duel (he doesn't slap him with a glove but instead politely gives him his card). Alas, the viewer's hope that there might finally be some action is dashed as the baron, having heard the whole story from Margit, visits Steltendorff and sets him straight. He also tells Eberhard about his visit to Trude but he no longer has any objection to their match. Both sets of couples are reconciled. The fate of the coat remains unknown.

Love between the rich and poor was a frequent theme in Hollywood movies, especially during the silent era, but it doesn't seem to have resonated much with German moviegoers considering how seldom it comes up (though you do have the occasional "royalty in disguise meets nice commoner girl" scenario). The Third Reich claimed that Nazism had made classes irrelevant. Trude is certainly a passive character; an American heroine would have had a little more spunk. The little shop girl just seems to accept her low place on the totem pole. She has no reason to do Margit any favors but she does, even though she ends up getting fired as a result. Apparently, when one of your betters asks you to do something, you meekly comply. Again, when the baron comes calling, she caves in to his demands almost immediately. In the end, the whole issue is just shrugged off with the baron acknowledging what a sweetheart Trude is, mainly because she knows her place and is willing to give Eberhard up.

The casting of Viktoria von Ballasko as Trude pretty much seals the deal: she often played put-upon wives and girlfriends. Here the camera lingers in soft focus on her face; her expression is often tearful and full of noble self-sacrifice. The *New York Times* reviewer got it exactly right (even though he misidentifies the actress): "She suffers in real Ann Harding style throughout the picture." The character's submissive qualities are perfectly in keeping with the Third Reich's idea of womanhood.

Ball im Metropol has an attractive cast of popular performers. Heinz von Cleve (Eberhard), the "handsomest man at Ufa" (according to his publicity), does well in his scenes with Heinrich George. This is not surprising given that they were friends and von Cleve very much admired the older actor. After *Ball*, von Cleve went on tour with George in the play *The Mayor of Zalamea*. In the postwar years, von Cleve did mostly radio work but did appear on German television as well, notably in adaptations of *The Picture of Dorian Gray* (1961) and *Dracula* (1972).

Hilde Weissner (Margit) was a singer and an actress on the classical stage. She made a number of important films in the '30s, including *Traumulus* (1936) with Emil Jannings, *The Grand Duke's Finances* (1934, directed by Gustaf Gründgens) and, perhaps best of all, *The Man Who Was Sherlock Holmes* (1937) with Hans Albers.

If there is an American actor comparable in type to Franz Schafheitlin (Steltendorff), it might be George Macready, a specialist in cold-blooded characters and imperious authority figures. Schafheitlin had a very long career, starting in silent days and ending in the 1970s. Steltendorff was a typical part for him: not quite a villain but not exuding much warmth either, officious and unbending and casting a jaundiced eye at his inferiors.

Karl Platen appeared in six of Wisbar's films. A onetime stage actor, he had a busy career in silent film with conspicuous supporting roles in Fritz Lang's *Destiny* (1919, as the creepy apothecary) and Lubitsch's *Madame Du Barry* (1919, as the heroine's brother). By the '30s, he was invariably cast as household servants and spent more time than Arthur Treacher and Brandon Hurst combined opening doors, answering the phone and announcing dinner. He brought a certain warmth and loyalty to those roles, always suggesting the kindly long-time family retainer (or at least the cinematic version of same). He was given a slightly larger role in *Ferryman Maria* playing the old ferryman who is claimed by the Grim Reaper.

On March 5, 1938, *New York Times* reviewer Frank Nugent described the film as "far from original in subject matter [but] excellent acting by a competent cast, headed by Heinrich George, and some nice city and country scenes in the Germany of about 1900 combine to make it fairly interesting."

Although Hitler reputedly liked the film, Dr. Goebbels was not impressed and described it in his diary: "Idea good, actors good too, but weak, excessively insistent direction. No pace."

In spite of the quote at the beginning of this essay, Wisbar's direction seems detached as though he's not particularly interested in the story. He dwells on the singing and dancing at the ball, the splendid setting of the hotel, the fancy cafés and later even the equestrian show. He doesn't seem in a hurry to get back to the unimaginative storyline. Overall the film is like many made during the Third Reich: superficial, somewhat frivolous entertainment meant to distract the mass of German moviegoers from what was happening around them and issues far more serious than the contrived misunderstandings and inter-class romance that make up the plot of *Ball im Metropol*.

Petermann ist dagegen!
(Petermann Is Against It!)

Aka *Er ist dagegen* (*He Is Against It*)
Neucophon-Tonfilm Produktion/Terra Filmkunst
Censored on November 19, 1937
Premiered on January 14, 1938
76 minutes

Cast: F.W. Schröder-Schrom as August Hartmann; Ernst Waldow as Julius Petermann; Fita Benkhoff as Hanne Krüger; Johannes Barthel as Gretner the chauffeur; Olaf Varnhorn as Karl the apprentice; Berthold Ebbecke as Hans Merk; Walter Gross as Hubert Herbert Horn; Hilde Schneider as Lotte Kern; Beppo Brem as Sepp Stadler; Hugo Fischer-Köppe as Wily Scholz; Karl Platen as "Uncle" Ernst the steward; Franz Jan Kossak as Fredrichs; Marjan Lex as Miss Hüttel; S.O. Schoening as Neffke.

Credits: Director: Frank Wisbar (as Frank Wysbar); Script: Alf Teichs, Otto Bernhard Wendler, Frank Wisbar (as Frank Wysbar); Based on the 1936 play *Petermann fährt nach Madeira* (*Petermann Goes to Madeira*) by August Hinrichs; Producer: Fred Lyssa; Line Producer: Hans Tost; Art Director: Erich Czerwonski, Music: Wolfgang Zeller; Photography: Erich Claunigk.

Frank Wisbar's last film in Nazi Germany was a "message" movie in the guise of a comedy. It is one of the relatively small number of Third Reich films that was intended as out-and-out propaganda. As such, Wisbar was unhappy about making it, a feeling shared by his wife Eva. It was certainly a preview of the kind of projects he would be faced with if he elected to stay in Germany. Nevertheless, while he had little choice in the matter, the location shooting at sea and off the coast of Norway gave Wisbar an excuse to delay the forced divorce proceedings against Eva.

The movie is largely an advertisement for the KdF, Kraft durch Freude program (Strength Through Joy) sponsored by the German Labor Front, the union to which all German workers were obligatory members after Hitler banned the trade unions. The Labor Front's main function was not to represent its members but rather to ensure that production went smoothly. However, this did mean at least attempting to make sure the labor force was not too discontent. The KdF, started only ten months after Hitler came to power, was aimed at giving workers something to do in their leisure time (workers got five vacation days a year, generous by the standards of the day). The KdF arranged day trips and excursions to museums, plays, sporting events and concerts. Trains were even sent to remote areas to pick up people and bring them into town for a day of recreation. All of this was done at little or no charge to the beneficiaries. Millions participated and many clearly appreciated that, for once, government—which had hitherto ignored them—seemed to be concerned about their needs.

Of course, the

Er ist dagegen!—Petermann (Ernst Waldow, top left) is against it but Hilde Schneider (top right) and Fita Benkhoff (bottom) are all for it.

motivation behind the program was not entirely benign. There was concern that workers, given unstructured leisure time, might get into political trouble. Giving them something tangible and fun to do would certainly ingratiate them to the Third Reich. Also, the productivity of the average worker was surprisingly low so it was thought that vacations and holidays would re-energize people once they returned to their jobs. And of course, participation in the KdF was not a matter of choice; abstainers would risk finding themselves on a list of troublemakers and end up making a trip of a very different sort than the ones promoted by the KdF.

The KdF jackpot was getting a cruise to Scandinavia or Madeira (off the coast of Portugal). The fees for such trips, while modest, were still beyond the range of many workers so relatively few were able to take advantage of them (one in 20 according to one estimate) and there was some cynicism that such cruises were still just for "big shots." The notion of rich and poor mingling together on a cruise was in keeping with Nazi propaganda that they had achieved a society where class distinctions were irrelevant; there was only the "Volk," the people. The program was extensively advertised and the subject of newsreels and magazine articles. Two workers who had been lucky enough to win a Madeira cruise wrote a glowing article about their vacation and also noted that the workers of Madeira lived in wretched conditions, unlike their German counterparts.

The play *Petermann Goes to Madeira* was written by August Hinrichs, whose rural comedies were very popular. His *Krach um Jolanthe* (*The Fuss About Jolanthe*), a favorite of Hitler's, was made into a 1934 film that won awards and was touted as "outstandingly cultural" even though the title character was a pig. Hinrichs, a loyal Nazi, occasionally did serious work like the anti–Christian blood and soil epic *De Stedinge* which was staged outdoors and was well-liked by the SS.

According to articles in the *Hamburger Anzeiger* (August 21 and 22, 1937), Wisbar and scenarist Otto Bernhard Wendler prepared for *Petermann* by going incognito on an actual KdF cruise to Norway. Wisbar wondered what would happen if he behaved like the curmudgeonly Petermann does in the story. At breakfast, Wisbar found a note on the menu: "8 AM—Report for the deck march." Wisbar declined, saying, "I don't exercise on vacation." No notice was taken of his refusal. He did eventually go on deck and, taken in hand by a little girl, marched around the deck several times as the band played on. The music then turned into a waltz and the deck became a dance floor with hundreds of couples participating. The film was later shot on another cruise with the 900 guests acting as extras.

Wisbar's movie begins with Julius Petermann walking to work. A huge crowd waits docilely on a street corner for the traffic cop to give them the signal to cross. Petermann ignores them and steps out into the street, where he nearly collides with a bicyclist. The policeman gives him a ticket but Petermann is not sorry; after all, the day before there was no traffic officer and he crossed at will, so why should things have changed? This is one of a number of scenes that depict Petermann as a stubborn man totally and unreasonably out of step with the times.

Petermann is the chief accountant for a large firm. He dresses formally and conservatively, no matter what the circumstances; not a hair is ever out of place and his moustache is always neatly trimmed. While his co-workers are enthusiastic about the KdF, Petermann doesn't see the point. "Joy," he grouses, "is a private matter," and this emphasis on recreation interferes with work. The firm's employees regard Petermann's attitude with a certain bemusement but he has an ongoing battle with Hanne, the woman who runs the canteen. Of course, in Germany, as in Hollywood, this means they will fall in love as any regular moviegoer will easily guess.

The KdF sponsors a day trip to the country and a dance for the workers. Petermann attends but sits by himself and doesn't join in the fun. To his surprise, he gets a winning raffle ticket for one of the cruises. To no one's surprise, Hanne also gets a ticket. Petermann is unhappy about having to go on the cruise at all, much less with Hanne, but his supervisor convinces him to participate. Petermann insists that he will take his work with him.

Petermann boards the huge cruise ship (it's actually *Der Deutsche*, the very first KdF liner) and meets his bunkmates, all of whom are good-natured and looking forward to the trip. The passengers are from all walks of life: workers, librarians, chauffeurs, secretaries. The only notable on board is the business tycoon Hartmann, accompanied by his secretary and accountant. Petermann runs into Hanne and is a bit scandalized that her shipboard outfit reveals her thighs. Petermann of course is still dressed for work.

In the film, the cruise is actually headed for the coast of Norway, not Madeira. Presumably, Madeira would have been a budget breaker and almost certainly would have had to include at least a sequence or two on land. No matter as getting there is all the fun. There is constant activity aboard ship ranging from organized games to marching bands. The passengers are forever singing and dancing and holding hands in one big love fest. All the cruise lacks are Mickey Mouse and Donald Duck. In reality, the cruises weren't quite so lavish. Bathroom and shower facilities were not in proportion to the large number of guests and there were also complaints about favoritism and the fact that Party lapdogs were given the choice rooms.

In any case, nothing dampens the enthusiasm of the movie's passengers even when some turbulence causes sea sickness. Everyone quickly bounces back and good humor is restored even without the aid of Dramamine. In the midst of all the joy, there's also a subplot about a secretary's romantic encounter with a young man, which, in spite of a few minor obstacles, ends happily.

Petermann, still uncomfortable and grumpy, tries to do his accounting work but all the music and hoopla distract him. He loses his way in the ship and can't find the dining hall. When he finally does get his bearings, dinner is over and—in an image that perfectly (and amusingly) captures Petermann's situation—the accountant has to struggle through the crowd going upstairs while he is attempting to go down. He finally succeeds and ends up eating in the vast hall all by himself. If this were one of the "great man" movies so beloved by Dr. Goebbels, Petermann's refusal to become one of the herd would be celebrated. But Petermann is not Diesel or Carl Peters but a little man, and his "greatness" must consist in conforming to the norms of the new society. We know that in the end he will be like "Hot Lips" Houlihan after she sheds Frank Burns in *MASH*.

As the ship approaches the rugged and stunning coast of Norway, the passengers gather to watch a life-saving demonstration. A dummy is thrown into the water to be "rescued." Petermann, as usual, is not with the group and when, from another part of the ship, he sees the dummy in the water, he mistakenly thinks it's a real person and dives in to save him. Of course, then it's Petermann who must be rescued by the crew. The passengers all have a good laugh at the accountant's expense, but Hanne loudly points out that Petermann is really a hero as he risked his own life to try to save another. The jeers quickly become cheers and Petermann becomes the toast of the ship.

Since his usual outfit is drenched, Petermann is obliged to put on some slightly ill-fitting but cruise-appropriate white clothing. Suddenly he is Scrooge on Christmas morning, a totally new man. He good-naturedly participates in all the hijinks aboard ship including a competition in which Hanne feeds him milk from a baby bottle (Freudians take note). Petermann later declares his love for Hanne and the last shot of the film is of the Nazified Love Boat, all lit up, making its way through the night.

Petermann, of course, is not a serious critic of Nazi society. He doesn't object that there are no Jews aboard and that individual liberties have been suppressed and the labor unions dismantled. His complaints are basically trivial, the harrumphing of a curmudgeon, the sort of character who would have objected to automobiles replacing horses. Had this been a more serious film, Petermann perhaps would have been depicted as a burnt-out case watching helplessly from the sidelines as the new order marches past him. But this a comedy—and propaganda—so it must only be a matter of time until Petermann joins the crowd and is no longer "against it."

Dr. Goebbels was generally opposed to specific references to the Nazi Party in film, fearing that audiences would be turned off by too-obvious propaganda, but *Petermann* appears to be an exception. One of Petermann's bunkmates introduces himself with a cheery "Heil Hitler." The Nazi flag is very much in evidence on the ship and a large swastika is in the foreground when the captain makes a speech encouraging the passengers to be respectful of each other and cooperative in participating in the on-board activities.

One Nazi reference you do not see in the film is the portrait of Adolf Hitler that was on display during the dinner room sequence. During filming, Wisbar removed it but after lunch it was back up again. Wisbar took it down a second time and was confronted by a Gestapo agent who had been posing as an extra. The spy threatened Wisbar with arrest for insulting Der Führer. However, Wisbar thought fast and, summoning up even more indignation than the Gestapo man, spoke directly to the 500 cast members who were gathered for the scene and who had witnessed the confrontation: "Don't you realize that if the portrait would hang there the audience would concentrate on it, and if so, they would not be able to capture the sense of this important scene? And furthermore, we would do our Führer wrong because he would not have our undivided attention. Do you really call it an offense if I insist on that?" The crowd responded with a loud *"No!"* The discomfited spy had to apologize but it was another reminder for Wisbar how little the authorities trusted him.

Ernst Waldow's performance as Petermann is undoubtedly the most enjoyable part of the film though it wasn't much of a stretch for the actor as he became known in the '30s for his comic portrayals of fussbudgets and pompous, officious characters. Waldow had a long career on the classical stage and made his first film in 1916 as the tutor in Paul Wegener's *Rübezahl's Hochzeit/Rübezahl's Wedding*. In films he was invariably cast in supporting roles. Indeed, there are no real stars in *Petermann* though it is populated with well-liked character performers. According to *Der Spiegel* (October 6, 1964), Waldow had played in almost 200 films by the time of his death in 1964.

Fita Benkhoff (Hanne), like Waldow, had essayed serious roles (Desdemona, Marguerite) on the stage but played mostly comic supporting parts in film. She was also a singer and does one tune in *Petermann*. She had a very long postwar career on stage and screen as well. One of her last parts was as one of the dotty Brewster sisters in *Arsenic and Old Lace* and she was preparing to do *Madwoman of Chaillot* when she died in 1967.

No Wisbar film would be complete without Karl Platen, here playing a ship's steward.

When *Petermann* premiered in St. Pauli at the Schauberg Theater, Waldow and Wisbar were in attendance and received applause from the audience. Waldow, who was well-known there from his appearances on the Hamburg Kammerspiele stage, made a speech about the film and paid tribute to actor Hugo Fischer-Köppe (who played Willy the bus driver in *Petermann*), who had just died.

The reviewer for the *Altonaer Nachrichten* (January 29, 1938) found the film to be a "warm-hearted, sentimental little story" that Wisbar inserted unobtrusively into a realistic depiction of a KdF trip. Carl Düsterdieck of the *Hamburger Nachrichten* described it as "lively and moving, both cheerful and serious." The reviewer was grateful that Wisbar filmed during a real cruise and did not attempt to do the movie in a studio. "The audience will feel this plot is taken from reality and it will echo in their hearts." The writer also praised Wisbar, Waldow and Fita Benkhoff ("natural and spirited").

According to Eva Wisbar, Dr. Goebbels was very dissatisfied with *Petermann Ist dagegen* and might even have banned it if not for the money that had already been spent on it. Perhaps he needn't have worried as other sources say the public stayed away, perhaps wary of sitting through something that was supposed to be good for them.

Women in Bondage
Monogram Pictures
Previewed on October 16, 1943
Released on January 10, 1944
72 minutes

Cast: Gail Patrick as Margot Bracken; Nancy Kelly as Toni Hall; Bill Henry as Corp. Heinz Radtke; Tala Birell as Ruth Bracken; Gertrude Michael as Gertrude Schneider; Alan Baxter as Otto Bracken; Maris Wrixon as Grete Ziegler; Rita Quigley as Herta Ruman; Felix Basch as Dr. Mensch; H.B. Warner as Pastor Renz; Anne Nagel as Deputy; Mary Forbes as Gladys Bracken; Frederick Brunn as District Leader; Ralph Linn as Corporal Mueller; Francine Bordeaux as Litzl; Aune Franks as Blonde; Gisela Werbiseck as Herta's Grandmother.

Credits: Director: Steve Sekely; Screenplay: Houston Branch; Original Story: Frank Wisbar (as Frank Bentick Wisbar); Executive Producer: Trem Carr; Producer: Herman Millakowsky; Associate Producer: Jeffrey Bernerd; Photography: Mack Stengler; Art Director: Dave Milton; Editor: Richard Currier; Assistant Directors: William Strohbach, Eddie Davis; Dialogue Direction: Harold Erickson; Music: Edward Kay; Sound: Tom Lambert; Makeup: Fred Walker; Technical Advisor: Frank Wisbar.

> You'll want to scream STOP as they wantonly destroy an innocent girl!"
> —tagline for *Women in Bondage*

Frank Wisbar's first solid American movie credit was this low-budget anti–Nazi film for which he wrote the original story and acted as technical advisor. The movie's producer Herman Millakowsky had worked in Germany but, being Jewish, left for Paris when the Nazis took over. When France fell to the Third Reich, he and his family fled to Casablanca and from there to the United States. Hungarian director Steve Sekely, who had made films both in his native land and Germany, was also Jewish and left Europe for the safety of America. Publicity for *Women in Bondage* emphasized that it was the work of people who escaped the Nazi terror and could be expected to draw upon their own experiences for a realistic look at life and love under Hitler's Germany: "The men who produced this film actually saw it happen. The picture was written and directed by refugee eyewitnesses." Millakowsky was quoted as saying, "We are not fictionalizing; we are telling the truth," and it was alleged that he gathered material for the film in Germany, Austria and France. It was sometimes mentioned that Wisbar was able to get out of Germany by "a ruse." In spite of all these bona fides, what ended on the screen smacked more of Hollywood than Nazi Germany.

As recent film histories have pointed out, Hollywood was slow to rally against the Nazi banner in the '30s. The German market was lucrative. Isolationism—and hence reluctance to take sides—was a real force in American politics, and censors argued that if anti–Nazi films were allowed, then pro–Nazi films would have to be tolerated as well. There was leftish opposition in LaLaLand to Nazism but it waxed or waned according to what was happening in Moscow. Anti-Fascist films were often disguised as period pieces. William Dieterle, an ardently anti–Nazi German director, helmed three such films, *The Life of Emile Zola*, *Juarez* and the 1939 *The Hunchback of Notre Dame* (wherein gypsies pretty much stand in for the Jews as victims of racist oppression). And of course, there was the notable exception of Warners' *Confessions of a Nazi Spy*.

However, it wasn't until the U.S. entered the war that American movies suddenly discovered how awful the Nazis were and the wheels of propaganda began grinding out diatribes against the Third Reich via war movies, espionage thrillers and melodramas of all descriptions. In the latter category is RKO's *Hitler's Children* (1943), made for a little under $200,000 but grossing three million. Producers took note. If *Hitler's Children* drew people to the theater, why not use the even more salable title *Hitler's Women*? Reputedly, Herman Millakowsky beat out producer Walter Wanger by a mere two hours in copyrighting the title.

Even though Monogram didn't want anyone else using the title *Hitler's Women*, there were some doubts about how long it would remain viable. Right after the film wrapped on August 23, 1943 (after a two-week shooting schedule), it was reported in *Film Daily* that Monogram wanted to take out a $100,000 insurance policy just in case Hitler was overthrown before the film was released. The article reported that the studio was having trouble finding an underwriter even though the movie was just a few months away from being shown and Monogram feared that if Der Führer met his end before that, the movie's title would no longer be "timely." The studio spent $14,000 on additional scenes just in case and picked *Women in Bondage* as an alternate title. The idea that Hitler's generals would continue the war even after his death turns up in *The Strange Death of Adolf Hitler* (1943). Even though Hitler would survive another two years, Monogram still ended up using *Women in Bondage* as the movie's final title. "Hitler's Women" was often used as a tagline and in publicity.

Wisbar had sold couple of stories to Herman Millakosky around the same time as *Women in Bondage*. The stories, *Desert Comedy* and *Immortal Spring*, did not go before the cameras. Possibly Wisbar and Millakowsky knew each other from their film careers in Germany.

Both *Women in Bondage* and *Hitler's Children* deal with *Lebensborn*, the Nazi program to ensure that as many "pure-blood Aryan" children as possible be produced for the Third Reich. Women were told that their greatest duty to the Fatherland was to propagate and that marriage, however desirable, need not be the sole context for motherhood. Single women were encouraged to get pregnant by SS men and, if they decided they didn't want the children after all, other SS families or special orphanages would take them. A 1961 German film, *Lebensborn* (aka *Ordered to Love*), dealt with the same subject. Both *Hitler's Children* and *Women in Bondage* seem to skirt around facing the program squarely even though it's central to their stories.

In reviewing *Women in Bondage*, the *Variety* critic remarked: "the original story of Frank Bentick Wisbar, who produced *Maidens in Uniform* in Germany, is faithfully transferred to the screen by Houston Branch." We might doubt whether the reviewer did actually read Wisbar's story but, in any case, it's not available to us so we can't be sure how closely Branch followed Wisbar's work.

This synopsis comes from a viewing of the film:

After a long absence, Margot Bracken returns to her native Germany to live with her husband Ernst's family while he serves on the Eastern Front. Ernst's mother is the same kindly soul as ever but his sister Ruth and brother Otto are fanatical Nazis and expect Margot to be a "Hitler woman." Against her will, Margot is appointed to be section leader of a group of girl Nazis by Party loyalist Gertrude Schneider. (The group is not named but is perhaps meant to be the Bund Deutscher Mädel.) The girls seem to spend most of their time marching, listening to Hitler on the radio, practicing first aid and identifying model airplanes of Allied bombers.

Margot becomes fond of her charges, especially Toni Hall, a servant in the Bracken household and engaged to marry her SS sweetheart Heinz Radtke. Margot is less enthusiastic about the arrogant Herta, who has been encouraged by Schneider to hang out with the SS even though her grandmother heartily disapproves of her wanton behavior.

Before she can marry an SS man, Toni must undergo a physical to see if she's worthy of being mated to one of Hitler's finest. The extremely unpleasant lady doctor informs her that the distance from her ear lobes to chin indicates that she has no Semitic tendencies but then she is disqualified when she flunks the eye test. Toni and Herta's grandmother appeal to Margot for help. Schneider angrily berates Margot for trying to interfere with Nazi family policy.

When Toni discovers that Heinz is quite willing to switch his affections to someone else since she is imperfect, the girl becomes hysterical. Her angry denunciation of the program causes Schneider to order her arrest but Margot successfully helps her get out of town. Toni gets captured anyway and, though tortured and whipped, she refuses to tell who helped her escape. Schneider strongly suspects Margot. Toni is ordered sterilized but when the ambulance comes for her, she sees Heinz passing by with his new sweetheart and breaks away. The guards shoot her.

Nancy Kelly is about to become one of the *Women in Bondage*.

When Herta's grandmother persists in objecting to her dalliance with SS men, the authorities declare her senile and she is euthanized. Margot gets into further trouble with Schneider when she arranges for SS widow Grete Ziegler to have her newborn baptized in church rather than in a SS ceremony (which involves copies of *Mein Kampf* instead of the Bible and a sword replacing holy water). The SS tries to do things their way but the courageous priest still manages to invoke Christ at the blasphemous ceremony.

Ernst Bracken returns from the war but he is physically broken and spends much of his time in bed. The local doctor examines him and determines that he is incapable of having sex. Schneider decides that since it is Margot's duty to bear children for the Reich, she is to be impregnated by Otto instead. Ernst overhears the conversation and shoots himself. Margot launches into a diatribe against the whole rotten Nazi system.

Strict blackout conditions are mandatory in the little town, which is frequently bombed by the Allies. (In case any tender-hearted soul in the viewing audience has qualms about this, we are told that there is a factory hidden in the village.) When the (stock footage) bombers come again, Margot turns on the lights in her house and opens the skylight. The house is bombed and Margot and Otto are killed. As a bonus, so are a quartet of SS men who have come to turn out the lights.

A closing recap of events reminds us that, in spite of Nazi oppression, human decency has not been extinguished in the Third Reich.

Interestingly enough, only the male bad guys and SS people get killed. The awful Schneider and Margot's fanatical sister-in-law are allowed to survive.

The similarities to *Hitler's Children* are many (and duly noted by the critics). Both deal with Nazi family policy, sterilization of "undesirables" and the need for Third Reich women to procreate. Both have scenes where a woman is whipped and both feature heroic clergyman (played by H.B. Warner in both films; if you're doing holy, you might as well hire the King of Kings) and in the end the anti–Nazi Germans sacrifice their lives in opposition to Hitler. On the plus side, *Women* lacks the "inspiring" speeches that bog down *Children*. While American viewers were fed a steady diet of Nazi villains, *Hitler's Children* and *Women in Bondage* were reminders that there were "good Germans" and not everyone in Deutschland supported Der Führer.

Frank Wisbar had seen the Nazi racial policies first-hand and suffered under them since he was obliged to divorce his Jewish wife to continue his career. The Jewish racial laws and the trouble they brought to couples where one partner was Jewish could have made for a very powerful indictment of the Nazi system but nothing like that is brought up in the film. While it's tempting to speculate that Wisbar omitted this because his own behavior at the time was less than heroic, it should be noted that even the most fervent anti–Nazi films of the day rarely mentioned the Jews at all.

Perhaps a more serious fault—at least from a historical perspective—is the role of Gertrude Schneider. The SS did indeed have a women's auxiliary but they did mainly office work, answering the phone and other mundane secretarial chores for the SS (though some were employed as guards in the death camps). They certainly did not have any kind of command positions and would not have been in charge of ordering the men around like Schneider does in the film. Even the character of the woman doctor is dubious as the Reich had driven most women from the professions. Wisbar was well aware of all this but perhaps found the idea of an SS villainess on the silver screen offbeat enough to be engaging (the same could probably be said of Lina Wertmüller's *Seven Beauties*). However, the story gets other things right; even the bizarre Nazi baptism is based on fact (Himmler's elite could not marry without his permission and SS babies were indeed christened wrapped in a Nazi banner).

Reviews were overall favorable, especially when you consider that the film hailed from lower echelon Hollywood. The *Los Angeles Times* critic had much praise for the film when it previewed on November 11, 1943:

> A strong brief for the fortitude of women under great stress is promulgated in *Women in Bondage* which is an exceptionally fine study of conditions under the Nazi rule in Germany. The picture abstractly and almost coldly presents the whole problem of their subjugation, which takes no account of their sentiment and inner yearnings, but forces the dedication of their lives to the Reich.... The action is so unmoviesque that you become oblivious to all else except what goes on in the picture itself, no matter what the distractions. In fact, this picture reaches far beyond such a film as *Hitler's Children*, a feature of similar theme, in its earnestness and sincerity.

When the film opened in Los Angeles, another reviewer was also impressed: From the March 3 *Los Angeles Times* review: "Subjection of love and decent family relations to creation of the "master race" is shown without too many melodramatic trimmings which fact gives the picture an almost documentary quality."

At Los Angeles' Hawaii Theater, the film broke all records. The theater's huge electric roof sign announcing *Hitler's Women* was no doubt helpful in drawing the crowds.

Marjorie Kelly of *The Washington Post* found the film melodramatic and not fit for children even though it carried out its theme "with all possible delicacy" (September 3, 1943). However, Kelly opined it could have taken a more sophisticated approach:

> It would be interesting to have more films of this sort, particularly if emphasis were put, not upon melodramatic plot, but upon characterization, upon the attempt to

explain what makes a Hitler woman tick, how race persecution and moral laxity are rationalized and how decent Germans feel about the abuses. Of all the aspects of this world conflict, the least explored in the films has been the position of people inside Germany who do not like the Nazis. That is what makes *Women in Bondage* important.

The *New York Times* wasn't sold. From their March 27, 1944, review:

> A somewhat belated film about conditions inside Germany. Incidentally, and in fairness to the producers, this Monogram production is by no means as cheaply sensational as the exploitation display which adorns the marquee and outer lobby of the theater.... In rather flat reportorial style, this film is hardly a startling revelation since *Hitler's Children* did the same. Nor have the producers of *Women in Bondage* treated with dramatic conviction the romantic theme involving an SS trooper and his sweetheart.

Motion Picture Herald (November 20, 1943) thought the film "a painstakingly produced melodrama [with] all performances taking a somewhat measured pace from Steve Kelly's [sic] direction which is geared to a script heavily underscored for purposes of documentary effect. The film reflects extreme care and an expanded budget. Should be adults only." *Harrison's Reports* (November 6, 1943) likewise considered the picture not for children even though the barbaric Nazi practices "have been handled in an inoffensive manner." According to *Showmen's Trade Review* (November 20, 1943):

> Endowed with fine direction and splendid characterizations, this is a top offering for many situations. Though slow in tempo it will nevertheless provide entertainment for those patrons who like dramatic fare. The title is a natural, especially to attract women[!]. The story though lacking in romance as we know it will keep the spectator absorbed.

Variety (November 21, 1943) did not think Sekely's direction showed much originality but predicted that the film would do well and had a number of exploitable angles. Some of those angles were taken to the max when the film was shown at Milwaukee's Palace Theater. The hoopla was worthy of a Hollywood premiere: Usherettes were garbed as Hitler Youth and ushers as storm troopers. In the lobby, patrons were treated to the sight of a disheveled young lady lying prone on a dais under a large swastika and the words "She has served the Reich."

Scenes showing Toni and the other girls walking around the examining room only covered by sheets go on for longer than strictly necessary and seem geared to invoke a sick prurient interest. In other circumstances, the censors would have worked their blue pencils to the nub over the subject matter but because it was wartime and the story anti–Nazi, the film was given a pass. Its posters and ads were often very lurid and anticipated those men's magazine covers showing nubile young women being tortured by Nazis. Even though the '40s were more innocent times, the use of "bondage" in the title may have been meant to have a sexual undertone as well. However, the term was found to have other uses too and war bond sales in connection with the film sometimes used the line: "Save our men and women from bondage. Buy bonds."

Reviewers praised the film's acting. Gail Patrick convincingly goes from someone initially willing to give the Third Reich the benefit of the doubt (she thinks Toni surely must be mistaken about not being allowed to marry Heinz because of her myopia) to a growing horrified realization that the Nazis have abandoned all morality. Patrick was a grade A actress at Paramount in the '30s; when she left to freelance, she sometimes found herself doing films like *Women in Bondage*. Due to health reasons and other interests (including designing children's clothing), Patrick largely quit acting in the late '40s. She later produced the popular TV series *Perry Mason*.

The *Los Angeles Times* was particularly impressed with Gertrude Michael's performance as Schneider and lamented that she didn't turn up in the movies more regularly. Michael frequently played dubious characters and outright villainesses (as in the 1936 version of *Forgotten Faces*). Her Schneider is a typical Hollywood Nazi: cold-blooded, almost automaton-like in her lack of emotion and constantly spouting Third Reich propaganda. She later appeared in a number of episodes of Wisbar's *Fireside Theater*.

A pig-tailed Nancy Kelly is more cloying than poignant as poor Toni. She reputedly hated the part—and gets stuck with the clunkiest lines. A scene where she wanders the street attempting to prove she's not Mr. Magoo and really does have good vision is unintentionally funny. An actress from childhood, Kelly was more stage than film thespian as an adult. Her biggest success was probably in the Broadway and movie versions of *The Bad Seed* wherein she played the mother who probably would have preferred sterilization to giving birth to a soulless murderess.

Viennese-born Tala Birell (Ruth Bracken) had considerable success on the stage in Germany in the early '30s. She made a few films, perhaps most notably E.A. Dupont's *Menschen im Käfig* (*Caged Men*) with Conrad Veidt. Universal's Carl Laemmle, Jr., signed her in 1932 and it was announced that a variety of projects were being planned for her: *She*, *Revolt* (in which she would play a spy in India), *The Red Pawn* by Ayn Rand and *Russian Woman*. None of these projects came to pass and the only films Birell ended up doing for Junior Laemmle were *The Doomed Battalion* and the bizarre *Nagana* (from all reports, a wildly melodramatic yarn about the search for the cure for African sleeping sickness which somehow involved Birell getting sacrificed to the crocodiles!). Birell left Universal for Columbia where she played mostly supporting roles. By the '40s, she was doing bottom-of-the-bill pictures like *The Frozen Ghost*, *Isle of Forgotten Sins* and *The Monster Maker*. Her postwar career was considerably more distinguished and involved organizing theater for American G.I.s and refugees in Berlin.

Women in Bondage came in with a budget of $104,000, a superproduction by Monogram standards, and it earned at least a million dollars. Nineteen forty-three proved to be a good year for Monogram as their exploitation picture *Where Are Your Children?* also did very well.

While *Women in Bondage* was hardly a prestige picture, it did get noticed and no doubt was helpful in moving Frank Wisbar along on his modest American film career.

Strangler of the Swamp
PRC
Released on January 1, 1946
60 minutes

Cast: Rosemary La Planche as Maria Hart; Robert Barrat as Christian Sanders; Blake Edwards as Chris Sanders; Charles Middleton as Ferryman Douglas; Effie Parnell as Martina Sanders; Nolan Leary as Pete Jeffers; Frank Conlan as Joseph Hart; Theresa Lyon as Bertha; Virginia Farmer as Anna Jeffers; Chris Drake as George.

Credits: Director: Frank Wisbar; Original Story: Frank Wisbar, Leo J. McCarthy; Additional Dialogue: Harold Erickson; Dialogue Director: Harold Erickson; Assistant Director: Harold Knox; Associate Producer: Raoul Pagel; Photography: James S. Brown, Jr.; Art Director: Edward C. Jewell; Editor: Hugh Winn; Set Decorator: Glenn P. Thompson; Music: Alexander Steinert; Sound: Frank Webster; Director of Makeup: Bud Westmore.

> [I did] mostly horror pictures…. The kind where a loft opens and a host of bats fly out. My wife wanted to watch a dandy on television the other night. It was called *Strangler of the Swamp* and I almost knocked the furniture over getting to the TV to turn it off. I knew all about the film because it was one of mine.
> —Frank Wisbar, interviewed by George Condon, May 11, 1953

> Obviously, *Strangler of the Swamp* is no masterpiece but it is a masterpiece of classy shoestring budget shooting.
> —William K. Everson, "Program Notes on *Ferryman Maria* and *Strangler of the Swamp*," May 8, 1987

Frank Wisbar's first Hollywood movie as a director was a reworking of his greatest film *Ferryman Maria*, not that anyone recognized it as such. *Ferryman Maria* had played briefly in New York City, opening on Christmas Eve of 1938 at the Casino Theater, one of the few venues left for German movies. It was reviewed only in the *New York Times* and *National Board of Review Magazine*. The January 4, 1940, *Times* announced that the Museum of Modern Art had acquired a number of foreign films for its collection, including *Maidens in Uniform* and the "lesser known" *Ferryman Maria*. Both films were subsequently shown at the Museum. I can find no evidence that *Maria* played anywhere outside of the Big Apple. No reviewer mentioned any connection between *Maria* and *Strangler*.

Wisbar's first problem in re-doing the story for American audiences was turning it from a fantasy into a horror film. Having Death as a character in the story was not going to fly. The personification of the Grim Reaper was common enough in the German silent era (and not unknown in Hollywood films of those days as well) but would hardly be viable for 1940 viewers. True, Fredric March in *Death Takes a Holiday* (1934) and Cedric Hardwicke in *On Borrowed Time* (1939) provided precedents but these were films based on popular plays. Death as a bogeyman in a second feature horror film was likely to seem comical. Wisbar decided to substitute a vengeful ghost, which was itself kind of a risky move. Ghosts were usually played for laughs and when they were part of a mystery film they often turned out to be fakes with the Scooby-Dos of their day ferreting them out. The one serious Hollywood ghost story of the mid-1940s, *The Uninvited* (1944), had no imitators. Indeed, some reviews of *Strangler* expressed pleasant surprise that there was no last reel twist revealing the supernatural events as having a human origin.

The notion of a person condemned to death cursing his executioners and returning from the grave to wreak vengeance became a staple of horror movies in the 1960s after *Black Sunday* and *Horror Hotel* but it was quite uncommon in 1946. (Wisbar did a variation on it for his script for *Rimfire*; see entry.) "God will give you blood to drink" was a curse on her judge uttered by a "witch" about to be hanged during the Salem witch hunts (Nathaniel Hawthorne borrowed the line for *The House of the Seven Gables*). We don't see the execution of the wrongly accused ferryman of *Strangler* but are told how he uttered his dire malediction just before he was hanged.

Ferryman Maria begins with a written (and sung) description of what the film is all about. *Strangler* likewise opens with a mood-setting explanation but one that is considerably less poetic than its predecessor:

> Old legends—strange tales—never die in the lonely swampland. Villages and hamlets lie remote and almost forgotten. Small ferryboats glide between the shores, and the ferryman is a very important person. Day and night, he is at the command of his passengers. On his little barge ride the good and the evil; the friendly and the hostile; the superstitious and the enlightened; the living and—sometimes—the dead.

The little (unnamed) village by the swamp has been under a curse ever since the execution years before of Ferryman Douglas, who was accused of fatally stabbing a farmer. The testimony of villager Joseph Hart was instrumental in condemning him. Douglas was lynched but before he died he pronounced sentence on the necktie party members: He proclaimed that he would return to strangle them all and their descendants. Since then, a number of those under the curse have died by strangulation though the circumstances are ambiguous enough for doubters to declare the deaths accidents. The latest victim was found entangled in the weeds while swimming. The women of the village believe he was killed by the Strangler but most of the men are skeptical, particularly Christian Sanders, the little town's most prominent citizen and himself a member of the lynching party.

Martina, Christian's wife, and a couple of the other women decide it's time to take down Douglas' noose, which has hung from the hanging tree as a warning ever since. Joseph Hart, who replaced Douglas as ferryman, brings them over to the spot but doesn't want them to remove the noose. However, it falls on him, causing him to collapse in fear. As the ferry returns to the village, we learn from the women that it is commonly believed that the curse will only end when one of the cursed individuals willingly offers himself to the Strangler. When the ladies suggest Joseph make the sacrifice because he's on in years, he dismisses the whole notion: "I'm only 70, not old for a man. I have plans for the future. My grandchild will come—take over the ferry and I'll have time to do what I've always wanted, plant sugar cane." The women of Swampville are not impressed by Joseph's hope to go from ferryman to farmer and lament the fact that none of their men have the nobility to do the right thing.

Later that night when he is alone in his small hut by the ferry, Joseph takes a piece of paper from his Bible and prepares to burn it. The sound of the gong announcing that someone wishes to cross from the other side interrupts him and he replaces the paper (which we later learn is a confession to the murder for which Douglas was executed). Joseph is confronted by the ghost of the ferryman: "Douglas, have you risen from the dead?" exclaims the old man, stating the obvious. Joseph is strangled when the ferry rope he has tossed toward the dock ends up around his neck, throttling him as the ferry continues on its way.

A few days later, Christian is going through Joseph's meager belongings with the help of Jeffers, the town misfit who seems to be the only male who believes in the curse. They are interrupted by the arrival of Maria, Joseph's beautiful granddaughter. They tell her that her grandfather died peacefully ("Just slipped over to a better world"). Maria spends a few days in Christian's house where she is fussed over by Martina. Martina has taken the hangman's noose to the ruined church the village is trying to re-build. She ties it to the bell rope in the hopes that being in a sacred spot will somehow work against the Strangler's power.

Maria decides to replace her grandfather as ferryman. Christian has convinced the rest of the townsfolk not to tell her about the Strangler legend or how the old man really died. He also finds Joseph's confession, which means that he and his companions lynched an innocent man.

Christian's son Chris comes back to the village having spent three years at agricultural school. (He's returned because he "misses the smell of swamp water.") He and Maria quickly fall in love. Chris expresses fear about Maria being alone at night but she tells him she likes her job and the swamp: "The swamp makes me think of fairy tales, so lovely. Any minute you expect beautiful old legends to come to life." Chris proposes and Maria accepts and they plan to announce their engagement at the upcoming Halloween dance. Maria doesn't want to give up her job as ferryman: "It's been too much like my life. Going back and forth from shore to shore, never resting, never stopping."

Christian, exasperated by all the talk about the Strangler, considers the possibility of draining the swamp, using the money allocated to restore the church. Martina is shocked by his suggestion but he tells her he is going to bring it up at his speech at the Halloween dance. Christian firmly rejects Chris' plan to marry Maria, telling the boy she has a murderer in her family. Chris responds that there's one in his family too, namely his father who helped hang an innocent man.

From her hut, Maria hears Chris cry out. She finds him caught in a noose intended as a deer trap. She rescues him and brings him to her cabin. Badly hurt, he babbles on about the Strangler. Maria gets on the ferry and heads for the other shore to get the doctor but she is joined by the Strangler, who pulls the ferry back to the village. Even though no one has told Maria about the curse, she exclaims, "I know now." The Strangler goes to Maria's hut to claim his victim but he has stumbled away. Maria rushes to the village to tell Christian what has happened. He tells her to get help while he goes to the swamp to find Chris. The Strangler supernaturally prevents anyone from hearing Maria and she rushes to the swamp. Christian has found his stricken son but the ferry has been sunk. Together with Maria, they head to the old church, knowing that a spirit cannot cross the threshold. "We must destroy him!" declares Christian, suddenly sounding like Prof. Van Helsing. He rings the church bell to summon help but the cord—actually the noose—falls off.

Chris can't breathe and is obviously dying. Maria leaves the safety of the church and willingly gives herself to the Strangler to end the curse. However, the Strangler, instead of taking her, walks away. At Maria's urging, he falls to his knees to make peace with God and is covered by a cloud of fog and disappears. Chris can breathe again and Maria joyfully tells him that the Strangler is gone forever.

In *Ferryman Maria* and the earlier Fritz Lang film *Destiny*, the heroine's sole concern is to save the life of her lover. This is to a large extent true of

Strangler but there is also the sense that the girl's sacrifice will also save the community. Such was the case in Murnau's *Nosferatu*. (In Werner Herzog's *Nosferatu* remake, the implication was that the community was perhaps not worth saving.) In *Strangler*, the ghost is not a monster of evil like Count Orlock but could be looked upon as an avenging angel out of the Old Testament, visiting the sins of the fathers upon the children. The little village labors under an unexpiated sin, the lynching of Ferryman Douglas. Even when Christian (is the name meant ironically?) discovers the truth, he does not acknowledge it before the community but instead shifts all the blame to Joseph Hart and makes Maria guilty by association, thus repeating the mission of the Strangler who makes the innocent suffer along with the guilty. As in some other Wisbar films, the women seem stronger and more righteous than their men. In offering herself to the wraith, Maria is making up for the village's guilt by making a Christ-like sacrifice. Fortunately, the Strangler—and presumably the Almighty—is satisfied by the gesture alone.

No doubt Wisbar found filming *Strangler* quite the contrast to his work on *Ferryman Maria*. For the latter, he had the magical Lüneburg Heath for a setting, the services of his favorite actress Sybille Schmitz and first-rate artists for camerawork and music. While *Ferryman* was shot almost entirely outdoors, there are only one or two simple exteriors in *Strangler* and the swamp is a soundstage with an overworked fog machine (though it's not quite true that you *never* see any water; there is one brief shot of the real thing). Instead of the exotic and mysterious Sybille Schmitz, Wisbar had beauty queen Rosemary La Planche, who looked more suited to sipping a malt in an Andy Hardy movie rather than pulling a ferry across a swamp. While we don't know the budget for *Ferryman*, it was no doubt considerably more than the reputed $20,000 for *Strangler*. According to the trade papers, *Strangler* started shooting during the first week of September 1945 and had wrapped by September 11, a very brief shooting schedule though no doubt typical of PRC.

The two Marias are of course very different. Sybille is a stranger without a homeland while Rosemary has roots in the community and seems to belong there. Wisbar managed to sneak a number of elements from *Ferryman* into his *Strangler* story. Both films have a scene where the old ferryman is alone with his thoughts in his little hut just before the gong summons him to his doom. There's no fiddler in *Strangler* but perhaps the town screw-up Jeffers is meant as a non-musical substitute. However, Carl de Vogt was a pleasant scamp in *Ferryman* while Nolan Leary's Jeffers comes off as some sort of village idiot. The scenes between Jeffers and Christian are almost excruciating to watch with the audience sharing Christian's exasperation with the fool. (It should be noted though that at least one critic praised Leary's inept performance.)

In both films, a villager makes a pass at the heroine and is rebuffed.

Much is made of the upcoming Halloween dance but then it doesn't happen. That was perhaps a budget issue but it's hard to imagine the Strangler dosey-doeing with Maria in any case. The bell sequence from *Ferryman* is repeated in *Strangler* but almost thrown away with the bell silenced not by supernatural power but because the rope has fallen off. The church in *Ferryman* is empty and gives the feeling of abandonment (even though that's not really the case; the villagers are all at the dance) but in *Strangler* the impression is one of desolation. It's not clear whether the church is merely under construction ("I want a roof over my head when I pray," complains one of the ladies) but it looks more like a ruin that's being restored. Why it would have been allowed to fall into that state isn't mentioned unless something is being implied about the spiritual aridity of the village. The two long shots we see of the church (a miniature?) don't quite match the close shots.

The overall horror atmosphere of *Strangler* is sufficiently creepy with the stylized set (fog, tree branches, weeds) working quite well, especially at night with all the swamp noises adding to the effect. It's not realistic, but succeeds in creating an eerie little world of its own (much like the village in *Horror Hotel*). The few daytime shots are less persuasive and the artificiality of the set more jarring. The film sags in the middle with only the occasional shots of the Strangler, balefully observing the romantic mush, reminding the viewer of the menace in the background. The finale with its tense pursuit of the main characters through the swamp makes up for it.

It's generally agreed by horror buffs that the Strangler should not have spoken; and, as William K. Everson put it, he just tells us what we already know. James Card, in his review of *Ferryman Maria*, had a similar complaint about the overly loquacious Grim Reaper: "Death is perfectly effective to an accompaniment of music and good lighting. When he speaks, the illusion fades. Pure horror is silent and always will be." It's sometimes said that the Strangler's lips don't move when he talks—a nicely eerie effect—but the film is not consistent in doing that. However, the camera often cuts away when he does speak, which gives the impression that his voice is coming from another world.

Reviewers generally thought the film was good enough for its type. Some typical critiques:

> Swamplands are excellent breeding places for film stories, with their eerie atmosphere and the odd characters that traditionally dwell near them. So, *Strangler of the Swamp* has a head start in these respects. In most ways, it completely lives up to its opportunities. One of the pseudo-spiritual ideas is introduced when the Strangler cannot enter the church and thus the youth is saved, its introduction seeming somehow out of key as well as hackneyed.... A serious criticism is that all the swamp dwellers seem to have accents apparently produced by teachers in Hollywood acting schools.—*Los Angeles Times* (December 31, 1945)

Strangler of the Swamp (1946)

[*Strangler*] is better in creating the eerie atmosphere of a fog-swept swamp than in maintaining suspense.... Occasionally this tale of witchcraft and an old curse becomes as foggy as the scenery when the spook of a ferryman is scaring the daylights out of natives. A couple of the murders are exciting, but it grows a bit tiresome after the "Shadow" chases Robert Barrat and his son for two reels. Although the ending seems to be one of those makeshift things, the lovely Rosemary La Planche is appealing as a pure-of-heart heroine who offers to sacrifice herself to end the ancient curse.—*Cleveland Plain Dealer* (May 25, 1946)

Routine program fare. It should serve its purpose as a supporting feature wherever audiences like spooky pictures, for it manages to give one the creeps. Since the story deals with the supernatural, it is, of course, a fantastic affair, the sort that will amuse rather than scare discriminating patrons. More than the story or the acting it is the dismal swamp settings, the low-key photography and the sudden appearances of a grotesque "ghost" character that give the picture its chilling effects. The constant danger to the heroine manages to hold one in some suspense.—*Harrison's Reports* (January 26, 1946)

Theaters which cater to the horror trade will find this picture a very satisfactory offering for their clientele. It will give their patrons their fill of spooks and eerie atmosphere with ample suspense, chills and thrills.... The acting is good and the direction by Frank Wisbar ... makes the story as believable as possible for this type of fare.—*Showmen's Trade Review* (January 5, 1946)

A fantastic story, told in horror fashion, for action fans. Robert Barrat suffers from a confusing role. Rosemary La Planche, in her first starring role, is "beautifully" miscast as the girl who returns to a swampland community to live alone and run a weird six-person ferry boat that operates on a pulley system. Direction: Fair. Photography: Falls short.—*Film Daily* (December 20, 1945)

An out-and-out ghost story that lends itself well to some emphatic theater front exploitation along "horror" lines. Wisbar's direction essentially aimed toward entertaining those audiences for whom spine-tingling incidents need not be set in a foundation of logic.—*Motion Picture Daily* (January 7, 1946)

A theater owner in Rivesville, West Virginia, was not impressed: "This is not a very good horror picture but the girl in the picture shows that she has personality. The music score was very good for a picture of this sort."

The girl, Rosemary La Planche, did indeed have a great deal of personality which she combined with her apple pie good looks to win numerous beauty contests, becoming Miss California in 1940 and 1941 in the Miss America pageant and winning the second time around. She said that her main interest in being a beauty queen was to get into the movies, thinking she'd have greater success as a somebody rather than a nobody. She later changed her mind about the wisdom of such a road to fame: "Winning a national beauty contest is a good way to get into the movies but you have a heck of a time living it down. Nobody wants to regard you as an actress." Rosemary's sister Louise, also a beauty contest winner, appeared in small parts in a number of films, beginning in 1923 with *The Hunchback of Notre Dame* (playing the little daughter of the queen), but never had any starring roles.

Rosemary—who had done bit parts as a child—won a supporting role in the hillbilly comedy *Prairie Chickens* (1943) and this led to an RKO contract. The contract, which her parents had to approve (Rosemary was just 19), called for "a salary graduating up to $1500 weekly with the stipulating that she invest 10% of her earnings in war bonds and place 25% in a trust fund." The contract didn't say RKO actually had to use her. While the studio wasn't shy about cashing in on the publicity of having Miss America as one of its actresses, La Planche ended up doing largely uncredited bits: "I never got a chance to do much over there but I learned a lot." One thing she learned was not to try to upstage the star. In *Mademoiselle Fifi*, the Robert Wise-Val Lewton film starring Simone Simon, La Planche was one of several bit players doing the laundry in the background of Simone's scene. La Planche pounded the petticoats with more enthusiasm than Gervaise paddling Virginie in *L'Assommoir* but it detracted from the main action and her scene ended up on the cutting room floor.

La Planche told John Todd Tipton, in an interview published on January 22, 1946, that she was happy to be working at PRC:

> They've given me the first opportunity to show that I can do dramatic acting. Now there will be some film to show what I can do. My agent got me the role in *Strangler of the Swamp*. It seems to have made a hit. It's been running a week downtown and already I have received 500 fan letters. I got the role in the second picture [*Devil Bat's Daughter*] because Frank Wisbar, producer and director, happened to see me walking across the PRC lot. Some folks seem to think I'm only a face and a body but Mr. Wisbar fought for me.

Reviewers were kind to La Planche's acting in her two PRC epics but it didn't lead to better things. She subsequently made a couple of serials before her film career petered out. She had a happy marriage to a radio-TV producer and busied herself with painting. In a 1977 interview, she noted "with pride" that her two starring films, *Strangler* and *Devil Bat's Daughter*, were included in a book titled *The Most Famous Horror Movies* (she probably meant William K. Everson's 1974 book *Classics of the Horror Film*). While her Maria certainly wasn't in the same league as Sybille Schmitz, she brings poignancy to her final confrontation with the Strangler and does a very moving reading of the line "Your cruel hands shall not touch him." (Unfortunately, she then reverts to her cheerleader-like persona for the admittedly lame line, "Give up the fight.")

While the Strangler was not clearly shown, no doubt moviegoers recognized his sepulchral intonation as belonging to the same actor who offered "10,000 Ming golds for the capture of Flash Gordon." Charles Middleton made countless film appearances (230 according to his *Los Angeles Times* obit), big and small, and was frequently cast as a villain, his most famous baddie being Ming the Merciless in the *Flash Gordon* serials.

Robert Barrat makes Christian likable in spite of his stubbornness and gruff manner. Barrat had a notable Broadway career in the '20s before becoming a reliable character actor in numerous films. He kept in top shape physically which no doubt served him in good stead in *Strangler* as he had to carry Blake Edwards (Chris) all around the set during the closing reels. Edwards is famous for his career as writer-producer-director of many hit comedies including the *Pink Panther* films, *Victor/Victoria*, *SOB*, *10* and *The Party*. His acting career was certainly negligible though his Chris (one of his larger film roles) is agreeable enough.

Strangler made the rounds, often paired with other PRC horrors like *Devil Bat's Daughter* and *The Flying Serpent*, before finding a niche on late night TV in the '50s and '60s. It was largely forgotten until Everson's *Classics of the Horror Film*. Everson admitted *Strangler* was far from a classic but used it as an opportunity to praise the unjustly neglected Wisbar, whose *Ferryman Maria* does indeed deserve the "classic" accolade. Everson found *Strangler* a commendable attempt to raise a Grade C horror film from the swamp of mediocrity to at least dry ground. Years later, Everson showed both movies and, in his program notes, expanded on his admiration of Wisbar. In *Poverty Row Horrors*, Tom Weaver sought to pull *Strangler* down from its modest pedestal, attacking the swamp set as palpably phony and fan admiration for Wisbar a pretentious preference for the European over the American. However, looking at the various websites and boards devoted to vintage horror, it's clear that *Strangler* has kept its admirers. It is certainly no more a great horror film than *Detour* is a great film noir but its reputation as an above-average and offbeat cheapie seems secure.

Devil Bat's Daughter

Producers Releasing Corporation
Released on April 15, 1946
67 minutes

Cast: Rosemary La Planche as Nina MacCarron; John James as Ted Masters; Michael Hale as Dr. Clifton Morris; Molly Lamont as Ellen Masters Morris; Nolan Leary as Dr. Elliot; Monica Mars as Myra Arnold; Edward Cassidy as the Sheriff; Eddie Kane as George; Frank Marlowe as the Taxi Driver; Frank Pharr.

Credits: Director and Producer: Frank Wisbar; Assistant Director: Louis Germonprez; Assistant Producer: Carl Pierson; Dialogue Director: Harold Ericson; Screenplay: Griffin Jay; Original Story: Leo J. McCarthy, Ernst Jaeger; Photography: James S. Brown, Jr.; Art Director: Edward C. Jewell; Editor:

Devil Bat's Daughter (1946) 121

Douglas Bagier; Set Decorator: Glenn P. Thompson; Costumes: Karlice; Music: Alexander Steinert; Sound: Earl Sitar; Special Effects: Ray Mercer; Makeup: Bud Westmore.

> After *Spellbound*, Hollywood fell all over itself going psychiatric. Even the quickies found gold in them thar psycho thrills and one outfit came out with this zany: *The Devil Bat's Daughter*. Why not just *Batty*?
> —Hedda Hopper's February 10, 1946 column

This film's lurid, campy title caused amusement in a number of quarters, anticipating the smirks that would greet *I Was a Teenage Werewolf* some years later. *Devil Bat's Daughter* is a sequel-of-sorts to 1940's *The Devil Bat*, a film that commands much affection in fans of vintage horror. His Daughter, however, does not. It is of course a delicious absurdity that the evil Dr. Carruthers of *Devil Bat*, a vengeful fiend who sics his monster bats on his enemies and is played to sardonic perfection by Bela Lugosi, is given a revisionist history which rehabilitates him as a misunderstood, well-meaning Henry Frankenstein type whose creation got out of control and eventually killed him as well as several others. However, no viewer in the '40s got too excited about the inconsistencies that abound in the horror films of the era. (Can *anyone* explain how Kharis the mummy sinks into a swamp in Massachusetts in *The Mummy's Ghost* only to resurface in the Louisiana bayou in *The Mummy's Curse*?) It's likely few remembered just what was what from film to film and didn't care about it any more than last week's popcorn. Modern fans of course can study these epics at their leisure on DVD and Blu-ray and pick them apart. However, the main problem today's horror mavens have with *Devil Bat's Daughter* is that it's pretty dull stuff in comparison with the original. And there's no monster.

The May 12, 1945, *Showmen's Trade Review* noted that Leo J. McCarthy, formerly the general sales manager at PRC, had been appointed producer and was planning three movies for the 1945–46 season: *Devil Bat's Daughter, Strangler of Paris* and *Lost Atlantis*. Subsequent articles reported all kinds of plans from PRC, including expanded studio facilities and more foreign sales. It was claimed that 38 features and 12 westerns had been slated for 1945–46 at a cost of $8 million, a figure that no doubt caused some mirth among those acquainted with the studio's threadbare production values and meager budgets. *Devil Bat's Daughter*, along with *Strangler of the Swamp, The Lost Continent* and *The Mummy's Daughter* (!) were all to be included in that line-up as well as plans for PRC's first color film, *The Enchanted Forest*. It was also claimed that PRC was going to do their first film with a million-dollar budget, *Her Sister's Secret*.

Obviously no million dollar budget was being planned for *Devil Bat's*

Daughter. The July 7, 1945, *Showmen's Trade Review* announced, "John Neville, who did the original story of *The Devil Bat's Daughter*, has been assigned to write the screenplay. Leo J. McCarthy will produce and the picture will start within two weeks." Actually, Neville did the screenplay for *The Devil Bat* and did no work on the sequel. He was instead assigned to PRC's *The Flying Serpent*, a reworking of *The Devil Bat* starring George Zucco in the Bela Lugosi role and a hilarious Mexican monster bird taking the place of the killer bats. Perhaps not wanting to rehash the same plot still again is one reason why *Devil Bat's Daughter* flies off in an entirely different direction. However, the original story outline, submitted to the MPAA in August 1945 (described in Tim Snelson's *Phantom Ladies*), reads like a full-fledged horror film: Dr. Carruthers is still lurking around but as a vampire and assisted by a mysterious woman. A stake through the heart destroys them both. (PRC had already done a vampire movie, 1943's *Dead Men Walk*.) It may well have been the release of Alfred Hitchcock's *Spellbound* in December 1945 that prompted PRC to take a radically different approach. *Spellbound* has a troubled main character framed for murder, nightmare sequences and the revelation that a psychiatrist is the guilty party, all elements that find a place in *Devil Bat's Daughter*.

The story credits for *Daughter* seem a bit of a mystery. Publicity and reviews credit Frank Wisbar with co-authoring the original story with Ernst Jaeger. However, Leo J. Mahoney ends up sharing the story credit with Jaeger. Actually, Mahoney resigned from PRC in August 1945 but, perhaps for contractual reasons, was given a writing credit on *Daughter* and *Strangler of the Swamp* (but no producing credit on either film). Ernst Jaeger was a German film critic who wrote for *Film-Kurier* in the 1930s and became press agent for his good friend Leni Riefenstahl. He accompanied Riefenstahl on her disastrous 1939 trip to Hollywood to find an American distributor for *Olympia*. Jaeger was married to a non–Aryan and, as a one-time Social Democrat, was no supporter of Hitler, so he was regarded with contempt by the Nazis. He then defected to America, much to Riefenstahl's furious displeasure, and scribbled gossipy articles about her relationship with Hitler. It's a bit hard to imagine what his contribution to *Devil Bat's Daughter* might have been. Possibly Wisbar let him have a writing credit as a favor to a fellow refugee. In any case, Jaeger later worked with Wisbar on *Fireside Theater*. The *Daughter* screenplay was the work of Griffin Jay, who had done a number of Universal's '40s Mummy movies as well as *The Return of the Vampire* and *Cry of the Werewolf* for Columbia and *The Mask of Dijon* for PRC. Shooting began on January 9, 1946.

The film begins in the little New York town of Wardsley as a young woman found unconscious in the road is brought to the hospital to be examined by Dr. Elliott. Her eyes are open but she is unresponsive. (This opening scene has slight echoes of the beginning of *The Unknown*.) The sheriff discovers that a cab driver brought her to the deserted home of the late Dr. Paul Carruthers, creator of the murderous Devil Bat. The sheriff and doctor visit the house and find the girl's luggage as well as an old newspaper condemning Carruthers as being responsible for the Devil Bat murders. The girl is identified as Nina MacCarron, recently arrived from England and the daughter of Dr. Carruthers.

Unable to awaken the girl, Dr. Elliott enlists the aid of Dr. Cliff Morris, a New York City psychiatrist recently arrived in the area with his wife Ellen, a wealthy semi-invalid. Morris gets some response from the girl and then leaves for the Big Apple to visit his mistress Myra. A frantic Nina flees from the hospital and finds her way to Dr. Morris' house where the kindly Ellen takes her in. Morris is not happy to hear that his wife is daring to act without consulting him first but accepts the situation as Nina promises to be an intriguing case.

Nina slowly recovers but the sight of a bird in the garden sends her into hysterics and she screams that it's a bat. She finally tells Morris that her mother married the Rumanian scientist Dr. Carruthers who left when Nina was four. Her mother then died of "some sort of anemia" but locals suspected that Carruthers was responsible as they feared he was a vampire (because of his experiments with bats). Nina subsequently had nightmares that she was a bat flying alongside her father. She worked in an office in London during the war and weathered the Blitz successfully. Then she came to America in search of her father; discovering the newspaper condemning him as a murderer sent her over the edge. Morris assures her that the dead cannot harm the living and that she needs to break free of the past. However, the doctor shows a rapt interest when Dr. Elliott rambles on about vampire legends and how, according to the stories, a living person can sometimes be possessed by the undead.

Ellen's son Ted returns home, having finished his military service. Ted has always disliked Dr. Morris because he suspects (rightly) that he married Ellen for her money. Ted and Nina are taken with each other and when the cutesy billing and cooing turns serious, Dr. Morris advises Ellen to send her son away lest he end up falling in love with a mentally disturbed woman. Ellen reluctantly agrees to get Ted to hurry off to Boston to secure work in a law firm there.

In Ted's absence, Nina's condition deteriorates. The nightmares grow more intense and she seems to be sleepwalking as well. Ted's little dog is found stabbed with the bloody scissors in Nina's room. Nina has no recollection of the night before and fears she may have killed him. Morris wants to send her to a sanitarium but the next morning it is Ellen who is found murdered after Nina awakens on the stairway, the scissors in her hand. Nina is arrested as newspaper headlines scream "Devil Bats' (sic) Daughter Confesses!"

Ted can't believe Nina is guilty. He becomes convinced that Dr. Carruthers' notes, recently stolen from the old house, provide the key to the mystery. Ted recovers the notes from Myra, who admits that Morris took them. Ted, in the company of Dr. Elliott and the sheriff, confronts Morris. Ted has read the notes and discovered that Carruthers never intentionally killed anyone; now Ted accuses Morris of withholding the notes both for personal profit and to prevent Nina from finding out she has not inherited criminal tendencies from her father. Morris smoothly rebuts his stepson point by point but then Ted produces the pills Morris has been giving Nina and reveals that a chemical analysis shows that they leave the user temporarily comatose and in no position to move much less walk down the stairs and commit murder. *Someone* else must have carried Nina down after killing Ellen. Morris has no answer for that one, pulls a gun and is shot by the sheriff while trying to escape. The dying murderer asks Ted to forgive him.

Ted visits Nina in the hospital and the following somewhat odd exchange occurs:

Devil Bat's Daughter—as usual, the poster promises more than the film delivers.

> TED: You must understand, darling. He made you think all those things.... You see, there's nothing to be afraid of any more.
>
> NINA: And I was so sure. Will I ever really believe in myself again?
>
> TED: What does it matter as long as you believe in me?
>
> NINA: You're right.... It doesn't matter at all.

If there's a subtext to the film—or as

much of one as a Grade C chiller is likely to have—it's in poor Nina's search for parental love. After the death of her mother and desertion by her father, she is bereft and in search of family stability (the script never tells us who actually raised her). Cliff and Ellen seem to provide a new family with Ellen being the nurturing mother figure and Cliff the strict paternal disciplinarian. The fact that Nina is being cared for in their home rather than a hospital adds to that impression. Cliff treats her like a stern father; he scolds her, makes sure she takes her medicine, censors her reading and sends her to bed. At one point, getting ready for the sack, she takes off her robe in front of him and is seen to be wearing a revealing night gown. But Nina is due for a repeat of her personal history: The mother figure again dies and the father turns out not to care. Is it something about her? In the end, Nina's only chance for reassurance and love is to submit to Ted, the round-faced boy detective whose boring stability guarantees her own.

It is very obvious from the get-go who will be revealed as the villain. Obviously, Miss America isn't going to turn out to be Miss Transylvania so that just leaves one serious possibility. Ads for the film had no problem giving away the "mystery": "Entrapped by a crazed psychiatrist!" "A melodrama of the mind with a psychiatrist as the villain!" It might have worked better for the film to have dispensed with the whodunit angle altogether and follow the story from Dr. Morris' point of view (especially as Michael Hale easily gives the movie's best performance) as he plots against Nina. Indeed, Nina is absent for much of the last quarter of the film and Ted's search for Carruthers' notes does not seem very well-motivated. Why does he think they will reveal anything? Ultimately they prove irrelevant since it's the pills that establish Dr. Morris' treachery.

Evil movie psychiatrists are as old as Dr. Caligari. When shrinks turn up in silent era Hollywood films, they were usually good guys though there were the occasional exceptions (1918's *Two-Soul Woman* and its 1923 remake *The Untamable*). Sinister hypnotists abounded but they usually exerted their nefarious powers without the benefit of a doctorate. Shrinks largely vanished from the big screen in the '30s but on the rare occasions they did appear (*Lady in the Dark*, *Blind Alley*) they were portrayed sympathetically. Villainous psychiatrists enjoyed a brief vogue in the '40s. One *Devil Bat's Daughter* reviewer noted, "The psychiatrist, apparently, has replaced the town banker as the source of all evil." *Shock* (1946) with Vincent Price actually aroused a great deal of controversy and drew some protests. However, the sinister celluloid shrinks were quickly replaced by the healers and exorcists of *The Snake Pit*, *David and Lisa*, *The Three Faces of Eve*, *Captain Newman, M.D.*, *I Never Promised You a Rose Garden* and numerous others. Only Hannibal Lecter seems to have carried on the tradition of the psycho analyst.

A few *Devil Bat's Daughter* reviews sound as though they could have been written by modern detractors of the film:

> Illogical proceedings accompanied by stilted dialogue provided director Wisbar and his cast with little to work with.—*Motion Picture Daily* (April 4, 1946)

> Minor program fare. It is a far-fetched tale, developed without new angles, and since the action is for the most part slow-moving, one's interest in the proceedings diminishes. The individual performances are passable but the players are handicapped by ordinary material and stilted dialogue. It may get by with audiences who are not too particular about plot construction or production values.—*Harrison's Reports* (April 13, 1946)

> Another murderous psychiatrist in formula mystery.—*Christian Science Monitor* (October 3, 1946)

Other reviews were overall positive. *Variety* hated the original *Devil Bat* ("Acting, directing, photography—all poor") but was pleased with its follow-up, which they reviewed on April 10, 1946:

> Frank Wisbar rates a bow as for his work as producer-director and partial story scribbler. Unpretentiously produced and all possibilities have been drained. Rosemary La Planche in the title role doesn't accomplish any miracles of character delineation but it's a tough part. Michael Hale's psychiatrist tops the cast; in great measure his acting lends the picture much of its credibility and interest.... James Brown's camera cleverly captures the mood sought. Terse dialogue keeps plot constantly in rein. Background music also helps intensify effects.

Some other positive critiques:

> Frank Wisbar who produced and directed the film and who shares with Ernst Jaeger credit for the original story certainly got every penny's worth out of the budget allotted him. Lack of marquee names is counterbalanced by an interesting story, expertly directed. Despite its title, it's not a horror film or sequel to the same studio's earlier *Devil Bat*. The acting does not quite come up to acceptable standards. Of the cast, only Rosemary La Planche and Molly Lamont perform with anything like finesse. Griffith Jay wrote the screenplay which is enhanced by Alexander Steinert's musical score.—*Motion Picture Herald* (April 13, 1946)

> In spite of its fumbling and amateurish performances this little mystery has the suspense and thrill needed to make a good minor shocker.—*National Board of Review* (April 1946)

> PRC has done a good job with this sequel to their original *Devil Bat* made some six years ago, and a strong enough offering to give the company its real first push toward success. *Daughter* should do even better than the original which was helped by Bela Lugosi's name. Musical background sets up the moods of the picture in fine style. Michael Hale is a splendid menace.... Very satisfactory horror offering for those who like to be scared.—*Showmen's Trade Review* (April 13, 1946)

Devil Bat's Daughter (1946)

Devil Bat's Daughter played on a double bill with Universal's *House of Horrors* in Oakland. Local reviewer Theresa Loeb (*Oakland Tribune*, June 12, 1946) was not enthusiastic about either film but preferred Rosemary La Planche to Rondo Hatton:

> Not too bad. This movie benefits from excellent direction and photography and better than average acting on the part of most principals. Michael Hale is especially fine as a mad psychiatrist. Rosemary La Planche is not only good to look at but handles her fairly difficult acting assignment exceedingly well.

Comments from local exhibitors were also favorable:

> A good picture and a good murder story.—Bearden, Arkansas

> Good little picture.—Flomaton, Alabama

In Chicago, during a particularly hot July week when movie attendance was low, one exhibitor featured a double bill of *The Devil Bat* and *Devil Bat's Daughter* and did excellent business. In the '50s, papa and daughter bat played together in a number of places. It would be interesting to know what audiences made of the discrepancies between the two stories. Elsewhere, *Daughter* was co-billed with *Strangler of the Swamp*, *Valley of the Zombies*, *The Catman of Paris* and *Mysterious Intruder* (an entry in the "Whistler" series). A *Daughter* ad promised "A bloodthirsty vampire" and "[T]he story of a lovely girl who is forced to live the life of a criminal!" In Burlington, Vermont, a newspaper ad announced a heroine "hungry for love but cursed by the brand of the vampires"—but, apparently too cheap to prepare a poster for the blurb, said the illustration was "too horrible to print (!)."

Alfred Hitchcock had the services of Salvador Dali (amongst others) for the dream sequences in *Spellbound* while Wisbar relied on low-budget special effects veteran Ray Mercer, who worked on countless cheapies and stayed in business right into the '60s, often for TV (*Adventures of Superman*), occasionally working on more expensive projects (the Roger Corman *House of Usher*) and running his own special effects-optical effects for hire company. It's pretty basic stuff in *Devil Bat's Daughter*: images going blurry, clips from *The Devil Bat*, some silhouette drawings, a moody skyline, close-ups of bats, all strung together rapid fire subliminal-style with Alexander Steinert's music boosting the eerie ambience. There's one barely glimpsed but startling shot of a bat pouncing on a bird that fits in well with Nina's earlier vision in Morris' garden. None of this is spectacular but it works well in creating a disorienting, uneasy atmosphere.

La Planche is easy on the eyes and tries hard as Nina, managing the hysterics reasonably well though her dialogue delivery smacks of high school play histrionics. At least her performance is superior to that of June Lockhart, who played a very similar role in Universal's *She-Wolf of London* released around the same time and with a plot much like the PRC film. From a bit of studio PR, we learn the following about La Planche:

> A sequence of PRC's *Devil Bat's Daughter* called for Rosemary La Planche to play a stenographer. A secretary on the lot was summoned to the set to instruct the beauty queen on the intricacies of shorthand and typing but Rosemary proved such an inept pupil that Director Frank Wisbar soon lost patience and called for a take. To everyone's amazement the actress performed with remarkable speed and accuracy both on the machine and in her notebook. "Why didn't you tell me you'd been a stenographer?" Wisbar asked tartly. "If you'd asked me," replied Rosemary, "I'd have also told you that I was California state typing and shorthand champion for two years."

No doubt she was but she didn't get to prove it on the set as there's no such scene in the movie (unless there was some sort of flashback to Nina's office work in England that ended up getting cut; not very likely). A brief look at the career of the former Miss America, bat girl, ferrywoman and keyboard maestra can be found in the essay on *Strangler of the Swamp*.

Michael Hale makes Dr. Morris condescending and supercilious, certainly arrogant enough to attempt a "perfect" crime. Still, there's an odd sympathetic dimension to his performance (he seems to genuinely want to cure Nina—at least at first). But of course we don't *see* him cut up the nice little dog or slaughter his wife. According to Hedda Hopper's January 11, 1946, column, Hale never intended to be an actor:

> Michael Hale, former *LA Times* ad man and husband of one of my assistants, were [sic] coming out of the theater one night when an agent buttonholed him and said "You ought to be in pictures." And two days later, by golly, he was. He got the lead in PRC's psycho-chiller *Devil Bat's Daughter*.

In spite of his good work in *Daughter*, Hale's career was very minor, consisting of a bit part in 1946's *The Killers* and some television roles that petered out by the late '50s. Perhaps he went back to selling ads for the *LA Times*.

Molly Lamont (Ellen) is best remembered by horror buffs for her role as the chatty corpse in *Scared to Death*. Like La Planche, Lamont was a beauty contest winner. Her success resulted in the South African native going to England where she proceeded to churn out mostly B movies and quota quickies. According to PR, she had done 40 of them by the time she was discovered by RKO and signed with them for the 1935 epic family saga *Jalna*. Lamont was announced for a starring role in 1935's *Seven Keys to Baldpate* but the part went to Margaret Callahan instead. In spite of being given the usual starlet build-up at RKO, Lamont's only other feature for that studio was the loopy satire *Another Face*. She did a few more films in England and freelanced in Hollywood, scoring a good supporting role in 1937's *The Awful Truth*. In

March 1937, Lamont wed aviator Edward Bellande, onetime co-pilot with Charles Lindbergh and a genuine hero who successfully landed a burning plane. (He later became a major player in the aerospace industry.) The marriage was apparently a very happy one and Lamont temporarily dropped out of films. When she decided to return a few years later, she found herself doing small roles, sometimes uncredited. She occasionally turned up in the news, doing her bit for the war effort or standing up for her friend Heather Angel at the latter's wedding. Lamont still looked chic and lovely supporting Joan Fontaine in *Ivy* (1947).

Nolan Leary, so annoying and inept in *Strangler of the Swamp*, is here a credible Dr. Elliott. Leary's career dates back to vaudeville and the early silent era. He did scores of small roles and bit parts (including playing Lon Chaney's deaf father in *Man of a Thousand* Faces) and extensive television work right into the '80s. Wisbar must have liked the actor because he used him frequently on *Fireside Theater*. Ed Cassidy, who bears a resemblance to William Conrad, plays the sheriff, a part that couldn't have been much of a challenge as he portrayed sheriffs dozens of times, usually in westerns though he occasionally shook things up by playing a marshal. John James (Ted) had a brief and undistinguished career, usually playing in westerns and war movies. He turns up as an air crewman in the risible prologue added to the 1944 reissue of *The Sign of the Cross*,

Devil Bat's Daughter became a fixture on early television. No doubt it was sometimes in competition with *Fireside Theater*.

Secrets of a Sorority Girl

PRC
Released on August 15, 1946
58 minutes

Cast: Mary Ware as Linda Hamilton; Rick Vallin as Paul Reynolds, Addison Richards as John Hamilton; Ray Walker as Whitey King; Marie Harmon as Judy O'Neill; Caren Marsh as Audrey Scott; Mary Kenyon as Barbara Chase; Marilyn Johnson as Jeanne Cooper; Rosamond James as Karen Miller; Mauritz Hugo as Charles Stevens; Emmett Vogan as Joseph Kellan; Frank Ferguson as Justin Farley; Anthony Warde as Nick Vegas; Bill Murphy as Andy Jones; Pierre Watkin as Dr. Harlan Johnson; Dewey Robinson as the Blue Parrot bartender.
Credits: Director: Frank Wisbar; Assistant Director: Ivan Volkman; Producers: Max Alexander, Alfred Stern; Original Story: George Wallace Sayre; Screenplay: George Wallace Sayre, Arthur St. Clare; Photography: Robert Cline; Art Director: Edward Jewell; Editor: Roy Livingstone; Set Decorator: E.H. Reif; Costumes: Klarice; Music: Karl Hajos; Sound: Buddy Myers.

Secrets of a Sorority Girl (1946)

> Secrets of campus cuties never before TOLD except in their DIARIES!
> —tagline for *Secrets of a Sorority Girl*

This often incoherent and badly acted farrago is undoubtedly Frank Wisbar's worst movie. Initially it wasn't supposed to be his movie at all as it was initially assigned to veteran B movie director Lew Landers. Something very last-minute must have happened as the Library of Congress entry for the film (dated August 20, 1946) has Landers' name crossed out and replaced with Frank Wisbar. The credits crawl on screen also lists Wisbar. We don't know what went down but it may be a reasonable guess that Landers fell ill and had to abruptly bow out. Nor can we be sure if he shot any footage before being replaced by Wisbar (the film's shooting schedule was from approximately April 20 to April 30). However, it would seem nobody got the memo as Landers' name still turns up as the director on the poster, in the publicity and in all the reviews. Given the poor quality of the film, I don't imagine Wisbar was inclined to fight for credit.

The suggestive title is meant to be titillating and the sorority girls show up throughout the film but have next to nothing to do. Viewers tempted by the title will search in vain for cat fights and sorority paddling (instead check out Roger Corman's *Sorority Girl*) as *Secrets* is basically a dull courtroom drama with a befuddled but chaste heroine whose behavior defies both logic and effective dramaturgy.

What ended up on the screen doesn't always match the Library of Congress synopsis which at least takes a stab at making the story comprehensible even though it still doesn't add up. I presume the Library of Congress entry follows the original script.

The film begins with the murder trial of Linda Hamilton, president of her college sorority. From a few flashes of newspaper headlines, we learn that she is the daughter of crusading D.A. John Hamilton, who is running for governor and has vowed to clean up the city's gambling racket. Linda is accused of killing a motorcycle cop with her car and fleeing the scene. As various people testify, the story slowly unwinds (or perhaps we should say unravels) in flashbacks.

First to testify is former reporter Paul Reynolds, who is doing some post-graduate work at Linda's college. He becomes acquainted with Linda at a sorority dance but just as sparks begin to fly, Linda faints. Apparently, this is not the first time nor will it be the last. She recovers and Paul takes her to the Blue Parrot, a gambling joint. Even though Linda apparently has a good relationship with her widowed dad, she doesn't seem very concerned about what this might do to his career if she is caught. Club owner Nick Vegas knows who she is and has the bartender (big lug and Preston Sturges regular Dewey Robinson) snap a few pictures. The joint is raided but Linda and Paul get out in time. Paul and Linda later visit Whitey King's gambling house but she only drinks ginger ale. Again the place is raided and again she and Paul get away undetected. Paul further testifies that on the fatal night, Linda again went to the King gambling house and got intoxicated. As still another raid commenced, the two fled in Paul's car but Linda insisted on driving. As the motorcycle cop gained on them, Linda abruptly slammed on the brakes, causing the officer to smash into them. Linda then drove away by herself, leaving Paul stranded, but he decided not to report the incident.

The psychiatrist Dr. Johnson testifies that Linda came to see him under an assumed name. In flashbacks, he tells her that a physical revealed she is just fine but Linda hysterically accuses him of hiding the truth from her. In the Library of Congress synopsis, Linda is told she has only a year to live but in the movie she *assumes*, because she has been getting headaches like her mother did before she died, that she is dying too. This is supposed to explain her reckless behavior and fondness for roadhouses. Pierre Watkin as Dr. Johnson continually plays with his glasses on the witness stand and is always looking down at them. Very likely he is reading his dialogue from cue cards.

Here Mary Ware does her best acting in *Secrets of a Sorority Girl* while Ray Taylor (left) and Rich Vallin wish they were elsewhere.

John Hamilton apologizes to Linda for neglecting her but promises to make up for it after the election when she'll be his "first lady." Linda's fainting spells get worse and she resigns as sorority president. On the stand, Linda tells how she visited Whitey's gambling house on the night in question but that he refused to serve her liquor. She tells the court she must have passed out as she has no memory of anything until waking up in Paul's car after the officer was killed. Via more flashbacks, we learn that someone has sent pictures of Linda gambling to her father along with a few pages from her diary in which she mentions killing the policeman. A letter accompanying the pictures warns the D.A. to lay off the gambling joints *or else*. Linda, who wanted to tell her father the truth the previous night when he was too busy to see her, then turns up at his office and confesses. He has her arrested. The Library of Congress summary is very different. Paul reveals himself as the mastermind behind the gambling operations (hey, graduate school is expensive) and tries to blackmail Linda to get her father to cooperate. When that doesn't work, Paul goes to a political meeting attended by John Hamilton and reveals the pictures and diary pages knowing that will scuttle his campaign for the statehouse. Hamilton orders both Paul and Linda arrested. The film jettisons all that and saves the revelation of Paul's true colors as a last-minute "surprise."

Dr. Johnson again takes the witness stand and testifies that Linda's blackouts are probably caused by stress at her fear of dying young. The prosecuting attorney offers a rebuttal that such blackouts are also consistent with heavy drinking. Linda is called to the stand again and denies being drunk, claiming the only time she had a drink was a glass of champagne at the races. ("And don't you think champagne is an alcoholic drink?" snarls the prosecuting attorney.) However, under prodding from her attorney and now convinced that she's not dying, Linda remembers what happened. She passed out during the raid and was carried to the car by Paul. (The Library of Congress summary has Paul and Whitey fighting and Linda getting knocked cold as the customers stampede out.) Whitey and Paul were in the car and it was Paul who was driving when the policeman was killed. Whitey left and then Paul put Linda behind the wheel. Whitey, who is present in the courtroom, suddenly decides it's time to confirm Linda's story. He also announces that Paul is the head man for the local gambling business. Paul grabs a gun and attempts to escape but is shot by the police. Linda, who has fainted again, wakes up smiling in her father's arms. The man who gives Paul the gun is listed in the credits as Justin Farley and according to the Library of Congress summary he's a crooked bail bondsmen who earlier tipped off Nick Vegas about the raid. In the finished film, we don't see him until the finale when, quite out of the blue, he hands Paul the gat. He's played by Frank Ferguson, a familiar face from TV (*Peyton Place*) and best remembered by horror buffs for his role as the irritating and irritable waxworks owner Mr. McDougal in *Abbott and Costello Meet Frankenstein*.

The film's deviations from the Library of Congress summary suggest that the production was particularly hasty, even for a PRC film. Continuity is certainly poor and often confusing with the awkward flashback construction making things even more muddled. The revelation that Paul is the villain is particularly unconvincing; he's a former reporter and current grad student but he's somehow found the time to take over the gambling rackets without anyone even suspecting him. Linda's predicament is likewise far-fetched and her dialogue often unintentionally funny. ("Are you awake now?" asks her attorney after she describes her nightmarish fainting spells. "I hope so," she responds.) The heroine's blackouts being used as a cover-up for another's crime is also part of *Devil Bat's Daughter*.

Reviews were uniformly bad:

> Using typical *True Confessions* material as the basis for a confusing, poorly motivated plot, *Secrets* is pretty much of a dud. With a cast devoid of marquee names, this quickie will make a weak supporting dualer even in minor neighborhood spots. The picture unfolds in a series of seemingly endless flashbacks.... As the psycho neurotic sorority girl, Mary Ware gives an extremely amateurish performance and Rick Vallin is little better. Except for Addison Richards and Ray Walker, most of the others conduct themselves like newcomers to the acting profession.—*Independent Exhibitor's Film Bulletin* (September 16, 1946)

> Lew Landers has attempted to create an air of suspense throughout the picture but the story is inclined to drag. Rating: Average.—*Motion Picture Herald* (August 24, 1946)

> This program melodrama has an exploitable title but as entertainment is just moderately interesting. The story, which unfolds in a series of flashbacks, is exceedingly thin and "choppy" ... [it] reminds one of one of the stories heard on daytime radio serial programs or published in the *True Confessions* type of magazine. At no time does the action strike a realistic note.... Not much can be said for either the direction and the acting; both are lacking in subtlety.—*Harrison's Reports* (August 24, 1946)

> This is a loosely woven story, directed not too carefully, in which the players are not convincing. The tenuous thread of story threatens to break completely at times. While the players struggle valiantly to overcome the difficulties of script, they just don't reach the bounds of credibility. Audiences which are not too discriminating may find some entertainment in it. The more sophisticated will probably find very little.—*Showmen's Trade Review* (August 24, 1946)

> Far-fetched plot pitched with psycho-neurotic theme. Should get by as fill-in. Mounted on a small budget, the film offers moderate entertainment.—*Film Daily* (August 22, 1946)

Mary Ware was sometimes billed as Mary Tucker but she didn't have much of a film career under either name, not surprising if her acting in *Secrets of a Sorority Girl* is any indication of her abilities. Even allowing for the ridiculous script, Ware is vacant-eyed and inexpressive throughout. B movie tough guy Rick Vallin can't do a whole lot with his role as Paul but it's not surprising as the part makes little sense. Addison Richards (John Hamilton) seems to be channeling Lewis Stone as Judge Hardy; usually Richards' performances have a sharper edge.

The music was done under the auspices of Karl Hajos, PRC's primary music man during this period. Hajos had a distinguished career; the Budapest-born conductor and composer studied under Johann Koessler and Richard Strauss and conducted in Vienna, Berlin and Cologne. He wrote hundreds of songs, composed operettas and did the music for the 1927 Broadway play *The Pearl of Great Price*. One can only imagine what he must have thought working for the cheapest outfit on Poverty Row. Nevertheless, he apparently gave it his all as his score for the 1945 PRC sleeper *The Man Who Walked Alone* was nominated for an Academy Award.

No such honor awaited Frank Wisbar for his direction of *Secrets of a Sorority Girl*.

Lighthouse

PRC
Released on January 10, 1947
62 minutes

Cast: June Lang as Connie Armitage; Don Castle as Sam Wells; John Litel as Hank Armitage; Marian Martin as JoJo; Charles Wagenheim as Quimby; Richard Bailey as Henry Simmons.

Credits: Director: Frank Wisbar; Screenplay: Robert B. Churchill; Original Story: Don Martin; Producers: Frank Gilbert, George Moskov; Music: Ernest Gold; Photography: Walter Strenge; Editor: Robert Jahns; Art Director: Glenn P. Thompson; Makeup: Carl A. Russell; Special Effects: Ray Mercer; Sound: Earl Sitar; Second Unit Director: Wallace Grissell; Assistant Director: Albert C. Schnee.

Lighthouses today are usually automated and have no need of regular staff. They are generally more scenic than mysterious but nevertheless they've been the setting for a number of thrillers with their keepers often depicted as being mentally unstable, driven to extremes by isolation and the tension inherent in their jobs. In the allegory *Thunder Rock* (1942), lighthouse keeper Michael Redgrave is troubled by the ghosts of the drowned. In *Tower of Terror* (1941), a blending of espionage drama and horror film, Wilfred Lawson is totally bonkers and keeps his wife's corpse buried under the lighthouse. *Horror on Snape Island* (1972) gives you two monstrous, crazed lighthouse keepers for the price of one. Best of all is the 1946 Finnish film *Cross of Love*, a bizarre combination of the 1925 *Der Turm des Schweigens* (*The Tower of Silence*) and *Street Angel* (1929).

Frank Wisbar's *Lighthouse* is quite tame by comparison. It's largely a drama–romantic triangle that teeters on the edge of film noir but never quite takes the plunge. It's modestly entertaining and well-acted and, with a running time of barely an hour, doesn't wear out its welcome.

The film begins with a flowery written introduction:

> Wherever ships sail and the sea and danger lurks, there is always one friend to guide the voyager to safety—the lighthouse. Standing staunchly against the storms and gales, the lighthouse sends its warning beam tirelessly into the night. And always, watchful, vigilant is the man who tends the lighthouse, living his life of oppressive loneliness and seclusion. He lives in his own little world so that other may live—it's a small world but things happen in it.

Hank, the head lighthouse keeper of our story, very much fills the above-mentioned bill. His assistant Sam, considerably less dedicated, always finds excuses to go to the mainland and leave Hank to tend the light by himself. A middle-aged bachelor, Hank is easygoing and lets his younger helper take advantage of him.

Sam has been romancing Connie, a young woman who works in a cannery in the small coastal town. Tired of the unwelcome advances of Simmons, her boss, Connie quits her job after slapping him. Connie's roommate JoJo, a blonde good-time girl and wisecracker, is appalled that her friend has been so impulsive. Connie is sure that this latest development will inspire Sam to finally propose ("I hit him because I love you," she tells Sam). Sam, who has represented himself as the head lighthouse keeper, not an assistant, tells Connie they have to wait until he can land a different job rather than spend their married lives on the little island.

Sam tells Hank that he needs to see his wife, who has been giving him a hard time about getting a divorce. After several weeks without seeing Sam, Connie becomes alarmed and takes a boat to the lighthouse island. There she meets Hank and discovers that her boyfriend is not the head man, and also that he's married. Connie doesn't tell Hank about her relationship with Sam but pretends she came to the island because her boat ran out of gas. Hank is quite taken with Connie, who decides to spite Sam by letting Hank romance her. The two end up getting married.

When the newlyweds come back to the island, Sam is taken aback at this unexpected development. Hank is deeply in love with Connie and fails to notice the tension between his assistant and Connie. Finally getting Connie alone, Sam tells her that it was always his intention to divorce his wife and marry her. Connie is appalled at her misstep in marrying Hank but then discovers that Sam is again lying and has a girlfriend in town.

Connie, who genuinely likes Hank, decides to make the best of their marriage. However, Sam suddenly finds Connie irresistible now that she's rejecting him. At a little housewarming party, Sam gets JoJo drunk and encourages her to blab about Connie's past and how she has gone from one man to another. Connie leaves the room in a huff but Hank follows her and tells her he doesn't care about her past. Overhearing the conversation, Sam breaks a bottle in frustration.

Hank continues to follow his usual custom of watching stars from a ledge on the island. Sam spreads some liquid on the precipice so that Hank ends up slipping and falling onto the rocks. Connie rescues him and brings him to the mainland to recover.

After a couple of weeks of recuperation, Hank returns to the island though he has to walk with a cane. They are visited by Quimby, an officious insurance agent who asks some sharp questions about Hank's accident, even insinuating that his wife and young helper may have had something to do with it to collect Hank's life insurance. Hank angrily orders him to leave but a seed of doubt has been planted in his mind.

Depressed and irritable, Hank falls into a troubled sleep. Connie confronts Sam, who tells her he will never let her go. Hank awakens to find that the signal light has gone out. He makes his way to the main tower and replaces the bulb. He sees Connie leave Sam's room and suspects the worst. Connie tells him the truth about her past relationship with Sam but insists that she has grown to love Hank. Hank believes her and tells Sam that he's through and must get out. A fistfight ensues but then Connie, brandishing a hitherto unseen revolver, gets the drop on Sam, who slinks off to the mainland, leaving the couple to find peace and happiness on their island.

The rivalry between an older man and a young one for the affections of a girl was standard fare in '20s melodrama. If *Lighthouse* were a silent, the youth would be played by William Haines and the oldster by Lon Chaney, perhaps with the young lady being portrayed by Anita Page or Loretta Young. By the last reel, the callow youth would have reformed and the Chaney character would be obliged to give up his life (perhaps during a raging storm?) to save the girl. The situation had become hackneyed by the '30s but Edward G. Robinson would occasionally assume the Chaney part in films like *Tiger Shark* and *The Hatchet Man*.

By the '40s, audiences watching a story about a young woman married to an older man would invariably anticipate a noir-ish development along the lines of *The Postman Always Rings Twice* with the girl and her lover plotting to knock off her husband. *Lighthouse* seems to flirt with that idea but then backs away and leaves all its characters alive at the end, though it remains an open question just how much Connie will enjoy her new life "of oppressive loneliness and seclusion." Then again, after sharing digs with JoJo ("Modern Rooms—75 cents a day" reads the sign on their building), the lighthouse might not look so bad by comparison. In any case, the relatively low-key finale represents something of a twist.

According to *Motion Picture Daily*, shooting of *Lighthouse* began on September 12, 1946, with location filming done on the coast at San Pedro where a number of lighthouses were to be found. By the time of the September 26 edition of *Showmen's Trade Review*, the film had already wrapped with a few interiors having been shot at H and H Studio. Filming at a genuine lighthouse with real water must have been a nice change for Wisbar after the studio set of *Strangler of the Swamp*.

Motion Picture Herald (February 8, 1947) found *Lighthouse* to be a "generally satisfying action film with a conscientious cast" but noted that the Broadway audience was "impassive." *Motion Picture Daily* (February 10, 1947) was unenthusiastic but not entirely negative: "Although this modest film is quite undistinguished in acting, direction and dialogue, its familiar straight-line story is within the bounds of probabilities, and the characterizations ring true."

Perhaps the latter words sum up both the film's virtues and its faults. The story is reasonably plausible but not too exciting. This is well illustrated in the business about the light going out. Early in the picture, Hank tells Sam that he has nightmares thinking about that possibility and often wakes up in a cold sweat (the background music builds in intensity as he speaks). But later when this does actually happen, nothing very dramatic occurs. Hank wakes up, sees that the signal is down, goes to the tower and simply replaces the bulb. It's every bit as mundane as it sounds. There's no storm at sea or accompanying shipwreck (though one imagines that would not have been in the budget) and nothing is made of it other than allowing Hank to see Connie leaving Sam's room. One might expect the subsequent fistfight to end with Sam plunging into his death from the top of the lighthouse but instead he just gives up and leaves. It's more realistic and less melodramatic but also makes things slightly dull. The lighthouse setting hardly suggests isolation or gloom. Walter Strenge's camerawork is open, bright and scenic and the characters don't seem to have any problem getting back and forth to the mainland on the always placid ocean. The only claustrophobia is provided by the cramped, cheap interior sets of JoJo's apartment or the local tavern. The film should have borrowed some *Strangler of the Swamp* fog for a little atmosphere.

June Lang (Connie) accurately described *Lighthouse* as a "C-Grader"; it was the last film for which she received any billing. Lang had done well at

Lighthouse (1947)

Don Castle expresses his sexual frustration by breaking a bottle in *Lighthouse*. Castle was the quintessential B movie anti-hero.

Fox in the 1930s; horror genre fans may recall *Chandu the Magician* wherein she appeared in a fetching harem outfit on the slave auction block. She was not a big star at Fox but, in spite of the occasional bump, she worked steadily in conspicuous roles in good solid programmers, a couple of times in support of Shirley Temple. Things went awry in 1938 when Fox sent her to England to make *So This Is London*. The clouds of war were hanging heavily over Europe and Lang was terrified of the prospect of being trapped there if war were declared. Fox insisted that she stay put but she refused. (According to one story the last straw was when she was told she needed to be fitted for a gas mask.) Fox cancelled her contract. To make matters worse, she married Johnny Roselli, a gangster who, with his mob compatriots, had been moving into the rackets in Hollywood. Lang divorced Roselli after just a couple of years, claiming he would disappear for weeks at a time and didn't like her Hollywood friends. She insisted she believed him when he said his business was insurance (I guess you could call extortion and the protection racket insurance of a sort). Lang found herself cast in uncredited bits and laboring on Poverty Row. Wisbar later used her a couple of times on *Fireside Theater*.

Don Castle (Sam) did bit parts in the '30s. After leaving the service at the end of World War II, he got better roles but largely on Poverty Row. His resemblance to Clark Gable was often noted in publicity but Castle had a scowl that suggested he might do better playing more ambiguous roles than the usual romantic leads. Film noir seemed a good fit but the films were all low-budget efforts, mostly from Monogram. In one of the better ones, *The Guilty* (1947), he appeared opposite Bonita Granville (playing twins) and struck up a lasting friendship with her. Jack Wrather, the film's producer and Bonita's sweetheart, had been Castle's college roommate. Wrather was an oilman who decided to get into movies and TV. He married Granville with Castle acting as his best man. When things got lean for Castle, Wrather came to the rescue and made him producer on the long-running *Lassie* TV series in the '50s and '60s. Castle was as troubled in real life as some of the parts he played and he died of a drug overdose in 1966.

Unlike his co-stars, John Litel (Hank) had no career problems whatsoever. He had originally planned to go into banking (like the rest of his family) but then the First World War intervened and Litel, eager to participate, joined the French forces and was twice decorated. He stayed in France for a while after the war, traveling with a company of doughboy actors. Returning to the U.S., he enrolled in the American Academy of Dramatic Arts and later achieved success on the stage, notably in Broadway productions of *Irene*, *The First Legion* and *Ceiling Zero* (Litel received particularly fine notices as the aviator Dizzy Davis). He made many movies and in the 1930s he was a member of the Warner Bros. stock company, playing a variety of supporting roles. He freelanced in the '40s and had a recurring part as Mr. Aldrich in the Henry Aldrich series. He did a great deal of TV and was acting right into the mid–60s.

Standing out in the tiny supporting cast is Charles Wagenheim as the waspish insurance agent Quigley. He appeared in scores of movies and TV roles, often in uncredited bits. While his most conspicuous part may have been as the assassin in Alfred Hitchcock's *Foreign Correspondent*, Wagenheim was more likely to be victim than killer and, in both *The Jungle Captive* and *The Brute Man*; he ended up getting strangled by Rondo Hatton. Still acting at age 84, Wagenheim was found bludgeoned to death in his apartment. Another elderly actor, Victor Kilian, suffered the same fate a week later. (Both just appeared in episodes of *All in the Family*.) In the end, however, there proved to be no connection between the two murders as it was discovered that Wagenheim was killed by his invalid wife's nurse when he caught her stealing.

The Prairie

Zenith Pictures, Inc./Screen Guild Productions, Inc.
New York opening: August 17, 1948
65 minutes

Cast: Lenore Aubert as Ellen Wade; Alan Baxter as Paul Hover; Russ Vincent as Abiram White; Jack Mitchum [John Mitchum] as Asa Bush; Charles Evans as Ishmael Bush; Edna Holland as Esther Bush; Chief Thundercloud as Eagle Feather; Fred Coby as Abner Bush; Bill Murphy as Jess Bush; David Gerber as Gabe Bush; Don Lynch as Enoch Bush; Chief Yowlachie as Matoreeh; Jay Silverheels as Running Deer; Beth Taylor as Ann Morris; Commentary by Frank Hemmingway.

Credits: Director: Frank Wisbar; Screenplay: Arthur St. Claire; Based on the eponymous 1827 novel by James Fenimore Cooper; Executive Producer: Edward F. Finney; Producer: George Moskov; Assistant Director: Ben Kadish; Photography: James S. Brown; Editor: Douglas W. Bagier; Art Director: Perry J. Smith; Production Manager: Leon Chooluck; Sound Engineer: Ferol M. Redd; Original Musical Score: Alexander Steinert.

While *The Last of the Mohicans* has gone before the cameras many times, James Fenimore Cooper's other Leatherstocking books have largely stayed on the shelf. This includes *The Prairie*, the third of the series of five novels that chronicle the adventures of frontiersman Natty Bumppo, perhaps better known as Hawkeye, the Deerslayer, La Longue Carbine and the Pathfinder. Cooper apparently ran out of cool nicknames so in *The Prairie*, he is just called "the old man." He dies at the end of the story even though two more books about him followed, covering his early years. Like *Last of the Mohicans*, *The Prairie* is full of action with characters getting chased, captured, rescued or escaping and battling with the elements and hostile Indians. There are "good" Indians and "bad" Indians, a respect and love for the wilderness and bittersweet regret at the inevitable encroachment of civilization. What is perhaps atypical for Cooper is that Ishmael, a main character, while not exactly a villain, is decidedly unsympathetic and lives up to his Biblical namesake ("His hand is against every man and every man's hand is against his").

To do a proper film version of Cooper, you do need a little money to capture the sprawl and scope of the adventures (think of the outstanding 1920 and 1992 versions of *Last of the Mohicans*). Cash was something in short supply for Zenith Pictures' adaptation of *The Prairie*. Zenith Pictures consisted of director Wisbar, scenarist Arthur St. Claire and Sidney Smith (later to work with Wisbar on *Fireside Theater*). Zenith was associated with distributor Screen Guild, which specialized in producing low-budget movies. Final cost for *The Prairie* came to roughly $200,000 (according to the movie's pressbook), definitely a Poverty Row sum. Supposedly, Wisbar sent his second wife Vera von Langen back to their native Germany to claim some family jewels (denied to her during the war) to help finance the production. Filming began on July 30, 1947, at the recently opened Nassour Studio and wrapped two weeks later.

In spite of publicity referring to Cooper's novel as a classic, St. Claire was not too impressed and described it as "terrible by contemporary literary standards." He did admire the extensive background: "Cooper went into detail about everything. He spent 30 pages describing the old man in the story—telling how he wore two watches, and how he dressed. And he described the Indian's costume down to the last bead." St. Claire apparently didn't make too much use of this as the character of the old man is one of many missing from the film. Obviously, with a small budget, a minuscule cast and a running time of little more than an hour, things had to be scaled down considerably: the sympathetic Pawnee tribe is reduced to one individual, Chief Thundercloud, whose buckskin outfit looks as though it just came back from the dry cleaners. The hostile Sioux raiding party consists of barely half a dozen warriors. All things considered, though, the script makes a serious effort at doing justice to the story.

This synopsis comes from the pressbook:

Determined to find a land where law and order could be of his own making, Ishmael Bush sets out from Kentucky with his wife and five strong sons to cross into the unsurveyed territory of the Louisiana Purchase.

A buffalo stampede wipes out a neighboring wagon train, killing all except beautiful Ellen Wade. Indians who follow the buffalo ride up on their pinto ponies and attempt to kidnap Ellen but Asa Bush, the eldest son, and Abiram White, his uncle, arrive in time to drive the redskins off.

Ellen is taken to their camp, where Ishmael tells her another mouth to feed is not welcome, but that she may travel with them. Esther, Ishmael's wife, befriends Ellen.

The party now suffers incredible hardships as the burning sun and seas of scorched grass torture them with thirst and hunger. They are about to give up when a mysterious buckskin-clad stranger appears. Ishmael has to humble himself and ask for help. The stranger, a government map maker, Paul Hover, guides them to water.

By now all of the sons and Abiram are in love with Ellen, who tries to keep them at a proper distance because she is in love with Paul. Ishmael scorns the Bible texts of Esther, and when, after Paul leaves and Indians raid his camp, he vows vengeance.

Asa and Abiram quarrel over Ellen. While hunting buffalo, Asa shoots at an Indian, but Paul fires first and deflects his aim, berating him for firing at Eagle Feather, a friendly Indian. Asa knocks Paul down and they have a terrific fight which is broken up by the arrival of Ishmael. Paul tells Asa that the next time they meet, he will finish it. Ishmael takes this as a threat upon Asa's life and later, when Asa is found dead with a bullet in his back, Ishmael plans to hang Paul. Meanwhile, Paul, Ellen, and Eagle Feather have been captured by the Sioux Indians. Ishmael and his sons rescue them, and prepare a rope for Paul. Abiram, insane with jealousy, urges the lynching. But Eagle Feather, having found the rifle ball that killed Asa, returns in time to prove it was fired by Abiram. Confronted with the evidence, Abiram breaks down and Ishmael, who has bragged about being his own law, is faced with the duty of hanging his own wife's brother. Leaving Abiram stranded on the knoll, with no prospect of getting off alive, the pioneers depart. The Bible flutters in the wind, Abiram stamps on the grave of Asa, the noose dangles from a gnarled limb, and Abiram goes completely insane, rushing headlong into the hempen loop he planned for Paul. Sadly, Ishmael, a changed man, and Esther ride back to the knoll to bury Abiram beside Asa. Paul and Ellen ride off together into the sunset.

Women's groups found the film's grim finale inappropriate for children and Wisbar does pull out all the stops for this sequence of Abiram's madness and suicide. In addition to actor Russ Evans' somewhat over-the-top histrionics, you have thunder and lighting, eerie voiceovers, blurred images, shots of the macabre hanging tree that would fit comfortably into a horror film, and a mysterious wind that opens the Bible, causing the pages to flutter and then scattering some of them. If that isn't enough, shots of the noose are superimposed over Abiram's face. The murderer's dash to his death is shown with the noose in close-up in the foreground. We don't see his actual demise or his body hanging from the tree but only the somber reaction of Ishmael and Esther as they return to the knoll.

Abiram's end in the book is perhaps even more sadistic. He is tied up on a narrow ledge with a noose attached to an overhanging tree and then tightened around his neck. He has the choice of ending things quickly by jumping off or holding out until he collapses from exhaustion; either way his family is spared the task of dispatching him directly. They do have him trussed up in such a way that he can read the Bible they've placed in his hands. Perhaps the Good Book is turned to the passage where Judas hangs himself.

The film has an ambiguous attitude toward the Bible, surprising for the time. Ishmael calls it "sanctimonious drivel" and complains to the very religious Esther that they need food, not parables. When the seemingly kindly Esther demands the life of Paul for Asa, Ellen calls her "a hypocrite—you and your Bible!" Ishmael only begins to recognize that the Bible can console when Esther assures him it supports taking a life for a life! And when the life demanded turns out to be her brother rather than Paul, Esther cites the "vengeance is mine" verse to convince Ishmael that they should not hang Abiram themselves but rather force him to be his own executioner. At the end, the narrator's rant seems to suggest that manifest destiny and the pioneering American spirit can be the only real guides to settling the wilderness.

In these days of anti-government militias and rebellious, gun-toting western ranchers, some of Ishmael's dialogue has a curiously modern ring. He accepts Hover's help but thinks the army should stay on the other side of the Mississippi rather than bring government to still unexplored territory. "I loathe the very thought of law and order," he grouses, adding that he despises the weaklings who pay taxes and are afraid to offend the "powdered wigs that run their lives." Ishmael has seen his own farm foreclosed back in his native Kentucky and dreams of finding a paradise beyond the grip of the feds. When government agent Hover falls under suspicion for Asa's murder, Ishmael is more than eager to lead him to the hanging tree.

For a minor film, *The Prairie* got an unusual amount of publicity, notably a lengthy piece by Philip Scheuer for the August 17, 1947, *Los Angeles Times*, part of which was incorporated into the movie's pressbook. Scheuer visited the *Prairie* set and was impressed by Wisbar's energy and by the fact that the entire prairie was on a 250-foot indoor stage covered by tons of buffalo grass shipped in from Nebraska. Wisbar described the filming to the journalist:

> We are shooting it that way—realistic but stylized. Camera treatment is modern, yet what I would call highly poetic. The lower half of the screen will always be grass, grass that is wonderful to sneak through, to hide behind, to play a half-glimpsed love scene through! In the distance [Wisbar waved toward the sky cyclorama that surrounded the prairie[is infinity. I swear you think you can see 15 or 20 miles instead of 250 feet or less. On the cyclorama, we are projecting clouds—clouds painted on glass!—that will actually change with the feeling of the story, that will convey a mood of despair, when our pioneers are starving, of ominous menace when a buffalo stampede is approaching and so on.... Even in Nebraska we couldn't get anything to match this.

Speaking from experience, Wisbar also complained that independent films were often poorly done because of low budgets and unsympathetic front offices: "An indie outfit throws a script at a director three days before shooting time and expects him to shoot 12 pages a day—never mind what they are!—it's 12 pages or he's fired. No time to concentrate on the actors, lighting or even what he's trying to say." Wisbar hoped that *The Prairie* would prove to be a trailblazer for good independent productions that would have artistic values comparable to more mainstream efforts.

While Scheuer perhaps admired Wisbar's intentions, he was not thrilled with the results when he reviewed *The Prairie* in the October 12, 1949, *Los Angeles Times*:

> I wish I could say the film makes some claim on artistry. Occasionally, as in the toiling climb of the pioneers to a knoll and the villain's dash into the noose he hoped

would hang another, it almost does. But on the whole it struck me as more darkly stylized than convincing.

Scheuer also had mixed feelings about the set:

It was shot on an indoor prairie, which gives it the effect of a monochrome print. In a sense this was good, because it conveys the feeling of an unbroken trek through high grass. It was bad because the sameness of set works on the spectators as well as well as the characters, getting everybody down.

On August 25, 1948, *Variety's* Jose was considerably more positive:

The novels of James Fenimore Cooper have provided excellent screen fare for several decades. They usually have action, broad sweeps of motion and well defined storylines and *The Prairie* follows form. It is good frontier fare, a bit more adult than the general run of western and should fit on dual bills rather than those presented on Saturday matinees.... Frank Wisbar's direction is a good blend of action and restraint. His introduction of set-tos is invariably timed after slow passages so that greater impact is registered. The screenplay by Arthur St. Claire is in a manner that lets the camera have greater say in the matter.

Russ Vincent is thinking Lenore Aubert still looks pretty good even though she was just run over by a herd of buffalo in *The Prairie*.

The Prairie (1948)

The Prairie is in some ways comparable to Wisbar's *Strangler of the Swamp*, an attempt to do something out-of-the-ordinary with a very tired and predictable genre. Instead of the constant, otherworldly fog of *Strangler*, you have the endless grasslands, alternately monotonous and menacing, suggesting both a hellish, neverending journey and hidden dangers, often the only sounds being the perennial whistling of the wind (at least when Alexander Steinert's music doesn't get in the way). It's noteworthy that by the end of the picture, the pioneers haven't found any place to settle and are still trudging along through the ocean of grass.

One of *The Prairie*'s drawbacks is that the low budget just can't meet audience expectations for the action. (Early notices about the film made it sound like more of a murder story than an epic.) This is particularly obvious during the buffalo stampede. Publicity claimed that 30 buffalo were shipped in from Alberta, Canada, and then herded to the film set. However, this surely would have been a budget breaker for such a modest production and neither the pressbook nor the *L.A. Times* article mention anything of the sort. What you see in the film looks like stock footage of buffalo on the move intercut with shots of the doomed settlers reacting, falling down and ducking for cover before this onslaught of celluloid bison. It's not convincing and is too obvious a reminder of the film's meager production values.

The acting is, at best, uneven. Russ Vincent and Alan Baxter (who has some of the silliest bits of business, including having to flirt with Ellen while they're being held captive by Indians!) seem like actors who would be more at home in a speakeasy than on the prairie. Charles Evans just can't muster up the sort of fire that would make Ishmael both incorrigible *and* perhaps worthy of grudging admiration in his stubbornness. It's a part that would have suited Lionel Barrymore well—not that he would have been caught dead in such a lower-rung effort. The Indian actors don't come off too badly. Chief Thundercloud, whom some would credit with softening the Hollywood image of Native Americans in westerns, doesn't have a lot to do other than recreate the faithful Indian companion he essayed as Tonto in two Republic serials, *The Lone Ranger* (1938) and *The Lone Ranger Rides Again* (1939). Jay Silverheels, who would play Tonto on TV with Clayton Moore, is one of the bad Indians and gets drowned by Alan Baxter. Chief Yowlachie, a trained opera singer, doesn't get to sing but projects appropriate menace in a small part as one of the Indian raiders.

John Mitchum, Robert's brother, plays the ox-like Asa. (*All* the Bush sons seem a bit slow on the uptake.) He says he was wandering down Santa Monica Blvd. when he was spotted by a somewhat inebriated agent who asked him whether he wanted to be an actor. John, having nothing better to do at the moment, answered in the affirmative and was brought to meet Wisbar, who approved him for the part. John had a few other recollections about *The*

Prairie in his autobiography *Them Ornery Mitchum Boys*:

> One scene called for me to fight Alan. The assistant director asked if I could fight, and I assured him I could. The stunt coordinator told me to throw a left and told Baxter to throw a right. We were then to go into a clinch, after which the fight would be broken up. I threw a left all right, putting a gash above Alan's eye that required six stitches. I hadn't been told I was supposed to "pull" my punches in accepted film fighting style. Later, in a scene with Charles Evans, I found out why I had been chosen for the part. Evans sighs, "Asa, you're a very dull lad."

Dull or not, Wisbar liked Mitchum and used him frequently on *Fireside Theater*.

No doubt the best performance in *The Prairie* is delivered by the much underrated and underused Lenore Aubert (who also has a nude bathing scene). The pressbook claimed Aubert was thrilled with her role: "All my life I have wanted to play a pioneer American woman.... You see, I have just a tiny Viennese accent left so it is possible for me to play a French-Spanish Creole girl of 1803." One might be skeptical about the authenticity of the quote but, in her later years, Aubert did tell a fan that she loved *The Prairie*. She's certainly the most sympathetic character in the story and her part is in keeping with Wisbar's predilection to depict strong female characters.

Born in Slovenia and raised in Vienna, Aubert doubled for Claudette Colbert in long shots in European scenes in *Bluebeard's Eighth Wife* (1938). After the Nazis took over Austria, Aubert fled to France and when that too fell to Hitler she trudged across the border to Lisbon and eventually made it to the U.S. She worked as a model and then appeared in local theater in Los Angeles where a Goldwyn talent scout spotted her in *The Man Who Came to Dinner*. Though given a big publicity build-up, Aubert appeared in only one film for Goldwyn, the Bob Hope comedy *They Got Me Covered* (1943). She had good roles in a few RKO pictures: *Passport to Destiny* (1944), *Action in Arabia* (1944) and *Having Wonderful Crime* (1945), and got to sing in Fox's *I Wonder Who's Kissing Her Now* (1947). Considerably less prestigious were her appearances for PRC in *The Wife of Monte Cristo* and Republic's *The Catman of Paris*, both from 1946. Her hopes to land a British contract as well to star in a film version of *The Romantic Heart* came to naught and her career pretty much fizzled in the '50s. She's best remembered today as the sexy, sinister Dr. Sandra Mornay in *Abbott and Costello Meet Frankenstein* (1948).

After on *The Prairie* wrapped, it was announced that Wisbar and Arthur St. Claire would reunite do *The Red Witch*, to be directed by *Prairie*'s editor Douglas L. Bagier (née Wolfgang Löe-Bagier; he fled Germany almost at the same time as Wisbar). Nothing came of the project. Wisbar did work with Robert Lippert, the guiding light of Screen Guild, two more times.

Madonna of the Desert
Republic Pictures
Released on February 23, 1948
60 minutes

Cast: Lynne Roberts as Monica Dale; Donald Barry as Tony French; Don Castle as Joe Salinas; Sheldon Leonard as Nick Julian; Paul Hurst as Pete Connors; Roy Barcroft as Buck Keaton; Paul E. Burns as Hank Davenport; Betty Blythe as Mrs. Brown; Grazia Narciso as Mama Baravelli; Martin Garralaga as Papa Baravelli; Frank Yaconelli as Peppo; Maria Garnardi as Mrs. Pasquale; Renee Donatt as Maria Baravelli; Vernon Cansino as Enrico.

Credits: Director: George Blair; Assistant Director: Joe Dill; Screenplay: Albert DeMond; Story: Frank Wisbar; Producer: Stephen Auer; Music: Mort Glickman; Photography: John MacBurnie; Camera Operator: Herb Kirkpatrick; Editor: Harry Keller; Art Director: Frank Arrigo; Set Decorators: John McCarthy Jr., George Milo; Special Effects: Howard Lydecker, Theodore Lydecker; Makeup: Bob Mark.

The February 8, 1945, edition of *Film Daily* announced that Republic had purchased Frank Wisbar's original story "The Fighting Madonna" and that he had been assigned to do the screen treatment. A June article in the same journal also listed Wisbar as one of 50 writers employed by Republic. However, the film did not go into production until late 1947 and without Wisbar doing the screenplay. Perhaps concerned that audiences might think the film was about lady wrestlers, Republic changed the title to the more peaceful-sounding *Madonna of the Desert* by the time of the film's release a few months later. It was sold largely as a western or action picture ("[T]he desert flames with violence when evil threatens the Madonna of the Desert" exclaimed one ad). Wisbar has no other credits at Republic.

I don't have Wisbar's story to compare to the film. He had managed to smuggle elements of his masterwork *Ferryman Maria* into *Strangler of the Swamp* but it's not likely he was able to work his earlier film about miracles, *Anna and Elisabeth*, into *The Fighting Madonna*. If anything, *Madonna of the Desert* seems like a variation on *The Miracle Man* wherein crooks reform when confronted by genuine holiness. Modern-day miracles may have been treated as reality in the silent era (*The Patent Leather Kid*, *The Confession*) but the '30s and sound engendered a more ambiguous attitude (except for Biblical epics). Perhaps typical is *The Miracle of the Bells*, released around the same time as *Madonna of the Desert*, wherein the title miracle might be genuine but could be explained as having natural causes as well. Though he had not been in America very long, Wisbar had been become savvy enough about public taste to know what would be acceptable to the general audiences and what would be condemned by the Legion of Decency.

Madonna of the Desert (1948)

The Madonna of the Desert is a beautiful statue owned by rancher Joe Salinas. An article about the Madonna appears in an art magazine and attracts the interest of hoodlum Nick Julian, who is interested in the jewels embedded in the statue, not its supposedly miraculous powers. When his attempt to buy the Madonna from Joe is rejected, Julian hires an expert art forger to make a copy of the statue. He then enlists Monica "Legs" Dale (played by Queen of the B's Lynne Roberts) to seduce Joe and substitute the fake statue.

Monica arrives at Joe's ranch claiming car trouble. Joe's cantankerous partner Pete (a scene-stealing performance by Paul Hurst) is skeptical but the good-natured Joe accepts Monica's story and even invites her to go with him to a friend's wedding that day while Pete fixes her car. Joe has loaned the Madonna to the bride and groom for good luck. The wedding is attended by a bunch of Italian stereotypes that make *Life with Luigi* look like something out of neo-realism. Lynn is charmed but she still needs to attend to business so, while everyone is busy dancing, she attempts to steal the statue and substitute the fake. However, her dress catches fire from one of the candles (a pretty harrowing scene). Joe saves her and everyone is astonished to find that she had not suffered any burns.

Monica is still skeptical about the statue's power. "Nobody believes in miracles any more!" she snorts. Joe tells her that he returned from the war crippled in mind and body but thanks to the support of his friends and the power of the Madonna, he has made a complete recovery. Monica is still not convinced; "You might have gotten well anyway." Meanwhile, Tony French, Julian's old enemy, has also been tipped off about the Madonna and, posing as a laborer, shows up at the ranch looking for a job. Joe hires him but Monica guesses what he's really there for.

In spite of her tough talk, Monica is becoming open to the possibility that the statue's power is genuine. She buries what she thinks is the phony statue but gets confused and buries the real one instead. She tells Julian that she won't go through with his scheme and the furious thug slaps her around and heads for the ranch. He runs into Tony, who has copped the fake Madonna. Tony and Julian end up killing each other. Joe is convinced of Monica's sincerity and the former con lady settles down to life on the ranch with Joe, Pete and the Madonna.

Only in a Republic picture would spiritual conflicts be settled by fisticuffs and a shootout.

The film seems to embody the typical Hollywood version of miracles: They *might* be true—no sense alienating millions of American churchgoers—but even if coincidence and natural causes *could* provide the explanation, faith is a good, character-building thing and a sensible alternative to cynicism (which can lead to crime). Of course, only Monica reforms but then again, she's had some exposure to the real thing, unlike Julian and Tony.

The casting is a little offbeat with Don "Red" Barry, usually a good guy, turning up as lowlife punk Tony French while Don Castle, more often than not a villain, plays Joe, the decent man of faith. Sheldon Leonard does his usual tough guy shtick as Julian but I've always found even his serious gangster portrayals bordering on self-parody. Betty Blythe, Queen of Sheba in the silent era, is supposedly somewhere in the cast but I didn't spot her. Director George Blair and writer Albert DeMond have an endless string of credits but nothing exceptional, just good solid Saturday matinee fare. Blair did direct the 1960 cult horror film *The Hypnotic Eye*. Both men ended up in television.

The trade papers found *Madonna of the Desert* unremarkable but good enough. The comments in the March 6, 1948, edition of *Harrison's Reports* were typical: "Fair program entertainment, suitable for neighborhood theaters.... [T]he action is slow in spots.... The romantic interest is pleasant, the photography sharp and the production value pretty good." "Brog" of *Variety* (March 10, 1948) was a little more enthusiastic:

> Neat, clean-cut melodrama that will hold up well in the programmer department.... Plot is slightly off the beaten path, the pace is good and interest sustained.... Production values sustained on a small budget are expert. Camerawork by John MacBurnie, art direction and other technical contributions are good in shaping this one for neat payoff in its market.

While *Madonna of the Desert* is a passably entertaining melodrama, it's a far cry from *Anna and Elisabeth*.

The Mozart Story
Patrician Pictures, Inc./Screen Guild Productions
Released on November 13, 1948
94 minutes

Cast: (of Austrian original *Wen die Götter lieben* [*Whom the Gods Love*]): Hans Holt as Wolfgang Amadeus Mozart; Walter Janssen as Leopold Mozart; Rosa Albach-Retty as Mrs. Mozart; Annie Rosar as Mrs. Weber; Winnie Markus as Constanze Weber Mozart; Irene Meyendorff as Aloysia; Thea Weis as Sophie; Susi Witt as Josepha; Curd Jürgens as Emperor Joseph II; Paul Hörbiger as the valet of von Strack; Richard Eybner as Baron von Gimmingen; René Deltgen as Ludwig van Beethoven; Fritz Imhoff as Albrechtsberger.

Credits: (Austrian original): Director: Karl Hartl; Screenplay: Eduard von Borsody; Based on the novel by Richard Billinger; Photography: Hans Staudinger, Günther Anders; Production Designer: Julius von Borsody, Walter Schmiedl; Set Designer: Julius von Borsody; Costumes: Erni Knipert, Albert Bei; Editor: Henny Brünsch, Karl Hartl; Sound: Alfred Norkus; Music: Aloise Melichar; Source Music: Wolfgang Amadeus Mozart; Production Company: Wien-Film GmbH.

The Mozart Story (1948)

Cast: (American version): Wilton Graff as Antonio Salieri; William Vedder as Franz Josef Haydn; Tony Barr as Ruffini; Carol Forman as Catherine Cavallieri; John Siebert as Duke of Mannheim

Credits: (American version): Director: Frank Wisbar; Writer: Arthur St. Clare; Producer: Abrasha Haimson; Editor: Axel Hubert, Sr.; Special Effects: Ray Mercer; Camera: Paul Ivano

In 1942, the semi-independent Austrian film company Wien-Film produced a biography of Wolfgang Amadeus Mozart. It was originally supposed to be directed by Eduard von Borsody but he fell ill and was replaced by Karl Hartl, best known for the 1937 comedy *Der Mann, der Sherlock Holmes war/ The Man Who Was Sherlock Holmes* and the 1934 sci-fi thriller *Gold*. Hartl was not happy about the project but soldiered on with popular Austrian matinee idol Hans Holt in the lead. The film's title *Whom the Gods love* (*Wen die Götter lieben*) had also been used by a British company for their 1936 bio of Mozart which proved to be a huge critical and financial disaster.

Hartl's film has some scenes devoted to Mozart as a child prodigy but mostly covers less happy times. The young composer falls in love with the beautiful singer Sophie but she rejects him. He ends up marrying her sister Contstanz though he continues to carry a torch for Sophie. Mozart is unable to achieve financial success or win the court appointments that would guarantee stability and the story depicts the dire circumstances under which he was obliged to produce what become his most famous works (including *The Magic Flute*). The film also shows him meeting Beethoven, which is historically true though misleading as Ludwig von was only a teenager at the time. A mysterious, sinister figure in black contracts with Mozart to write a requiem and the very ill composer comes to think it is his own requiem that he is producing. He is proven right and he dies surrounded by his loving family but with no recognition from the world.

Dr. Goebbels, delighted with the film, praised it repeatedly. The Nazis were making propaganda use of Mozart and his music, as well as the other great composers from the glory days of Germany and Austria. Unlike (say) Wagner, Mozart was a somewhat dubious choice to further nationalistic hysteria but history was hardly an important consideration for Goebbels and company. Actually, it's been noted that the story is something of an uncomfortable fit for the "great man" genre so beloved by Nazi filmmakers. After all, Mozart doesn't triumph over his adversaries but dies a pauper; his music doesn't win the day until much later.

The April 14, 1945, issue of *Showmen's Trade Review* announced that producer Herman Millakowski was planning to film *The Immortal*, a life of Mozart, for Republic and Frank Wisbar was to do the screenplay. A 1943 piece in the trades had mentioned that Millakowski—then working for Monogram—had purchased the story *Immortal Spring* from Wisbar. Whether the two *Immortals* are connected or not, Millakowski's venture did not come to fruition.

In 1947, MGM announced that they would produce a film that would combine the life of Mozart with that of fellow Austrian Dr. Franz Mesmer, described as the "father of hypnotism." Robert Walker would be portraying the composer with Kathryn Grayson playing opposite him as a blind pianist. No doubt the gods of bad movies wept when the project did not come to pass.

Nineteen forty-seven also saw the American release of another Mozart picture, *Eternal Melodies*, hailing from Italy and starring Gino Cervi, perhaps best remembered for his ongoing role as Fernandel's nemesis in the Don Camillo movies as well as appearances in innumerable spear and sandal epics. The film, which had been made in 1940, got mostly good reviews but was hardly a blockbuster.

In 1948, Screen Guild Productions announced they would be doing a new version of Mozart's life and it would be their first "class" film. Since Screen Guild specialized in bottom-of-the-barrel westerns and continual reissues of Hopalong Cassidy movies, "class" may be taken with many grains of salt. What they ended up doing was cutting 40 minutes from *Wen die Götter lieben*, adding about 22 minutes of new footage directed by Wisbar and dubbing the whole thing into English.

Perhaps concerned that viewers might not take well to a film produced by the enemy during wartime (something that apparently didn't bother the makers of *Eternal Melodies*), Screen Guild tried to pass the film off as having been made after the war. When this didn't fly, they claimed it was okay because they had taken care to be sure the film's actors had been "de-Nazified." They must have somehow overlooked René Delgeten (Beethoven) who did some jail time for collaborating with the Nazis in his native Luxembourg. It all seems a bit of an unnecessary bother considering that *Wen die Götter lieben* had actually played in America (in a very limited release) a couple of years earlier.

Wisbar's new footage is almost entirely devoted to Antonio Salieri, played with sinister pomposity by Wilton Graff. Screen Guild claimed the character had been omitted from *Wen die Götter lieben* so as not to offend Germany's ally Italy but that's another fib: Goebbels didn't approve of the Salieri legends and suppressed them. And Salieri does turn up in the Italian *Eternal Melodies*. In real life, Mozart and Salieri were not pals and sometimes in competition for the same jobs but no historian today believes that Salieri devoted himself to undermining Mozart, much less killing him (as in *Amadeus*).

The Mozart Story begins with Joseph Haydn sharply questioning Salieri as to why he has been buying up all of the late Mozart's music. Does he intend to destroy Mozart's legacy? Salieri admits that he hated Mozart and we then move on to *Wen die Götter lieben* as a kind of flashback (though Salieri isn't present for most of the events depicted). Graff turns up periodically, trying to ruin Mozart's job prospects, and complaining about him to friends. Obviously, Graff and Hans Holt can't be in the same scene together so Graff lurks around by himself in the background, "watching" Mozart as he performs. At one point, someone impersonating Holt enters a scene with his back to the camera but there's no attempt at any kind of interaction between Mozart and Salieri. We learn that Salieri thinks Mozart's revolutionary approach to composing will ultimately destroy the music world and therefore must be suppressed. Salieri later comes to pity Mozart and goes to visit him on his deathbed but arrives too late (though in time to hear the *Requiem* being played). Back in the present, Salieri tells Haydn that he is buying Mozart's music to preserve his great accomplishments.

The new footage couldn't have posed much of a problem for Wisbar. There are never more than three actors in one shot so the set-ups must have been quick and easy. The simple backgrounds (a drawing room, a tavern) don't need to match the lavishness of *Wen die Götter lieben* and work reasonably well. The actors speaking in their own voices, rather than being dubbed into English, is also an advantage. The photography is in the capable hands of Paul Ivano, a good cinematographer whose work was primarily in B pictures but with the occasional classier production. Perhaps his main claim to fame is shooting the footage no one living has ever seen: the screen test for Bela Lugosi as the Monster in *Frankenstein*.

On December 6, 1948, G.K. of the *Los Angeles Times* had some good words to say about *The Mozart Story* including praise for the musical selections and the acting. Aware of the film's origins, he felt the dubbing was "cleverly accomplished" though the "voices are not as cultured as the subject calls for." It is of course a bit hard to take seriously a period piece in which one character chirps "'Bye, Mozart, have a good time" as the composer heads for Vienna.

A.H. Weiler of the *New York Times* was scornful and wrote in his November 15, 1948, review: "Although English dialogue has supplanted the original German and new scenes have been added to *The Mozart Story* which was first turned out in Vienna in 1939 [sic], Mozart and his coterie have not been helped much." The critic went on to describe the film as "dull and listless" and its depiction of Mozart "unconvincing and uninteresting." Weiler was not moved by the acting either and noted that Graff "plays the glowering 'heavy' Salieri with few flourishes." "Wear" of *Variety* (November 17, 1948) was equally critical:

> Dialogue suffered in the translation; it is well spoken by uncredited American voices, verbiage being often stilted and too often not in keeping with the plot devel-

opments. The additional footage intended to explain more fully why Mozart's genius was so little appreciated in his lifetime not only runs too long but looks like the padding that it is. Appeal limited. Too leisurely in pace.

After noting that *The Mozart Story* was a dubbed version of an old German film, Theresa Loeb in the October 18, 1948, edition of the *Oakland Tribune* was particularly critical:

> This fact alone makes makes most of the movie rather ridiculous. Add to that some of the most unbelievable pompous dialogue, composers acting and talking as if they were aware of posterity every minute of their lives and you have a boring film indeed. Why this movie was released at this time we cannot understand.

Wilton Graff had a notable Broadway career in the '30s, including playing James Stuart, treacherous brother of Mary (Helen Holmes), in *Mary of Scotland*. He didn't enter movies until the 1940s and while he had supporting roles in *Another Part of the Forest*, *A Double Life* and *The Dark Past*, he was more likely to be found in second feature fodder like *Pillow of Death* and *Valley of the Zombies*. His only starring role was as the mad hunter of human beings in the (gory for its day) drive-in cheapie *Bloodlust!* (1961). He also found a niche on television and turned up in a number of episodes of Wisbar's *Fireside Theater*.

Though he had been reluctant to do *Wen die Götter lieben*, Karl Hartl gave his Austrian countryman another whirl in *The Life and Loves of Mozart* (1955) with Oskar Werner but it wasn't until the historically dubious *Amadeus* (1984) that a Mozart film scored a resounding critical and box office success.

Rimfire

Screen Guild Productions
Released on March 25, 1949
64 minutes

Cast: James Millican as Tom Harvey; Mary Beth Hughes as Polly; Reed Hadley as the Abilene Kid; Henry Hull as Nathaniel Greely; Victor Kilian as Sheriff Jim Jordan; "Fuzzy" Knight as Porky Hodges; Chris Pin Martin as Chico; George Cleveland as Judge Gardner; Margia Dean as Lolita; Ray Bennett as Barney Bernard; Glenn Strange as Curt Calvin; John Cason as Blazer; Jason Robards as Elkins; Stanford Jolley as Toad Tyler; Ben Erway as Deputy Sheriff Harry Wilson; Stanley Price as Lamson; Lee Roberts as Jesse Norton; Don Harvey as Rainbow Raymond; Cliff Taylor as Bartender; Dick Alexander as Weber; Introducing Marjorie Stapp as Mary.

Credits: Director: B. Reeves Eason; Assistant Director: Herb Mendelson; Dialogue Director: Gloria Welsch; Producers: Robert L. Lippert, Ron Ormond; Associate Producers: Ira Webb, June Carr; Writers: Arthur St. Claire, Frank

Wisbar, Ron Ormond; Photography: Ernest Miller; Camera Operator: Archie Datzell; Stills: James Doolittle; Art Director: Fred Ritter; Editor: Hugh Winn; Set Decorator: George Milo; Women's Wardrobe: Nevada Penn; Men's Wardrobe: Alfred Berke; Music: Walter Greene; Special Effects: Ray Mercer; Script Supervisor: Dorothy Yutzi; Production Company: Lippert Productions, Inc.

An offbeat western, *Rimfire* takes a very curious turn about halfway through. Frank Wisbar was one of the three writers and while I can't be sure what his contribution was, it's not unreasonable to surmise that he may have been responsible for the macabre plot twist that bears a decided resemblance to *Strangler of the Swamp*.

Not wanting to waste any time, the film begins with a stagecoach robbery under the credits. The robbers stop the coach but the heist is interrupted by Tom Harvey, who shoots one of the stick-up men from a nearby rock and causes the other bad men to scatter, thinking they're faced with a posse. The coach is headed for Stringtown, New Mexico, and the grateful driver offers Tom a lift (Tom's horse was killed by a rattlesnake). Also on board is a card sharp known as the Abilene Kid and Polly, a young woman who has come to visit her uncle, Jim Jordan, sheriff of Stringtown.

The robbery was planned by Barney Bernard, who owns the Stringtown saloon. The Abilene Kid is acquainted with Bernard and knows he's behind the robbery but isn't interested in turning him in. Tom confides in Sheriff Jordan that he's really an undercover Secret Service man on the trail of a gold shipment that disappeared in the area a few years earlier. Jordan deputizes him so as to avert any suspicion from the townsfolk when he starts nosing around.

In the midst of this rather busy plot, two local yokels provide some painfully unfunny comedy relief, mostly involving a slot machine (something of an anachronism). A lackluster romance develops between Tom and Polly. The judge seems a bit ambivalent about his role in this wild and woolly town and the newspaper editor is always grousing about the lack of law and order in the community.

Following a barroom brawl, the Abilene Kid is framed for cheating at cards. After a farcical trial, he is sentenced to be hanged. (Perhaps the judge studied law under Roy Bean.) At his hanging, the Kid proclaims his innocence and warns of a dire fate that awaits a community based on injustice and greed for gold. It's right after this that we see the *Strangler* influence as the Kid's enemies get knocked off one by one by a ghostly killer. We see the murders though not their perpetrator, who is represented by an eerie voice before he starts shooting. The victims are all found with a playing card by their corpses, done in by bullets made of gold. Bernard and his thugs are among the victims and as the body count rises, the townspeople become convinced that the spirit of the Abilene Kid has returned for revenge. The killings become more and more indiscriminate and even the stagecoach driver ends up dead. Tom concludes that a rimfire gun is the murder weapon and suspicion is cast both on the newspaper editor (who we see hiding his rimfire gun) and the judge, who you would think would be the first victim if there was really a vengeful ghost afoot. Not wanting to overlook any whodunit clichés, there is a scene where one character has a moment of revelation and proclaims, "I know who the ghost of the Abilene Kid is!" only to be immediately shot dead. In the end, unsurprisingly, we discover that the culprit is flesh and blood, the idea of a gun-toting spook perhaps being a bit too outlandish. The serial killer turns out to be Sheriff Jordan, who engineered the gold theft and is using the ghost stories to eliminate his partners in crime. At least I think that was the motive but so many people have been killed that either half of Stringtown was in on the gold heist or the sheriff's real plan was to scare everybody out of town. The gold is discovered in a cave by one of the comic buffoons (apparently Tom isn't much of a detective) and there is a climactic fistfight between Tom and Jordan just as the latter, for no particular reason, is about to kill his niece. The sheriff is knocked out but his ultimate fate is unspecified, though given the town's curious priorities, he might have gotten off with just a warning.

The *Showmen's Trade Review* of April 9, 1949, was positive:

> A mystery story that turns out to be a real mystery. To bring this interesting element into the story, the producers ... had to sacrifice some of the action, a condition that might not sit well with the younger followers of this type of fare. But for the average moviegoer, there are good characterizations in an interesting, entertaining story. [Director Eason] gave the picture as much action as the story would take.

Variety's Borg (March 30, 1949) was likewise favorable though not without reservations:

> [F]isticuffs, gun battles and chases which B. Reeves Eason directs with a solid punch. His production is less sure when yarn includes a slowly paced western trial, an unnecessary hanging and mental reactions of townspeople to a series of ghostly killings.... Production is above average for western filmfare but [the producers] tried to cram in too much story.

The principal actors are uninteresting except for Reed Hadley, who makes the Abilene Kid such a sharp and likable rogue that we sorely miss his presence in the second half of the picture. There are plenty of familiar faces in the supporting cast, including Henry Hull as the cantankerous newspaper editor. It's nice to see western and horror veteran Glenn Strange with his arm casually draped over the shapely shoulder of a dance hall girl (Margia Dean).

Initial scenes for *Rimfire* were shot at Iverson's Ranch and then the crew moved on to Republic. Originally, Ford Beebe was assigned to direct but he fell ill. Beebe, who had a certain talent for horror films (like *Night Monster*) as well as horse operas, might have brought a little more panache to the murder sequences. As it stands now, they are a bit too rapid-fire and repetitious to generate any real tension.

Fireside Theater

Anthology programs have largely vanished from the airwaves today but in the early years of television, they were as much a part of the Boob Tube as sitcoms and reality shows are at present. *Kraft Theater* was the first in 1947 and as the number of TV sets across America multiplied, so did the variety of weekly anthology programs: *Armstrong Circle Theater, The Bigelow Theater* (known as *The Listerine Summer Theater* during reruns; can you guess who sponsored them?), *Chevron Theater, Broadway Television Theater, Ford Television Theater, Pepsi-Cola Playhouse, Studio One in Hollywood, Goodyear Playhouse* and a score of others.

And *Fireside Theater*. Not to be confused with the mail order play subscription service of the same name or the comedy group Firesign Theater or the many local theater groups who appropriated the title. TV's *Fireside Theater*, which started in Hollywood in 1949, is virtually unknown today but has two main claims to fame: In the days of mostly live television, it was the first *filmed* series (preceding *I Love Lucy* which is sometimes mistakenly given the credit) and it consistently got ratings among the Top Ten, much to the annoyance of its many detractors. It also brought recognition and a good deal of cash to Frank Wisbar who became the series' guiding light during most of its run. Wisbar, whose work in the humble vineyards of Poverty Row Hollywood had been largely ignored in the press and his German films forgotten, suddenly found himself in *Life* magazine and the subject of interviews, accolades and puff pieces.

Wisbar told an interviewer that his interest in TV started as early as 1942 but, as he said elsewhere, it actually began even before that, in mid–1930s Germany. The Third Reich, as a matter of national pride, had beaten Britain and America to the punch in producing regular television broadcasts in 1935. Hans-Jürgen Nierentz, who had collaborated with Wisbar on *Ferryman Maria*, was an important figure in the development of German television, and Wisbar assisted him in that area. However, the Nazis were divided on the best way to use the new medium and the industrialists who saw TV as the new radio and anticipated making a fortune with the mass production of TV sets ended up disappointed and frustrated when the Third Reich opted to treat TV like a modest version of the cinema. Instead of people watching in their homes, they would gather in halls or "parlors" to watch intermittent broadcasts on the small number of sets the Reich produced. Propaganda, music and little comedy sketches provided most of the programming though Nierentz tried to vary things a bit with some dramatic playlets. The 1936 Olympics were also broadcast. According to Wisbar, the Nazis also developed another, less known use for it: "Later the Nazis confiscated the entire TV system in Germany and used it as a kind of private party line, a private communication system between Adolf Hitler and his followers." This brings up images right out of *Metropolis* with the ruthless master of the great city talking to his henchman via television.

We note, in passing, that the IMDb credits Wisbar as the director of the 1939 BBC television presentation of *The Tell-Tale Heart* but this is surely an error. Wisbar was in America in 1939 and certainly would not have been brought to England to do a 25-minute television show. Dallas Bower, the program's producer, probably directed as well.

As the number of TV sets in America soared (there were six million by 1950), Wisbar desperately wanted to get in on the action. Most television was live and much of it centered in New York but Wisbar decided to do a half-hour story on film in Hollywood and try to sell it. He had to mortgage his house and spent $7500 on the movie (another source says it was only $3000 but $7500 sounds far more likely). "I decided to film either a dramatization of the 23th Psalm or an anti–Nazi suspense story about a time bomb. I flipped a coin and came up with the suspense yarn." The result was "Time Bomb" with John Mitchum (who had appeared in Wisbar's *The Prairie*), Robert Stevenson and Robert Bice, not exactly a big-name cast. No matter since Proctor and Gamble bought the film for *Fireside Theater* (which had premiered in April of 1949) and Wisbar signed on as producer-writer-director, eventually starting his own production company to make a series of films for the show.

Initially, Wisbar was not sure of the best approach to *Fireside Theater*, which originally had been a variety show. He attempted a couple of different things: "I tried a one-act play and it didn't work. Then a blown-up story followed by a condensed drama and neither one of those worked." Wisbar found himself scrambling to put things together: "No one thought that television would work on film. I couldn't get name actors. I couldn't get experienced writers. Agents wouldn't talk to me.... You had to lie, brag and exaggerate to get backing. You would go to a money man and tell him what you think the situation would be with TV films. You could talk about reruns but he would ask: 'Does anyone know what reruns will bring?' You had to admit, no, no one had ever tried it."

Season 2 focused on drama and horror, usually two 13-minute stories per episode. "I stood on street corners and asked writers if they wouldn't turn out scripts for $45 a copy. I had no trunk full of stories so I had to raid the public domain classics. I looted Chekhov, plundered de Maupassant and stripped Robert Louis Stevenson." However, *Fireside Theater* was given one huge advantage: It played on NBC Tuesdays at 9 p.m. following Milton Berle's variety show *The Texaco Star Theater*, the most popular show on television. Of course, not all of Uncle Miltie's fans necessarily stayed tuned for *Fireside Theater* but it certainly provided a formidable lead-in. *Television Daily* felt the latter was probably the only reason *Fireside Theater* thrived; from its November 17, 1949, review:

> Safely ensconced in the NBC timeslot following the top-rated Milton Berle show, *Fireside Theater* continues to offer film programs that are so far below quality of live video that its shadow of mediocrity is being cast on the entire field of TV films. Each week, two shorts, about 12 minutes each, are aired. With few exceptions, these films have been almost amateurish in script, acting and photography. The weakness of the story material is primarily due, we think, to the difficulties in developing characters and plot in such a short time. When occasionally a good story is used, the adaptation is so poor that the production and acting suffer as a result. (Once the show attempted to squeeze Cooper's novel "The Spy" into a quarter hour, less time for commercials). And photography for the most part has overlooked the rigid requirements of the video system and the ten-inch screen in both lighting and composition. Many of the Hollywood movie boys have been touting themselves as the salvation of TV programming. Their efforts, as demonstrated thus far on *Fireside Theater*, indicate they should acquaint themselves of the fundamentals of the new media before trying to save it.

Critics were far more appreciative of live shows like *Robert Montgomery Presents* which had classy adaptations of Fitzgerald and Hawthorne with big-name actors, high production values and one-hour running times. While it seems comically absurd to try to condense a whole novel into a film that runs less than 15 minutes, short stories, particularly of the horror variety, might have worked well with such a brief length. Some of the titles from *Fireside* certainly sound intriguing:

- "Germelhausen": An American GI in Germany runs across a cursed village that only appears every once every hundred years.
- "Mardi-Gras": When one of his guests dies of the Black Plague, a hotel manager devises an elaborate plot in order to prevent a panic in Mardi-Gras–thronged New Orleans.
- "The Scream in the Night": An artist, strangely inspired, depicts a scene of murder with such exactness that he is accused of committing the crime.
- "Vampire": A young girl, the victim of a vampire, is saved by her father's desperate action.
- "The Imp in the Bottle": based on the Robert Louis Stevenson story.

- "A Terribly Strange Bed": based on the Wilkie Collins tale about a gambling house with murderous proprietors.
- "Heartbeat": an adaptation of Edgar Allan Poe's "The Tell-Tale Heart."

The latter two films, both directed by William Cameron Menzies, were not done for *Fireside Theater* but fit into the show's format. It is also perhaps worth mentioning that two of *Fireside*'s better known shows, an adaptation of Shirley Jackson's *The Lottery* and Charles Dickens' *A Christmas Carol* with Sir Ralph Richardson, weren't really part of the series but replacement programs.

By the 1950 season, Wisbar largely abandoned the horror tales (though he did do a version of *The Amber Gods*) and focused on drama. Wisbar had decided that a one-story, 30-minute film worked the best. Proctor and Gamble joined with Bing Crosby Enterprises to produce the series and the January 30, 1950, *New York Times* noted that Wisbar "will produce one film every two days for the next three weeks at the Hal Roach studios with a budget of $12,000 per program." Shooting on film was very appealing to the sponsors because it meant there was good money to be made in reruns. Kinescopes of live performances were usually of poor quality, quite inferior to film. And film meant that retakes could be done if mistakes were made on the commercials. (Errors made during the film were obviously less important.) However, according to Wisbar, putting this all together was no mean feat:

> A TV producer must realize this, he must have a thorough understanding of mass psychology. He should be author, playwright and story editor in order to understand the stories he buys, to advise the writers on what he wants and to rewrite if he doesn't like what they give him. He must be a psychologist and diplomat in order to deal with the sponsor, agency, writers, actors and technicians simultaneously.

Columnist Buddy Mason, who visited the *Fireside* set, was impressed, writing in a July 1953 column:

> It's always a pleasure to watch Frank Wisbar direct this series. A master of stagecraft, Wisbar "paints" mood and tempo on film. We say "paints" because no other word is adequate. He transfers dramatic effect to celluloid like a painter creating beauty on canvas with ordinary oil colors. The same oils that become drab attempts to picture reality in the hands of lesser men. Ben Kline, veteran cinematographer, adds his skill to highlight the Wisbar "canvas." Right down to the longest speeches, Wisbar knows each player's lines by heart. His lips silently form each word as the actors speak. When the cameras roll, we never watch the players. It's Wisbar on the sidelines who gives the best performance. He does *all* the parts.

Critic John Crosby *was* watching the players and didn't much care for what he saw:

Frank Wisbar (right) watches Joan Blondell getting made up for "Sergeant Sullivan Speaking," an episode of *Fireside Theater*.

One of the paradoxes of modern television in its present state of infancy is that the acting in the film dramas imported east from Hollywood is atrocious. I'm not saying it's bad you understand. It's horrible. But the best of them (actors) are prevented from appearing on television by their studios. The rest of them are scared away by the curious social stigma which actors in the movie capital still attach to video.... Some episodes of *Fireside Theater* have been pretty good. Many have been very bad.

Nevertheless, in November 1951, Wisbar won the Sylvania Award for his work and *Fireside Theater* was cited as the best example of the use of film in television. (The Sylvania Awards were given by a 17-member committee led by critic Deems Taylor. There were no Emmys as of yet.) Still, *Swing* magazine groused that *Fireside Theater,* "which has maintained a consistent level of mediocrity, leads all television dramas in popularity—if you believe the ratings. There are at least seven other dramatic programs which are far better, have bigger budgets and greater box-office names in the cast."

If these critical brickbats bothered Wisbar, he didn't show it:

> I don't believe in being overly artistic. The arty picture is not what the majority of people want. On the whole, our audience seems to prefer its drama without violence. That's why all our shows are based on the same principle and they will continue to be.... The average man went to see Shakespeare and Christopher Marlowe They had everything in their stories that would appeal to all types of persons. They wrote of sex and funny situations and murder—and yet they had poetry and meaning for people who were looking for those things.

Wisbar joined the growing trend of anthology series of having the shows introduced by a host. This was not a development cheered by everyone. Milton Bass wrote on December 2, 1952:

> Even Frank Wisbar who has always done a pretty good job on *Fireside Theater* now feels it's necessary to introduce, break into and complete his filmed drama with a few choice words. He's about as welcome as Joe McCarthy would be at a meeting of the Civil Liberties league.

Wisbar hosted the show for several seasons and then yielded his chair by the fireplace to actor Gene Raymond. I regret not having seen any of the episodes hosted by Wisbar because I would love to hear him extol the virtues of Ivory Soap with his German accent and attempt to maintain his Teutonic dignity while demonstrating with a set of scales how Ivory is superior to Brand X.

Though critics were often scornful, *Fireside Theater* sometimes attempted to do something a little different. For example, "The Vigil" was shot almost entirely in close-ups while "Sergeant Sullivan Speaking" (with Joan Blondell and William Bendix) was done in long single-shot telephone conversations. "The Reign of Amelika Joe" was written by Afro-American actor James Edwards, who also starred in the episode. "Crusade Without Conscience," an anti–Communist thriller, won a Christopher award for Wisbar and teleplay writer Michael Foster. Wisbar also somehow found the time to direct a number of episodes of another anthology show, *GE Theater*.

Nineteen fifty-four brought a great deal of hoopla about the airing of the 250th episode of *Fireside Theater*. Cecil Smith wrote in *The Los Angeles Times* (November 12, 1954):

> It's high time that Frank Wisbar and his *Fireside* crew took a very deep bow for their long and continuing efforts to provide excellent entertainment for the televiewing public. They were pioneers in the field of filmed drama. They developed it from its very rude beginnings—one or two sets and a flighty camera—to its present technical excellence, which rivals all dramatic mediums.... Some figures: 7000 actors and extras have appeared on the show. Seven million feet of film exposed. Total cost of production, including air time, 14 million. Initially each episode cost about 7500 but now 26,000 is the average. Scripts used to be bought for $75 but now the cost is $1500 per script. For its first year, 2 million homes watched it once a week. Now it's estimated that 9,500,000 families tune in.

Wisbar and his crew had a big celebration on the set (now on the Eagle-Lion lot) with dozens of lovely actresses who had played in the series crowding into a big boxing ring center stage (to pose, not to fight). Many of the show's past stars were in attendance and Wisbar posed in front of a giant replica of a fireplace.

Wisbar often commented on the difficulties of producing a show like *Fireside* (or *any* series) and how important it was not to do predictable "formula" stories:

> The biggest problem facing TV dramas is one the movies never have to meet—holding on to an audience. We do not have a "captive" audience, one which must stay in the theater seat and watch or fall asleep. A story must be good or "click" goes the dial. Each week *Fireside* must hold the interests of families so completely they will stay with us for the entire half-hour.... In order to capture the audience, we start out with a climax—in other words, open the scene and cock the gun—then the audience will wait for the entire show for the gun to be fired.

Critic Lyn Connelly (*Eufaula Indian Journal*, March 11, 1954) suggested the producer-director take his own advice: "Wisbar is certainly correct which brings up the question, if he is so cognizant of this, how come *Fireside Theater* doesn't come up with better scripts? The ones in recent weeks have been pretty hackneyed and the acting leaves much to be desired."

Perhaps part of the problem was that Wisbar saw himself as doing nothing more than wholesome family dramas and he sometimes sounded like he was running for president of the PTA. Wisbar as quoted in the *Tyrone Daily Herald*, February 12, 1954:

> Too many children and teenagers listen to every word and watch every move on the TV screen. They are easily impressed and these are their most sensitive and formative years.... TV in a home where there are children is plain dynamite—it can be loaded with beauty and the good things of of life or it can be just plain trash! My dramatic recipe is the simplest in the world. It is aimed at bringing simplicity and humility into the American home—not divorce, drunkenness, dope addiction, suicide or lecherous language.

Such self-imposed limitations don't often make for very scintillating viewing, at least if the four episodes of *Fireside* I've seen are typical. Some brief rundowns:

George Brent, a very stolid, uninteresting actor at this date, stars in "Return in Triumph" as Horatio—not Hamlet's best bud, but a state governor with bitter memories of a childhood spent in poverty. As the show begins, Horatio and his grown-up son Randy (who calls his dad "governor") are hunting on the Bellefonte estate (played by a few bushes on a soundstage). The once proud mansion on the grounds has fallen into disrepair and is inhabited only by Nancy and her aunt Faith (Gertrude Michael), sister of the deceased Southern belle Rosamund. Nancy scolds the two men for intruding but Horatio is struck by Nancy's resemblance to Rosamund, who once humiliated Horatio. Faith recognizes Horatio and invites him and Randy to stay for dinner and spend the night. It turns out that Bellefonte is in receivership and Horatio is about to become the new owner. The viewer's hopes that this will develop into a kind of *Wuthering Heights* scenario are quickly disappointed by the endless dinner conversation. We learn that Horatio, when a teenager, approached Rosamund during a party at her estate and asked to wear her colors for an upcoming debate. She laughed at him but the next day he received a package containing a ratty tie and he concluded she was playing a cruel joke on him. However, it turns out that Faith, then a gawky 13-year-old, had a crush on Horatio and sent him the tie. This revelation inexplicably makes everything all right and Horatio realizes that he and Faith could have loved one another. And ... perhaps it's not too late. To clinch the deal, Randy and Nancy declare that they are in love, their romance having apparently developed while they were doing the dishes.

"Afraid to Live" is equally contrived but at least has a few changes of scene. A rich woman (Dorothy Malone) arrives on the Fiji Islands with her fiancé, a diplomat. It turns out that the woman's old beau is also on the island, doing some kind of anthropological research which doesn't pay much but is his life's work. Malone meets beachcomber Thomas Mitchell but he turns out to be a respected member of the local society, not a bum. Also a philosopher, he guides Malone into realizing it's the anthropologist she loves while the diplomat discovers he'd rather till the soil than attend black tie dinners. While watching the program, I thought I would describe Mitchell's performance as "owlish" but then a real owl shows up and that somehow convinces Malone of the wisdom of her decision. Malone, who did three *Fireside* episodes, was impressed with Wisbar: "It's such a thrill to work with him. Even though we shoot a telefilm in three days, he's so methodical and thorough it's like making a $5,000,000 MGM spectacle. And it's fun!" (*The Evening Independent*, December 15, 1954).

Fireside switches to humor with the tongue-in-cheek "The Grass Is

Greener." Gene Raymond plays Bruce, once a big-time actor but now happy to be running a ranch with his wife Irene and two children. Television has arrived and the kids really want one but Bruce is reluctant. Irene connives to have a set brought to the house on a trial basis. At this point we expect the rest of the film to be about Bruce's gradual acceptance of the new medium but instead things take a twist when Bruce watches his old friend Charlie in a movie on the tube. Bruce has heard somewhere that Charlie has fallen on hard times and invites him to the ranch. Charlie, with a ditzy girlfriend in tow, shows up for a visit and seems to be just fine. In fact, he thought it was Bruce who was having trouble, unaware that his friend purposely gave up the Hollywood life. Charlie urges Bruce to get back into the movies. When Bruce seems willing to consider the idea, Charlie sends producer Richard Wilbur to call on him. Wilbur (a broad but amusing performance by Ralph Dumke, a *Fireside* regular) is convinced that Bruce and his ranch would be the perfect subjects for a new series (the first reality show?). In fact, the whole family can play a part! In the middle of all this planning, Bruce is called away by a fellow rancher who needs help delivering a calf. Wilbur is appalled to think that such interruptions of filming could be routine and suggests just using the ranch for background footage and shooting the rest in Hollywood. Knowing that would mean selling the ranch, Bruce refuses and tells the astonished producer that he likes his life just as it is. As the producer departs, Bruce, his wife and two kids watch from the doorway of their happy home like they're posing for a Norman Rockwell cover.

In "The Indiscreet Mrs. Jarvis," Angela Lansbury delivers a sharp, knowing performance as Brenda, wife of industrialist Paul Jarvis (George Brent again). Sam (William Lundigan) is hoping to get an important job in Paul's new planned community. Paul invites Sam and his wife Ellen (Martha Vickers) to dinner and offers Sam the position but Brenda reacts badly to Ellen's presence. They knew each other years earlier, before Brenda's marriage to Paul. At that time, Brenda had embarked on a scandalous affair with a married man. Brenda is uncomfortable with the idea of having to see Ellen regularly. Brenda's bitter, crippled sister Catherine (Ann Doran) urges her to dissuade Paul from hiring Sam. She does so, saying Ellen has always been a troublemaker. Sam is puzzled when he doesn't get the job but Ellen feels it might be her fault, that she lacks the necessary social graces. She contacts Brenda, whose sister convinces her that a blackmail attempt is coming. The reality is that Ellen never knew anything about the affair. When Ellen and Brenda meet, the latter realizes she's been mistaken. She confesses everything to Paul, who is glad that his wife finally loves him enough to trust him.

If there's a common theme to these episodes, it may be that you shouldn't let your past dictate your choices, that the here and now and future are what count. Such a moral may have had resonance for a generation that had survived the Depression and war and was entering into a period of prosperity (for many people at least).

Always looking for technical innovations, Wisbar did some color tests for *Fireside Theater*. "Of course, color is coming," Wisbar enthused to a reporter. "It is just around the corner. But it might be some time before we reach that 'corner' and the turn. For one thing, sponsors will regard it with caution. Color will cost an advertiser 30 percent more than black and white and, for the first four or five years, the number of viewers with color TV sets simply will not justify boosting production costs by 30 percent. It's as simple as that" (*Cedar Rapids Tribune*, December 17, 1953).

At the same time, Wisbar was even more enthusiastic about the prospect of videotape, a technology that Bing Crosby Productions was working on:

> My present budget for one *Fireside* film is $20,000. I estimate I can cut 8,500 to 7,000 from the budget through the use of magnetic tape. Magnetic tape for picture and sound will eliminate film and all of its expensive handling. Instead of waiting for the dailies to be developed, a director can shoot a scene on tape with his electronic camera and then play it back immediately on a monitor; if he doesn't like the way the scene plays, all he has to do is erase it from the tape and shoot it over again. We're living on the threshold of a revolution in TV one that will see the combining of all the best techniques from "live" and filmed production.

That revolution was a long way off.

Wisbar resigned from *Fireside* in mid–December 1954 over a "policy dispute." The show continued to run until February 1955 when it was cancelled. Then it was revamped and went back on the air in September as *Jane Wyman Presents Fireside Theater* with the actress hosting and frequently starring. Today, these episodes are the easiest to come by. The Wisbar years are much more elusive. The Library of Congress has a handful of them and every so often a 16mm copy of a show will turn up on eBay. Some of them were edited and put together with other '50s anthology shows, to be sold to TV different stations under titles like *Royal Theater* and *Plays of the Year*. Usually, these were fillers for odd hours but cable pretty much put an end to their syndication. In the early '60s, 11 of them were dubbed into German and played in Deutschland as *Leine Spiele Aus Ubersee* (*Little Plays from Overseas*). While there's plenty of love for Lucy, Hitchcock and Rod Serling, Wisbar's TV efforts constitute little more than a footnote in the medium's history. Perhaps if some of the horror episodes become available, that might change. But very likely *TV Guide's* description of the show as making "no attempt at artiness, profundity or significance" will remain the final word.

Haie und kleine Fische
(Sharks and Little Fish)
Willy Zeyn-Film GmbH
Released on September 26, 1957
120 minutes

Cast: Hansjörg Felmy as Teichmann; Sabine Bethmann as Edith Wegener; Wolfgang Preiss as U-boat Commander Lüttke; Mady Rahl as Dora; Heinz Engelmann as Erich Wegener; Horst Frank as Heyne; Thomas Braut as Stollenberg; Ernst Reinhold as Vögele; Wolfgang Wahl as Chief Engineer of the U-boat; Siegfried Lowitz as Lt. Pauli; Stefan Wigger as Prinz Wrathenstein; Peter Frank as Dr. Timler; Reinhold Brandes as Lt. Kerstein; Sascha Keith as Zebra; Friedrich Schütter as Lt. Brandsetter; Horst Fesel as the Chief Engineer of the *Albatross*; Hellmuth Kleinschmidt as Koch; Vicco von Büllow, Dirk Dautzenberg, Walter Laugwitz.
Credits: Director: Frank Wisbar; Screenplay: Wolfgang Ott, based on his novel; Script Editor: Alf Teichs; Photography: Günther Haase; Production Designer: Erich Kettelhut, Johannes Oot; Costume Designer: Irms Pauli; Editor: Carl Otto Bartning; Sound: Jan van der Eerden; Music: Hans-Martin Majewski; Producer: Alf Teichs.

According to Will Temper, Frank Wisbar once told him that if he had stayed in Germany during the Third Reich, he would have made "some solid war movies." Upon his return to Germany, that is exactly what Wisbar did though they might be labeled "anti-war" films and were certainly far from what would have been acceptable to Dr. Goebbels. *Sharks and Little Fish*, set on minesweepers and submarines, was based on the 1956 book of the same name by Wolfgang Ott, who served on a submarine in World War II.

As far as cinematic U-boats go, sympathy usually depended on what side of the periscope you were on. Hollywood movies of the silent era, mindful of the *Lusitania* and the merciless U-boat campaign against civilian ships, depicted German submarine commanders and their crews as vile, cowardly and sadistic in *Behind the Door, False Faces* and *Mare Nostrum*. There were really no German-made submarine epics during the Great War but in 1933, just as the Nazis were coming to power, Ufa released *Morgenrot (Red Dawn)*, one of the great submarine movies. It showed the U-boat warriors as honorable, devoted to each other and dutiful to the very end. There's a surprising near-pacifist speech by the mother of one of the characters, but more typical is the famous line "Perhaps we Germans do not know how to live, but how to die we know incredibly well." Far less effective was the 1941 propaganda film *U–Boote westwärts (U-boat Course West)*. The very slow first half shows the submarine crew on leave (and behaving very well; no brothels for these knights of the sea!). But there's some action later when the U-boat confronts a British destroyer. A few of the U-boat's crew had earlier been captured by the destroyer but the U-boat commander, though knowing this, still must torpedo the ship. (The prisoners cheer even though they are in mortal peril.) Happily, they are then able to rescue their comrades. Indeed, it seems as though the U-boat suffers only one fatal casualty (who is appropriately honored at a later ceremony). In reality, 75 percent of U-boat sailors died in combat but, obviously, at this point in the game, showing heavy military losses would have not have served the film's purpose.

Sharks and Little Fish gives a far more realistic depiction of submarine warfare though not as grisly as the book.

This synopsis is based on a viewing of the film:

Four young midshipmen report for duty on the *Albatross*, part of a flotilla of minesweepers. They're good friends but with very different personalities: Teichmann is cocky, Heyne a cynical intellectual, Vögele naïve and Stollenberg a conciliator. Teichmann gets into trouble with the captain of the *Albatross*, Lt. Pauli, who is both a martinet and inept. On a lazy Sunday, Teichmann goes sailing and yells at some women passing without warning on a motorboat. One of the women turns out to be an admiral's wife and when she complains, Teichmann has to report to Erich Wegener, chief of the flotilla. Wegener assigns Teichmann to help his wife Edith with some domestic chores. Teichmann is delighted to find that she is pretty and much younger than her husband. A mutual attraction develops but when he steals a kiss, she orders him to leave.

After a long period of inactivity, the minesweepers finally see some action. When enemy planes attack, Lt. Pauli doesn't order his ship to return to port and the *Albatross* suffers some damage. Pauli panics, fearing the ship is sinking, and orders the hatches battened down, trapping Teichmann and other sailors in the boiler room. Stollenberg defies the lieutenant and opens the hatches. A furious Teichmann punches Pauli, who promises to report him. However, the ship is far from sinking and when Wegener boards her, he immediately dismisses Pauli for incompetence.

The flotilla suffers much destruction in a major battle. Wegener's ship sinks and he is wounded. Teichmann saves him and the two cling to some wreckage until they are rescued. Wegener is blind as a result of his injury. When Edith comes to visit them both in the hospital, Wegener's good friend, U-boat commander Lütke, is uneasy about Edith's attention to Teichmann.

Teichmann is assigned to Lütke's U-boat but the commander seems to have it in for him and continually belittles him. During a night out at a local brothel, Lütke tells him that he has no respect for him as an officer or a gentleman. However, after several harrowing experiences on the submarine where Teichmann proves his worth, Lütke's attitude softens. As the German navy continues to suffer reverses, Lütke becomes convinced that the

British planes have new tracking devices that reduce the U-boats to sitting ducks.

Teichmann is still carrying a torch for Edith, who now has to care for her invalid husband. In the course of time, the couple adjusts to their new situation and Teichmann realizes he has no chance with Edith. Teichmann later meets with a despondent Heyne, who tells him that his father, a professor, has died in a concentration camp for expressing skepticism about the war. It also turns out he had Jewish grandparents. Heyne tells his friend that they are all little fish at the mercy of the greatest shark of all. Then he shoots himself.

Lütke's submarine is damaged while submerged during a battle. The crew must leave the submarine and swim to the surface. Lütke, the last to leave, is killed when his protective jacket is torn. Teichmann makes it to the surface. He is the last of his friends to survive, Vögele and Stollenberg having also died in the conflict.

The last shot of the film shows the survivors treading water and waiting to be rescued. The book adds the grisly detail that they are surrounded by the floating corpses of their comrades, whose dead eyes are being pecked out by birds.

Most of the film's battle scenes are provided by stock war footage. Wisbar does reasonably well with integrating it with the rest of the action but it certainly wouldn't fool anyone. It's all too obvious when you go from a shot of an actual ship blowing up to a studio tank with a few floating wooden planks to represent wreckage. Neither is there a real sense of claustrophobia in the submarine's interior; it comes off as being just a cheap set, not a functioning engine room (especially when compared to the excellent 1981 *Das Boot*). Another problem is that, given the episodic nature of the story, some of the action sequences are too brief to build up any real suspense.

The tension in the film comes more from the interaction of the different characters, a kind of father-son conflict between commanders and men that runs throughout the picture. You go from bad fathers (Lt. Pauli) to stern but just ones (Wegener) to the kind that mean well but just don't get you (Lütke). There's something Oedipal about Teichmann's attraction to Edith which can't possibly end with him actually possessing her so the film's one romance seems foredoomed from the start. His three friends aren't given any love interest and the other women in the film are whores, though very nice. Dora, who runs a brothel, even becomes a mother figure to Teichmann, attempting more than once to keep her bad boy out of trouble. In the end, the four friends have only each other to depend on, a situation not unlike that in *All Quiet on the Western Front*. But it's not enough to save their lives.

Like Wisbar's other war epics, the film has been criticized for dissolving the political background of the conflict. Throughout the film, there's no sense of the cause the characters are fighting for. No one says "Heil, Hitler" and there doesn't seem to be a bona fide Nazi in sight. Lt. Pauli, the film's only "villain," is a strutting fool always insisting on the proper salute, but even he doesn't spout Third Reich slogans. A writer for the Propaganda Ministry who comes aboard to write about the sailors' heroism is an absurd little man whose character is played for laughs, hardly an appropriate representative of the efforts of the fanatical Dr. Goebbels. The only time politics come into play is with the death of Heyne's father. Heyne can no longer fight for a cause that has murdered his father, but prior to that he had expressed no concern about all the other fathers who ended up in concentration camps. It's become personal rather than political and he doesn't have enough belief in the cause to surmount his loss. But we don't really know about his beliefs in the first place, only that he has a gloomy philosophy based on the fatalistic Schopenhauer so presumably he never could have been a devout Nazi. He and his friends have simply been caught up in the tidal wave caused by the Third Reich.

The film's political stance can perhaps be found in the agonized words of Lütke when he realizes the war effort is doomed: "I never wanted this goddamned war but I've done my best!" That seems to sum up Wisbar's attitude about the soldiers who fought for the Reich. Whether that truly reflects the reality is another matter. However, this is not unique to German war films of that era. An American submarine thriller, the excellent *The Enemy Below*, released at about the same time as *Sharks*, depicts the captain of the U-boat and his first mate as "good" Germans, giving their all to their duty but not believing in the cause (they roll their eyes when they see one of the crew reading *Mein Kampf*). Of course, all this may be something of a reaction to Hollywood war movies in the '40s where the German side was represented by jackbooted fanatics.

Hansjörg Felmy is perfectly cast as Teichmann. In his teen years, he was unfairly punished by a teacher and promptly socked him in the jaw, just the sort of reaction you'd expect from Teichmann. Felmy briefly aspired to be an opera singer but then switched to acting and did a number of plays. His first film, the World War II epic *Star of Africa* (1957), was followed by *Sharks*. He then played in still another film set in the Nazi era, *Unrühige Nacht* aka *The Restless Night*, this time portraying a rebel against the Reich who is eventually executed. Felmy subsequently won several Bambi awards (given by the movie magazine *Film Journal*) and played a variety of roles (including a couple of Edgar Wallace thrillers) in movies and on TV.

Horst Frank (Heyne) had worked with Felmy in *Star of Africa*. His portrait of sad, world-weary disillusion in *Sharks* got him the Best Actor award from the German Film Critics Association. Frank then settled comfortably into playing villains in westerns and spy thrillers, becoming something like a cross between Richard Widmark and a less wild-eyed Klaus Kinski. Horror fans will recall his sublimely creepy Dr. Ood from *The Head* (1959); if Monogram ever made an Expressionist picture, it might have looked like this one. Frank worked with Wisbar again in *Dogs, Do You Want to Live Forever?* and *The Officer Factory.*

The rest of the cast is uniformly excellent. Wolfgang Preiss (Lütke) and Heinz Engelmann (Wegener) seem to be the same character: a tough-minded, no-nonsense skipper devoted to his men and making the best of an increasingly unwinnable situation. Engelmann also brings real poignancy to his later scenes where he's blind and frustrated. Sabine Bethmann is a lovely Edith and would soon be playing in the Fritz Lang remake of *The Indian Tomb.* Mady Rahl's performance as Dora makes the character seem more than the typical whore-with-a heart-of-gold cliché. A major star for the Third Reich, she may have been intimate with Hitler himself. She played in the odious anti–Semitic film *Jew Süss* but at least had the honesty to later admit that she campaigned for her role (the rest of the cast made lame excuses for their participation after the war). She also worked for Wisbar in *Darkness Fell on Gotenhafen.*

Hans-Martin Majewski's score for the film is a mixed bag. Too much of it is jazzy and inappropriate. One notable credit in the film is art direction by Erich Kettlehut, whose outstanding career stretches all the way back to *Metropolis*. Kettlehut also worked with Wisbar on two telefilms, *Der Feuerzeichen (The Fire Sign)* and *Willkommen in Altamont (Welcome to Altamont).*

Sharks and Little Fish got mostly good reviews and was a box office hit, making for an auspicious beginning to the last phase of Frank Wisbar's movie career.

Nasser Asphalt (Wet Asphalt)

Inter West Film GmbH
Released on April 1, 1958
88 minutes

Cast: Horst Buchhoz as Greg Bachman; Martin Held as Cesar Boyd; Maria Perschy as Bettina; Gert Frobe as Jupp; Heniz Reinke as the Blind Man; Inge Meysel as Gustl; Peter Capell as Donnagan; Renate Schacht as Wanda; Richard Münch as Dr. Wolf; Ludwig Linkmann as Tanek; Aranka Jaenke as Mrs. Adorf; Nikolai Baschkoff as Cepinek.

Credits: Director: Frank Wisbar; Story and Screenplay: Will Tremper; Producer: Wenzel Lüdke; Original Music: Hans-Martin Majewski; Photography: Helmut

Ashley; Editor: Klaus Dudenhöfer; Production Designer: Albrecht Becker, Herbert Kirchoff; Costume Designer: Helga Reuter; Makeup: Herbert Greiser, Trude Weinz-Werner; Production: Emil Hess, Peter Homfeld, Heniz Karchow, Gert Weber; Assistant Director: Wieland Liebske; Sound: Hans Abel; Assistant Camera: Wolfgang Hoffmann, Nicolas Fexis.

> The press is going to have a field day!
> —a line from too many films to enumerate

In June 1951, the Associated Press reported a very strange story from Poland, wherein a German soldier supposedly survived for six years in an underground Nazi supply depot. "According to reports the soldier said he and five other soldiers were imprisoned in the concrete bunker when German troops, retreating from Poland, dynamited the entrance in 1945 [...] Authorities said the bodies of four men, encased in sacks of flour and almost completely mummified, were found in the depot." There are two different stories of what happened to the surviving soldier: In one, he completely recovers and leaves the hospital never to be heard of again. In the other, he dies of scurvy.

In spite of what it says in the article, Polish authorities disclaimed any knowledge of the story. The consensus today seems to be that the story was likely a hoax but alas there was no Snopes.com in the '50s and it's impossible to know at this juncture who would have perpetuated the fraud and what their motives might have been. But more on that later.

The story, true or not, inspired Rudolf Hagelstang's 70-page narrative poem *The Ballad of the Buried Life* (1952). Margarete Hohoff's play *The Legend of Babie Doly* (Babie Doly is a village near Gdynia) and the 1955 novel *Le Blockhaus* which became the basis for a 1973 Peter Sellers film, *The Blockhouse* (which changed the protagonists from Wehrmacht soldiers to slave laborers). Frank Wisbar's *Wet Asphalt* takes the position that the story was just a fraud meant to sell newspapers.

This synopsis is based on a viewing of the English dubbed version of the film:

In 1947, Greg Bachman, who has spent several years in a Berlin prison for sneaking into Spandau and interviewing Nazi prisoners, is surprised to find that his sentence has been reduced by six months. At the prison gates, he is met by Jupp, chauffeur to newspaper magnate Cesar Boyd. Jupp tells him that his boss wants to see him. Though puzzled, Greg agrees to be taken to Boyd's house.

Boyd, flamboyant and charismatic, tells Greg that he arranged for his sentence to be shortened because he wants the talented journalist to work for him. Bachman will find the sensationalistic stories that Boyd sells to the different newspapers and Boyd will rewrite them in his own style. The money is good and Bachman quickly agrees. During the next four years, Boyd sends him all over the globe in search of stories. Greg is content with this arrangement though he sometimes complains that he would like the occasional byline for his work.

Bettina, the young daughter of one of Boyd's old friends, arrives in Berlin after the death of her father. Boyd is to be her guardian and see to it that she enrolls at a university. Boyd's interest in the beautiful girl soon becomes more than paternal but he has a rival in Greg.

With the weekend approaching and with it the commitment to provide weekly big stories for the Paris newspapers, Boyd is irritated to find that Greg has not come up with anything appropriately exciting. Just to pass the time, Jupp tells his boss of an unusual experience he had in Poland during the war. He and some friends discovered a vast storage bunker in Gdynia (the English-dubbed version mistakenly has Göttingen—a German city!—as the place) that had enough supplies to last for years. He and his pals raided the bunker but before they could return for more plunder, the Wehrmacht dynamited it. Boyd tells Jupp to keep quiet about this event.

Shortly afterwards, Boyd gives Greg a story for the French press: Polish authorities clearing out the rubble in front of an old storage bunker have discovered that five Nazi soldiers have been living in the place since the war. Only one of them is still alive. Greg is fascinated by the story, which soon becomes a worldwide sensation.

The publisher of an American newspaper is furious that Donnagan, their man in Poland, has not reported any such story. Donnagan is told by his government contact in Poland that the story is bogus but he requests permission to visit Gdynia anyway. It turns out that Gdynia is the site of some rocket experimentation by the Russians. The communist authorities suspect the survivor story is a ruse to check out the rocket site ("All newspapermen in Poland are spies!" complains one official). When his request to go to Gdynia is denied, Donnagan travels there secretly and arrives just in time to see a British journalist on the same errand arrested by Russian soldiers. Donnagan, thinking that maybe something is up, tells the story to his newspaper and is promptly expelled from Poland.

Greg is exasperated by his boss' reluctance to provide more details about the story to the eager newspapers. He finally corners Boyd at the latter's favorite restaurant and insists that he comes across with further information. Boyd says he will immediately call his Polish contact and excuses himself to do so. When he returns, he tells Greg that the one survivor is totally blind. A picture of the stricken soldier promptly turns up in one of the tabloids. Boyd tells Greg to write an impassioned public appeal to the Polish authorities to release the name of the man and send him home to Germany. Boyd tells

Greg he can take the byline on this one. Greg's appeal further excites interest in the soldier's fate.

The Berlin Red Cross is besieged by people convinced that the survivor is their son or husband or brother or father. One old lady dies of a heart attack from overexcitement. Greg notices that Jupp is unusually affected by this event. The two of them go to the tabloid to find the source of the picture. Jupp mutters that the photographer is a liar. They quickly discover that Jupp is right and the picture is a fake (the photographer's assistant posed for it). Greg questions Jupp about his attitude but the chauffeur clams up.

At Boyd's restaurant hang-out, Greg asks to make a phone call. He is told that there is no phone nor has there been one for weeks. Greg realizes that Boyd lied about making a call from there to his Polish contact. Greg confronts Boyd, who says he's crazy. Greg's plea that the soldier be freed results in demonstrations in front of the Polish embassy. Greg and Bettina go to the chaotic scene but Greg's denunciation of the story as a fraud makes the crowd more restive and authorities have to use water cannons to drive them off. Greg and Bettina return to Boyd's home just as a truck driver shows up with a blind passenger. The driver says the blind man stumbled off a freight train from Poland and claims to be the bunker survivor. Livid, Greg insists the man is a phony. His vehemence alienates Bettina, who thinks the pathetic man may be telling the truth. Boyd interrogates the man privately and tells him that he knows he's lying.

Greg goes to Dr. Wolfe, publisher of a major paper, and tells him the story. Wolfe is interested but wants proof. Greg comes up with a plan: He will tell the press that Boyd is inviting them to his house the next morning so they may interview the survivor. Greg is convinced that the sham will be revealed when Boyd refuses to allow the interview.

The next morning Boyd, in Bettina's presence, is concocting a news item about the blind survivor. The reporters turn up and Boyd promptly changes stories and says he has discovered that his blind guest is lying and not really the soldier. The reporters leave but Dr. Wolfe tells Greg he now believes him and urges him to write the truth. Boyd tells Greg that if he does so, his own career as a reporter will be ruined. Nevertheless, Greg informs Boyd he is going to tell all and leaves in the company of Bettina.

American films have had a love-hate relationship with newspaper people. In the silent era, reporters were often portrayed in a heroic light in films like *The Cub*, *Go and Get It* and *Dinty* but even in the Age of Innocence there was occasional skepticism about the honesty of journalists and you get a movie like *The Lying Truth* (1922) wherein a small-town newspaper editor, desperate to increase circulation, invents a murder, a fabrication that has dire consequences.

By the '30s, you had a more skeptical attitude toward the ladies and gentlemen of the press who were often portrayed as fast-talking, profane, irreverent and willing to do anything to get the big scoop. The depiction was still somewhat sympathetic but you do get denunciations of tabloid journalism and the harm they could do the innocent in films like *Five Star Final* and *Scandal Street*. However, the ultimate in cynicism when it came to the press found a showcase in Billy Wilder's *Ace in the Hole* (1951) to which *Wet Asphalt* is sometimes compared (unfavorably). A man trapped in a cave is used by ruthless reporter Kirk Douglas for a big news item that turns into a circus as Douglas manages to delay the rescue of the man just to extend the life of the sensationalistic story.

All this changed after Woodward and Bernstein's exposé of Watergate and Nixon and the film about it, *All the President's Men* (1976). No longer were reporters seen as money-grubbing shills out to sell papers but as prophets devoted to challenging corrupt political and social establishments at the risk of their jobs or even their lives. This has largely remained the case though you get occasional mild exceptions like *Absence of Malice* (1981) and *Shattered Glass* (2003).

It's rare to find a vintage German film with journalists as important characters. If they turn up at all, it's usually as comic figures. In the Nazi era, there *were* no real journalists, just propagandists. It wasn't until the '50s that German filmmakers looked at the Fourth Estate and it was usually with a jaundiced eye. *Wet Asphalt* manages to have it both ways: You have the cynical, deceitful and ruthless publisher Caesar Boyd who cares not a hoot about the truth and the courageous young reporter who ultimately exposes him.

Asphalt producer Wenzel Lüdke told *Der Stern* the following: "Our story will portray an obscure newspaperman who invents the bunker story in the early postwar years. The film attacks certain types of asphalt journalism and shows how in the tense East-West atmosphere it was possible to put false messages into circulation."

However, in the film it's not a little-known reporter—which might be a bit more credible—but a newspaper tycoon who creates the tale. It's only the good luck that the story supposedly took place in an area restricted by the communists that saves it from being quickly discredited. It seems a very risky move for a man like Boyd to take just because it's a slow news week. Of course, tabloid journalism routinely creates outlandish stories just to sell papers but, judging by Greg's outraged reaction, we have to assume that while Boyd rewrites the news to make it more appealing to his readers, he's not in the habit of simply making things up out of whole cloth.

But Will Tremper, the writer of *Wet Asphalt*, claims that's pretty much what happened. Tremper, whom we have encountered earlier in the Wisbar biography, was something of a notorious character who alternated between respectable journalism and scandal-mongering tabloids. In *Mein wilden*

Jahren (1993), Tremper writes about his days as a ghost writer for journalist-historian Curt Riess. Riess, just like Boyd in the movie, had contracts with several magazines and newspapers to provide sensational stories. One of the papers was the French newspaper *France Soir*, whose publisher Pierre Lazareff paid Riess $1000 for each weekend scoop and wanted stories strong enough to sell out each of the five Saturday editions. French readers couldn't get enough tales about beastly German behavior and Tremper claims many of these scoops were simply invented by Riess. Riess told Lazareff the Gdynia bunker yarn which became a sensation and was picked by the Associated Press. When Tremper asked Riess where he got the story, his employer winked and said it was from the British Secret Service. Tremper was uncertain whether any of the tale was true but life is not the movies and Tremper did nothing to expose Riess. Perhaps *Wet Asphalt*, written some seven years later, is meant as payback.

Tremper also wrote and directed movies and at one time was considered something of a forerunner of the young rebel auteurs of the '60s. His script for *Die Halbstarken* (*The Hooligans*, 1956), a drama about juvenile delinquency, helped launch Horst Buchholz on his career of playing troubled youths. While working for the magazine *Stern*, Tremper received $100,000 from a Swiss patron to direct his first movie, *Flucht nach Berlin* (*Escape to Berlin*, 1960), one of the few German films to address the division of the country. Tremper often ran into trouble securing financing for his films and had to mortgage his house to bankroll his movie *Die Endlose Nacht* (*The Endless Night*, 1962). Later he convinced actors Paul Hubschmid and Eva Renzi to defer their salaries to help finance his *Playgirl*; they sued him after Tremper's unsuccessful attempt to distribute the film on his own. His film career as a maverick largely fizzled as younger directors came on the scene. Tremper continued to be a respected figure in the film world even though his many articles often attacked the German movie industry and resulted in the occasional lawsuit.

According to Tremper's account of the shooting of *Wet Asphalt*, the original title was *Preis der Warheit* (*The Price of Truth*) but *Wet Asphalt* was considered more commercial (the exact meaning is obscure; it may have meant something disparaging like "street journalism"). Tremper picked Wisbar up at the Hamburg airport and they both stayed at a hotel during the filming. Wisbar read about 20 pages of Tremper's screenplay and, quite taken with the story and dialogue, agreed to do the movie. Tremper was equally impressed with Wisbar's professionalism and his wholehearted dedication to the film. Though Wisbar was no stranger to alcohol, Tremper noted that he was a teetotaler while the film was being shot, drinking nothing stronger than a Coke (with a side of aspirin). Wisbar's regimen was Spartan, starting work at 6 a.m. and finishing at 10 p.m. Tremper can't recall even seeing him eat. In contrast to his later comments (see the bio), Wisbar stressed the longevity of film: "You folks seem to forget that you're working for eternity. Your movies will be shown on television a hundred years from now and you could disgrace your names. I despise actors and crew who sit around drinking at night instead of preparing themselves."

Wisbar was certainly prepared, mapping out in detail plans for the daily shooting. Tremper thought that Wisbar's method of dealing with the actors was more American than European: As long as the actors were prepared, Wisbar's guidance during filming was usually minor, such as: "Herr Held, a bit louder please." "Not too fast." "Once more, please, but take your time." "Horst, please do not turn around in this scene." No doubt this was the influence of Wisbar's years on Poverty Row and in TV.

Tremper noted that the film cost 1.1 million marks and did not do as well as his two other Horst Buchholz films. Hans-Martin Majewski's music won the German Film Critics' Award for best score.

Obviously, it's impossible to critique the acting in *Nasser Asphalt* given that it's the dubbed version, though it seems safe to assume that since Maria Perschy (Bettina) only manages one expression throughout the entire film, her performance would not have been helped by her speaking with her own voice. (Tremper said she was not in the original script but the producer insisted that there had to be a love interest.) Perschy went on to scream her way (presumably using her own tonsils) through films like *Hunchback of the Morgue*, *Castle of Fu Manchu*, *House of Psychotic Women* and *Horror of the Zombies* while occasionally side-tripping into exotic thrillers such as *Kilma, Queen of the Jungle* and sex comedies like *My Husband Prefers Virgins*. Her attempt at a Hollywood career (*Man's Favorite Sport*) failed to win her an American following.

Horst Buchholz and Gert Frobe are also dubbed by other actors even though both spoke English (in Frobe's case with a heavy accent). Buchholz became famous as a James Dean-Sal Mineo–type in his early career but is best known to American audiences for his performances in the Western classic *The Magnificent Seven* and the frenetic Billy Wilder Cold War spoof *One, Two, Three* (in which he plays a Communist zealot; the authorities torture him by making him listen repeatedly to "Itsy Bitsy Teenie Weenie Yellow Polka Dot Bikini"). Toward the end of his career, Buchholz had a good supporting role in *Life Is Beautiful* (1999).

Frobe knew what it was like first hand to be the victim of bad press. After his portrayal of the title villain in the James Bond thriller *Goldfinger*, he was interviewed by the London *Daily Mail* and quoted as saying, "Naturally, I was a Nazi during the Third Reich." Frobe insisted that what he had actually said was "During the Third Reich I had the luck to be able to help two Jewish people even though I was a member of the Nazi Party." Israel nevertheless banned his movies, but eventually one Mario Blumenau came forward and informed the Israeli embassy in Vienna that Frobe had indeed hidden him and his mother from the Nazis, and the ban was lifted.

Frobe, a classically trained violinist who later switched to cabaret comedy, was initially seen as a comic actor, a "German Danny Kaye." While his Goldfinger is no doubt his best remembered bad guy, it's given full-blooded competition by his portrayal of the drunken, sadistic mountain patriarch in *Via Mala* (1961) and the child murderer in the 1958 *Es geschah am hellichten Tag* (*It Happened in Broad Daylight*; the story was filmed several times, most recently as *The Pledge* with Jack Nicholson).

One German critic noted that Martin Held's emphatic acting as Caesar Boyd caused the audience to laugh in the wrong places. Presumably, no one chuckled at Held's Claudius in Fritz Kortner's production of *Hamlet* or during *Krapp's Last Tape*, directed by Samuel Beckett. In film, he alternated between comic roles (the 1956 version of the classic *The Captain from Köpenick*) and villains (the 1954 *Canaris* where he played the infamous "Hangman" Heydrich).

The reviewer for *Der Spiegel* (4/16/58) was not impressed with *Wet Asphalt*, calling the production "tedious and threadbare" and of little relevance to the question of tabloid journalism given that the story was so atypical. The critic referred to Wisbar as "remergierten Hollywood director" and opined that his direction was "lame."

Erika Müller's comments in the April 10, 1958, edition of *Zeit* were more favorable. She found Wisbar's direction "realistic, nuanced and powerful" and a provocative appeal to the conscience of journalism. Müller did criticize Wisbar's handling of the crowd scene in front of the embassy as "too broad." She did like the fact that Wisbar did not settle for a simple black-and-white treatment of all the characters and mentioned Frobe's loyal but conflicted chauffeur as a good example of moral cowardice.

Like many of Wisbar's postwar films, *Wet Asphalt* did not play in America. Dark Sky Films released it on DVD in 2005, passing it off as film noir. Some reviewers of the DVD, besides being indignant that the movie hardly qualified as a noir, found the presentation terrible. There was much criticism of the visual quality of the print and the lack of a German-language alternative to the English dubbed version. *DVD Verdict* commented, "So far this ranks as the worst DVD of the year."

New York Times video reviewer Dave Kehr welcomed the release of the DVD (November 1, 2005):

> [...] the film offers further tantalizing suggestions of the range and nature of Wisbar's talent. The expressionist tendencies are still there, highlighted by Wisbar's treatment of the father-son conflict, a classic expressionist theme, but are now balanced by a fascinating, documentary-like view of postwar, pre-wall Berlin, haunted

by its Nazi past and cornered by its Communist neighbors. The Dark Sky print is, alas, dubbed into English, but given the ultra-rarity of the title (and the lack of any identifiable market for it), it's hard to complain.

The ending is a bit ambiguous as we never really learn whether Greg actually manages to convince the world of Boyd's duplicity but Greg's rejection of his boss is depicted as a moral triumph. However, the situation gets a bit muddled when Boyd tells Greg that he's been like a father to him but Greg responds that he doesn't want a father like him. The notion that Boyd has been some kind of father figure to Greg seems tacked-on and perhaps an attempt to capitalize on Buchholz's earlier juvenile delinquent movies. It actually might have been a good avenue to explore but as it stands now, nothing in the story leads up to it since Boyd comes off as an overbearing and manipulative employer and Greg a compliant worker rather than suggesting any kind of closer relationship.

The film is very cleverly plotted as it demonstrates how a lie can get devastatingly out of control with all kinds of unexpected consequences. The East-West conflict and the tendency of Iron Curtain countries to be excessively secretive is believably portrayed, especially when you recall that at the time of the bunker story, Poland, sensitive about stories of how a major purge of its communist party played out, had expelled all but two Western journalists. One was the near legendary Edward R. Murrow and the other Ormonde Godfrey, an obscure Brit who worked for the American Associated Press. Erika Müller speculated that it was Godfrey who came up with the bunker story but this seems unlikely. Possibly, Polish authorities were willing to let the far-fetched tale grab some headlines so as to distract from what was really happening in the country.

Stories of survival under desperate circumstances (at sea, trapped in a mine, crashlanded in the Andes), whether real or fictional, usually manage to work cannibalism into the mix. Happily, the Gdynia bunker was so well stocked that the soldiers were spared that grisly alternative.

Hunde, wollt ihr ewig leben? (*Dogs, Do You Want to Live Forever?*)

Deutsche Film Hans GmbH
Released on April 7, 1959
93 minutes

Cast: Joachim Hansen as First Lt. Gerd Wisse; Wilhelm Borchert as General Paulus; Wolfgang Preiss as Major Linkmann; Carl Lange as General von Seydiltz; Horst Frank as Staff Sergeant Böse; Peter Karsten as Corporal Krämer; Richard Münch as First Lt. Kesselbach; Günter Pftizmann as Kunowski; Sonja

Ziemann as Katja; Günnar Möller as Lt. Fuhrmann; Ernst von Klipstein as a General; Armen Dahlen as Major Stanescu; Paul Hoffmann as General Codrenau; Karl John as General Hoth; Alexander Kerst as Chaplain Busch; Hans Paetsch, Friedrich Schütter, Wolfgang Büttner, Klaus Behrendt, Josef Frölich, Klaus Hellmold, Tatjana Iwanov, Erich von Loewis, Peter Lühr, Karl Meixner, Jöns Andersson, Heinz Plate, Gothart Portloff, Joachim Rake, Günther Ungeheuer, Reinhard Kolldehoff.

Credits: Director: Frank Wisbar; Assistant Director: Carl Otto Bartning; Screenplay: Frank Wisbar, Frank Dimen, Heinz Schröter, Based on *Stalingrad-biz zur letzen Patrone* by Fritz Wöss, *Letze Brief aus Stalingrad* by Heniz Schröter and *Hunde, Wollt Ihr Ewig Leben* by Fritz Wöss; Script Editor: Alf Teichs; Photography: Helmuth Ashley; Camera Operator: Franz X. Lederle; Assistant Camera: Wolfgang Hoffmann, Dietmar Graf; Production Designers: Walter Haag, Wilhelm Vierhaus, Hans Kurtzner; Painter: Paul H. Koester; Property Master: Waldemar Hinrichs; Costume Designer: Irms Pauli; Makeup: Walter Wegener, Heinrich Weber; Editor: Martha Dubber; Assistant Editor: Ursula Reinforth; Sound: Heinz Martin; Music: Herbert Windt.

Today most historians think that the beginning of the end of Hitler's campaign in Russia came when his army failed to capture Moscow. However, some would say the turning point was the siege of Stalingrad which resulted in the destruction of the German 6th army. At the very least, Stalingrad offered a mortal blow to the myth of Nazi invincibility, a propaganda coup that demoralized the German people and gave great hope to the Allies. Wisbar was in the U.S. during Stalingrad and recalled, "Even the Americans stopped breathing."

Wisbar claimed he had wanted to make a film about Stalingrad for years and finally had his opportunity after he returned to Germany in the mid-1950s. Many German postwar films were strictly for domestic consumption, often *Heimat* pictures which were full of pastoral scenery, beautiful maidens in pigtails and young men in lederhosen. Eventually film producers began looking for more serious subjects and with an eye to the international market. Wisbar felt the time was right for an important film about a subject that was still very painful for Germany.

Der Spiegel (April 9, 1959) featured a lengthy article about Wisbar's attempt to do a Stalingrad epic. Wisbar said he had been working on a Stalingrad script for quite a while but he got serious about the idea during the filming of his earlier war movie *Sharks and Little Fish*. He began doing extensive research on the subject and was impressed with a novel by Fritz Wöss about his time in Stalingrad as a liaison officer working with the Rumanian fighters during the siege of the city. Wisbar didn't think much of the book's literary style but felt the story would be a perfect springboard for a script. He also used the somewhat controversial writings of Heinz Schröter, who had been sent by Goebbels to Stalingrad to come up with some propaganda pieces about the men of the 6th Army; he returned with stories so frank and downbeat that the Ministry of Propaganda couldn't use them.

Wisbar approached the Federal Ministry of Defense in West Germany for help on the production. The initial response was positive and Wisbar was promised six tanks, 120 extras and permission to shoot the film on a military training ground. However, a mere two weeks later, permission was rescinded (which actually led to a debate in the German parliament) on the grounds that the film would open old wounds and result in contentious public discussion for which the country was simply not ready. The military authorities did think the script was good though they didn't like the title. (The phrase— or something like it—was purportedly uttered by Frederick the Great as a taunt directed at soldiers who were fleeing a battle.)

In spite of this setback, Wisbar was determined to make the film as historically accurate and realistic as possible. He interviewed the surviving generals and chief officers who had been at Stalingrad and found that most of them approved of his project. Veterans from the campaign were used to train 200 students from the Bergakademie in Clausthal-Zellerfeld in street-fighting tactics. Maybe he couldn't use the army but Wisbar had a good deal of newsreel footage from German and Russian sources. That would have to compensate for a rather modest budget which allowed for only one real tank, a fake one made of cardboard and wood and three field howitzers.

Dogs follows the conversion of First Lieutenant Wisse from a believer in the Third Reich to a skeptic who disavows the whole system. Wisse initially goes to Stalingrad as part of military intelligence to work with the Rumanian soldiers. When that task is completed, he finds himself fighting with his besieged fellow Germans. They have captured the city but it is a matter of the flies conquering the flypaper as they are eventually surrounded by the Russian army and cut off from supply lines and the other Nazi forces. The plight of Wisse and his companions is interposed with discussions among the generals about what to do. Hitler insists that General Paulus, commander of the 6th Army at Stalingrad, remain firm. However, Paulus' ammunition and supplies are low and his men starving and demoralized as winter descends. An army led by General Hoth is nearby but can't really challenge the Russian pincers. Paulus' only hope is for his army to break out of Stalingrad to join Hoth's forces. (The English subtitled version I watched uses the expression "breaking ranks" but that's inaccurate and misleading.) However, Hitler won't allow it and wants the 6th Army to hold the city and fight until the end. Wisse's companions, one by one, end up dying. His cowardly commanding officer (the film's one truly unsympathetic character) tries to escape and is shot by his own men. Paulus realizes the situation is hopeless and surrenders. Ninety thousand German prisoners are marched off to an uncertain future, Wisse among them. His friend Chaplain Busch says, "Maybe we will learn from this." "Or maybe not," responds the now wised-up Wisse.

While the newsreel footage does not always match up well with the rest of the film, it does give the movie the documentary-like feel Wisbar sought. To bolster that effect, there is narration giving historical background and there are no opening or closing credits. When the film premiered, the audience was handed a program with cast and credits listed. While it was customary for the actors and director to take a bow after the movie, Wisbar did not allow it because in this instance "it would have been blasphemous."

Wisbar's main criticism of the whole situation seems to be that the army is being used as cannon fodder to glut the vanity of one man, Hitler. (Hitler is played by a cabaret comedian. Wisbar felt he captured Der Führer perfectly.) Thus, thousands are condemned to misery and death because the Dictator doesn't want to lose face. While Wisbar provides plenty of information about the Army's precarious position is one of the film's biggest strengths, he doesn't give an explanation of why they are there in the first place. There's not really any political context. Initially, Wisse doesn't like it when somebody criticizes Hitler's military leadership but is the Dictator's ultimate failure to conquer Russia the only reason to reject him? In one scene, Wisse is sent to the makeshift hospital to look for "slackers" to fill his decimated ranks but of course finds only wretched, wounded men huddled together in heaps and waiting in agony for medical treatment that isn't coming. Over a radio we hear a speech by Göring spreading the lie about victory in Russia. Busch wants it turned off and when that request is refused, he destroys the radio. Although this is technically treasonous, no action is taken. It's a poignant scene but the irony is a little too obvious and heavy-handed.

The very sympathetic depiction of Chaplain Busch is typical of Wisbar's respectful stance toward Christianity. At one point, Busch and Wisse have dinner with a Russian peasant family. Before the children go to bed, they pray before an icon. "I thought they got rid of all that," comments Wisse. Busch responds, "They tried to—just as they did in Germany, but some things are eternal." Busch later holds an impromptu Christmas service for the dazed and bedraggled soldiers standing like statues among the bombed-out, nightmarish ruins at Stalingrad. Wisse is skeptical about the worth of prayers in such a hell but Busch tells him that "sometimes God can manifest Himself even in Hell." Given their contempt for Christianity, the Nazis were actually wary of the influence of chaplains on their soldiers and sought to counter it.

There was some criticism of the film for not admitting that the Wehrmacht was guilty of numerous atrocities against the Russian people. Wisse is even shown helping a Russian girl get a job when she's threatened with deportation. (Later she returns the favor by aiding him when he inadvertently stumbles into a Russian enclave in Stalingrad; it is of course the most unlikely of coincidences that she turns up right there.) When his group takes a Russian prisoner, one of Wisse's comrades prepares to shoot him, saying, "Neither side takes prisoners." Wisse saves the man and returns him to his comrades. The Russian leader then suggests a truce so they can aid their wounded. During the brief ceasefire, one of Wisse's troops plays a piano that is right in the middle of the ruins. The war-weary soldiers on both sides are comforted by the music for a few minutes until they have to resume the slaughter (the pianist later turns up in the hospital minus his hands). It's a moving moment and the narration tells us that it actually happened but it was far from the typical interaction of Russians with the 6th Army. When the Germans surrender, they are shown being led away in a forced march with soldiers collapsing and being left to die in the snow—hardly a positive picture of their Russian captors. Of course, this was the time of the Cold War, and in West Germany there was little love for the Soviet Union.

The cast is uniformly good though no one performance stands out. Matinee idol Joachim Hansen (Wisse)—not to be confused with the martial arts champion—had earlier played in another war film, *Star of Africa*, a biography of ace pilot Hans-Joachim Marseille. Carl Lange (General von Seydiltz), Horst Frank (Böse) and Alexander Kerst (Busch) were also in the cast of *Star*. Wolfgang Preiss (the contemptible Linkmann) was a regular in Wisbar's postwar movies and Sonja Ziemann (the Russian girl Katja) would have a much bigger and better part in Wisbar's *Darkness Fell on Gotenhafen*.

The soundstage set in Stalingrad certainly has a studio look to it; it was made of wood, cardboard, gypsum, sackcloth and debris. They may not be completely convincing but they give the landscape a surreal, otherworldly aspect, most appropriate for characters trapped in a nightmare. (It netted production designer Walter Haag a German film award for best set design.) Hans Windt uses music sparingly but it was a treat to hear a few chords of the ominous "swamp music" from *Ferryman Maria*.

Wisbar's best known postwar film, *Dogs, Do You Want to Live Forever?* was a box office hit and got generally good notices. It won a number of German cinema awards, including Best Picture and Best Director. It was also up for Best Picture at the Venice Film Festival. It has its flaws but remains a stark portrait of the madness and futility of warfare. Wisbar himself said that the film was meant to show that "wars of conquest are insane and that those who sow the wind will reap the whirlwind."

Nacht fiel über Gotenhafen
(Darkness Fell on Gotenhafen)

Deutsche Film Hansa GmbH & Co.
Released on March 3, 1960
99 minutes

Cast: Sonia Ziemann as Maria Reiser; Gunnar Möller as Kurt Reiser; Erik Schumann as Hans Schott; Brigitte Horney as Generalin von Reuss; Mady Rahl as Edith Marquardt; Erich Dunskus as Father Marquardt; Willy Martens as Father Reiser; Edith Shultze-Westrum as Mother Reiser; Wolfgang Preiss as Dr. Beck; Tatjama Owampw as Meta; Christine Mylius as Mrs. Rauh; Aranka Jaenke as Mrs. Kahle; Dietmar Schönherr as Gaston; Georg Lehn as Pinkoweit; Hela Gruel as Miss Pinkoweit; Karl Lange as Captain Zahn; Peter Voss as Captain Petersen; Günter Pfitzmann as Lt. Dankel; Thomas Braut as Lt. von Fritzen; Wolfgang Stumpf as Officer Reese; Raymond Joob as Matrose Helbig; Carla Hagen as Monika; Ursula Herwig as Inge; Marlene Riphahn as Kubelsky; Til Kiwe as S.S. Officer Lothar; Karl-Heinz Kreienbaum, Melanie Aschenbrandt, Gerda-Maria Jürgens, Erwin Linder, Günther Ungheheuer, Max Witmann.

Credits: Director: Frank Wisbar; Assistant Director: Carl Otto Bartning; Screenplay: Frank Wisbar, Victor Schüller; Script Editor: Alf Teichs; Photography: Elio Carniel, Willy Winterstein; Production Designer: Walter Haaq; Costume Designer: Irms Pauli; Editor: Martha Dubber; Sound: Heinz Martin; Special Effects: Theodor Nischwitz; Music: Hans-Martin Majewski.

Everyone knows about the *Titanic* and some at least are familiar with the *Lusitania* tragedy but far less known is the greatest of maritime disasters, the sinking of the *Wilhelm Gustloff* by the Russians in the waning days of the Second World War. *Wilhelm Gustloff* was named after a prominent Nazi assassinated in Switzerland (the boat was originally to have been christened *The Adolf Hitler*). It was commissioned as a cruise ship in 1937 as part of the "Strength Through Joy" program the Third Reich initiated to give workers nice vacations (see the essay on *Petermann Is Against It!*). During the war, it became a hospital ship and then a navy craft but in 1945 it was put into service to help evacuate the many refugees fleeing the Russian advance in the East. Stories of Russian atrocities (some of them true) panicked the desperate crowds hoping to escape from Prussia to the Western part of Germany and they stampeded to the harbor of Gotenhafen (today Gdynia, Poland) on the Baltic Sea. The *Gustloff* was meant to hold about 2000 passengers but may have been crammed with as many 6000, half of them children. (Sources later than Wisbar's film think the number may have been closer to 10,000.) Some military personnel were also on board. The ship set sail on January 30, 1945, and was pretty much unescorted. In a matter of hours, it was torpedoed by a Russian submarine. Only around 1,000 survived the sinking and the frigid waters.

Wisbar's *Darkness Fell on Gotenhafen* is the third of his World War II trilogy, the others being *Dogs, Do You Want to Live Forever?* and *Sharks and Little Fish*. (*The Officer Factory* takes place during the war but doesn't deal with it directly.) It's more expensive than the other two (it reputedly cost two million marks) and is less reliant on documentary war footage to get the action across. It was also the first film to cover a tragedy which was not well known in Germany. Wisbar enlisted the assistance of Heinz Schön, who had survived the sinking; Schön was a 17-year-old purser trainee at the time and had written about it. Wisbar also consulted government sources and combed through some 180 documents. He wanted the sinking of the *Wilhelm Gustloff* to symbolize the fall of the Third Reich, particularly relishing the irony of the ship having at once been a "Strength Through Joy" liner. He dismissed as "boring" the 1958 film about the *Titanic*, *A Night to Remember*, which, interestingly enough, used some footage from the German 1943 anti–British *Titanic* (which, to bring things full circle, used the boat

Nacht fiel über Gotenhafen reaches its tragic finale as the *Wilhelm Gustloff* is sunk by the Russians. Pictured are Erik Schumann and Sonya Ziemann.

Cap Arcona, later also a refugee transport from Gotenhafen and likewise sunk).

Wisbar said the film was meant to be a tribute to the German women who had suffered so terribly during the collapse of the Third Reich: "Our women were incredibly heroic during the war, certainly no less so than the men." However, Wisbar stated other motives as well for making the movie. A lengthy article in the March 1960 *Der Spiegel* contained an interview with Wisbar, a look at the original script of *Darkness* and a visit to the Göttingen studio where it was being filmed. (There were also location shoots at Bremerhaven, Cuxhaven and the bay of Helgoland.) Wisbar mentioned that he had recently been to the Moscow Film Festival and was surprised at the "consistently anti–German movies, hate films." This inspired him to take a look at Russian atrocities against Germans during the war and incorporate them into his picture. When asked whether his film should thus be considered anti–Bolshevik, Wisbar responded "You could say that." However, as we shall see, that aspect of the film was considerably toned down. Nevertheless, the film was banned in East Germany.

The film begins with ominous music and shots of corpses frozen in their life jackets floating about the dark Baltic Sea. A narrator (an uncredited Horst Frank) notes that the temperature is -18 degrees C. We see an unconscious (or dead) Maria clinging to a life preserver marked "*Wilhelm Gustloff.*"

The film goes back in time to the inauguration of the *Wilhelm Gustloff* as a "Strength Through Joy" ship. Stock footage shows huge crowds waving farewell as the ship embarks and passengers play shuffleboard and relax in deck chairs. A dance is in progress and we meet Maria and her fiancé Kurt. Maria, Kurt and their good friend Dr. Beck work at a Berlin radio station. Hans Schott is flirting with Maria much to Kurt's annoyance. The captain receives word that the ship must immediately return to port. This means that war has been declared. We see dozens of Iron Cross medals that indicate the Wehrmacht's early victories followed by row after row of wooden crosses showing the disastrous defeats that followed. There are a half dozen close-ups of weeping women. Originally the narration for this scene was to give statistical detail on the human cost of the war along with some purple prose about the suffering of women but this rant was eliminated.

Fast-forward to December 1943. Kurt is at the Russian Front while Maria still works at the radio station broadcasting a program called "The Housewife's Hour" followed by Dr. Beck reading announcements of Wehrmacht triumphs that he knows are false. Maria, now Kurt's wife and living with his parents, is losing patience with his nagging, hypochondriac mother. Maria goes to a New Year's Eve party where revelers sing a highly unusual version of "Oh! Susanna." When a woman requests "Lili Marlene," she gets the response, "Stupid bitch, go switch on your volksempfänger" (Nazi radio). Maria runs into Hans, the cousin of her good friend Edith. Hans again makes a pass at Maria, who firmly rebuffs him.

Nineteen forty-four brings more setbacks to the German war effort. The *Wilhelm Gustloff* has become a training ship for naval cadets. Assigned to the ship are Hans, who has been wounded in action, and the cynical Lt. Denkel, who has lost an eye and previously worked on the *Gustloff* when it was a cruise ship. Edith (a fashion designer) has been told to report to a factory to help make armaments. Annoyed at the notion that guns are more important than dresses, she leaves Berlin and heads for the family farm in Laswethen in Prussia. She asks Maria to watch her apartment. Hans returns on leave and he and Maria are trapped in the apartment during an air raid and are obliged to put out a fire in the building as the bombs fall (some pretty frightening stock footage of the latter). Worn out by the constant bombing, and very lonely, Maria allows herself to be seduced by Hans.

The German army is pushed back as the Russians press westward. Just as word arrives that Kurt is coming home on leave, Maria discovers that she is pregnant. Kurt's mother throws her out and Maria journeys to Laswethen to join Edith. When Kurt hears the news, he is furious even though Dr. Beck asks him to consider the trying and dispiriting circumstances women must face during war.

Hans and Denkel attend a party at a private club run by a woman named Kubelsky. The Gestapo arrives and it is revealed that the woman is hiding her father, a Jew, in a secret room. The two are dragged off with Kubelsky's scornful plea for help shaming the onlookers, who are appalled but do not interfere.

Maria tells Edith she wishes nothing to do with Hans even though he wants to support her. "This is my baby and my baby alone," she declares as her time approaches. She is befriended by an aristocratic woman known as the Generalin (her husband, a general, has fallen in action) as well as the other locals, including Gaston, a French POW who works for the Generalin. Maria gives birth to a boy and asks the Generalin to be godmother. The proposed date of the christening is January 30.

Thousands of refugees are fleeing the triumphant Russians. As the Red Army gets closer, Maria, her baby and the Generalin and her people join the endless stream of refugees. When the local stationmaster and friend of the family refuses to leave his post, Edith and Gaston go to try to talk some sense into him but he has already been killed by the soldiers. They also shoot Edith and Gaston who, though seriously wounded, makes it back to the others in the Generalin's carriage only to succumb to his wounds a little later. Kurt is also in the area and, having had an apparent change of heart, reunites with Maria. However, he is subsequently wounded. Maria is told that his only hope of recovery is to go to Gotenhafen and the *Gustloff* which has good on-board hospital facilities and is about to depart.

Maria and her friends make it to Gotenhafen but the scene is chaotic. Discovering that Hans is an officer on the *Gustloff*, Maria enlists his help in getting Kurt on board. Even though the number of wounded soldiers on the ship has already reached the limit, Hans and Lt. Denkel succeed in getting Kurt a place in the hospital ward. Maria, her baby, the Generalin and their female companions are also allowed spots in the already overcrowded ship. Women and children are everywhere. The ship's swimming pool has been drained and several hundred young naval auxiliary women are camped out there. The ship departs on a bitter cold night. While the passengers wave to those left behind, the scene is quite different from the cruise ship's joyous maiden voyage many years earlier. All the passengers are told to keep their life preservers on. The hope is they will reach safety in a matter of hours.

The ship's three escorts are reduced to one which also ends up being unable to continue. A Russian submarine spots the *Gustloff* and fires its torpedoes, all of which score direct hits. Panic ensues as water rushes into the ship and people frantically try to reach the deck to board the lifeboats. The empty swimming pool full of women fills with sea water, drowning almost all of them. (This actually happened; over 300 perished.) One of the lifeboats capsizes while being lowered, spilling its passengers into the freezing water. Maria is separated from her friends but the Generalin has Maria's baby and they are safely lowered into the sea. Hans tries to rescue Kurt but they are both swept away as the sea floods the hospital ward. Lt. Denkel makes it to safety but Maria is thrown into the water. A rescue ship arrives to haul in the few survivors while the *Gustloff*, lit up like a party cruiser by its emergency lights, sinks into the depths.

Safe aboard a rescue ship and clutching Maria's baby, the Generalin is surrounded by weeping women and motherless children. The Generalin muses out loud that women bear a responsibility for the tragedy for not trying to restrain their men from warfare. She speculates that even this terrible event will be forgotten until the next ship sinks, "perhaps a ship as big as the whole world."

The film ends as it began with a shot of the frozen refugees floating in the water. Maria is among them but some reviewers seem to have assumed that she survived (though it looked to me that she was dead). That may have been in the original script as Wisbar commented in the *Der Spiegel* interview that showing the survivors as "a one-eyed man and a sinner" was to symbolize "that was all that was left of Germany." In the completed film, it is the one-eyed lieutenant and a servant girl who make it to the rescue boat while the "sinner" Maria perishes. However, there is a still showing the lieutenant and Maria clinging to each other after the disaster. Was this shot filmed and then eliminated? In any case, the prints I've seen of the film put Maria among the floating bodies in the sea. This is something of a contrast to the last shot of *Sharks and Little Fish*: There the sailors are circled together and treading water after their submarine has been destroyed. They have survived but the women and refugees of *Night* are not so fortunate, a situation that accurately reflects the casualties in World War II where the number of civilian fatalities by far exceeded those in the armed services. In fact, during the bombing raid on Berlin, Hans comments that it's more terrifying than the combat action he's endured.

As mentioned earlier, Wisbar had intended to emphasize the Russian atrocities in a series of scenes: "Women and children shot down by the Russians as they flee through the snow ... male prisoners executed while the women and girls are raped.... Old men and women huddled in a basement with the Russians throwing in grenades." The sequence was to end with a shot of a mass grave of German victims. None of this made it into the film. The only real atrocity we see is the murders of the stationmaster and Edith. The Russian soldiers clearly have rape on their minds for Edith but she pulls a gun and shoots one of them before being killed herself. The film does include a sequence in which two Russian soldiers are captured by the Germans and found to be carrying a letter by the famous Russian poet Ilya Ehrenberg urging the Red Army to show absolutely no mercy to the Germans. (This is true but Ehrenburg claimed he meant it to apply only to the Nazi soldiers in Russia, not the German civilian population.) The German officer is not nonplussed by this message and reflects that perhaps it's just payback: "An eye for an eye." At one point, Wisbar had said that facts are facts but too much grisly detail would alienate audiences so he apparently decided to opt for a subtler approach rather than emphasizing Red Army atrocities. The Wehrmacht cruelties in Russia that inspired this thirst for revenge get only a brief reference: As Kurt and his company retreat from the Eastern Front, an old woman remonstrates with him for burning her village and his answer is "How is that my fault?" Not surprisingly, a *Der Spiegel* reviewer (October 1960) felt that Wisbar "took ideological bows in all directions."

Wisbar's sympathy for the female victims of war also originally included a criticism of the wartime double sexual standard. There was a line about how soldiers visit brothels as often as they got deloused but their wives are supposed to remain chaste while their men are away. That line didn't make it into the film but Dr. Beck's plea to Kurt that he should forgive Maria because of the wartime conditions is a milder version of it. Maria is certainly not held up to scorn for what happened, with the blame being put squarely on Hans.

The film then, as well as more recently, came in for a fair share of criticism about its politics. (The writer of the aforementioned *Der Spiegel* could not resist the crack that Wisbar was chronicling a war he had sat out in "the

California sunshine.") There is practically no Nazi presence in the film. Women as well as men supported Hitler but there's no indication of any of this in the movie where women are portrayed entirely as victims of the madness of war. The sequence where Kubelsky and her father are arrested while the officers look on helplessly was thought awkward, out of place and irrelevant. Had they never seen Jews arrested before? A recent evaluation of the film in *Screening War; Perspectives on German Suffering* was equally critical of that scene:

> This self-flagellation leads nowhere, only to the horror of the expulsion. The witness' guilt is not purged but in a sense relativized by what is about to happen to the German expellees. The brief episode's scenic composition and the narrative positioning ensure here once again that the persecution of the Jews can be understood as a symbolic anticipation of German suffering.

The criticism is perhaps too harsh, especially when you consider that persecution of the Jews is seldom depicted in West German films of the '50s and '60s. There is little question that the officers, ironically described as "heroes" by the doomed Kubelsky, are seen as moral cowards for doing nothing to prevent the arrest; this could be taken as a reprimand to the complicity of the "average" German in the Holocaust.

The film has also been faulted for spending too much time on "soap opera" and not enough aboard the *Wilhelm Gustloff*. The narrator of Günther Grass' novel *Crabwalk*, a mixture of fact and fiction about the *Gustloff*, put it this way: "The plot was utterly predictable. Just as in all the *Titanic* films, a love story had to be brought in as filler, taking on heroic dimensions at the end, as if the sinking of an overcrowded ship weren't exciting, the thousands of deaths not tragic enough."

However, the *Gustloff* was at sea for only a matter of hours (unlike the four-day voyage of the *Titanic*) and it was deemed that such a brief excursion could hardly be the main setting of a lengthy fiction film. *Salt of the Sea*, a recent novel about the *Gustloff*, likewise spends most of the story on land as various desperate characters make their way through the apocalyptic landscape in hopes of finding safety aboard ship. *Darkness* is meant to emphasize the troubles of women during the war; from coping without their men to enduring constant bombing and finally losing everything and becoming homeless refugees. On this level, the movie is quite successful, whatever one makes of its ambiguous politics.

The sinking of the *Gustloff* is harrowing and the miniature work for the ship going under is expertly done. The scenes of horror and mass panic aboard ship made quite an impression on *Crabwalk*'s narrator:

> You see masses of people pushing, clogged corridors, the struggle for every step up the staircase; you see costumed extras imprisoned in the closed promenade deck,

feel the ship listing, see the water rising, see people swimming inside the ship, see people drowning. And you see children in the film. Children separated from their mothers. Children holding dangling dolls. Children wandering lost along corridors that have already been vacated. Close-ups of the eyes of individual children. But the more than 4000 infants, children and youths for whom no survival was possible were not filmed, simply for reasons of expense; they remain and will remain an abstract number....

No doubt *Night*'s best performance is given by Brigitte Horney as the Generalin. She makes her character tough, matriarchal, indomitable, a survivor, the Molly Brown of the *Gustloff*. Such roles were Horney's specialty from the 1960s on but she began her career as a Max Reinhardt actress and played temptresses on the screen. One critic wrote, "It was said she could say more with her eyes than the censors would ever allow her to say." She played opposite Conrad Veidt in *Rasputin, Dämon der Frauen* (*Rasputin, Demon with Women*, 1930) and Karl Ludwig Diehl in Paul Wegener's *Ein Mann will nach Deutschland* (*A Man Wants to Get to Germany*, 1934). Her most notable '30s role was perhaps as the cabaret singer Ruby in *Liebe, Tod und Teufel* (*Life, Death and the Devil*, 1934), a studio-bound but effective adaptation of Robert Louis Stevenson's "The Bottle Imp." She sang "This Way or That Way Life Goes" in husky, sensual Marlene Dietrich voice and the tune became a hit.

Ufa tried to sign Horney to a long-term contract but she declined, preferring to freelance. She went to England to do a couple of cheap and forgettable thrillers, then returned to Germany to star in a number of Grade A productions, perhaps most notably 1940's *Der Mädchen von Fanö* (*The Girl from Fano*), a love triangle set against the background of the North Sea. Her co-star was her friend Joachim Gottschalk, who soon came to a tragic end. His wife was Jewish, a fact he did not try to hide, much to Dr. Goebbels' anger. In 1941, Gottschalk's wife and son were scheduled to be sent to a concentration camp but just before the Gestapo came for them, Joachim and his family committed suicide. Dr. Goebbels, not popular in the *film welt* to begin with, was subsequently even more despised. Horney risked official displeasure by attending her friend's funeral. She made one more important film, *Münchausen* (1943), playing the lusty Catherine the Great. In 1945, as the chaos described in *Darkness* came fearfully alive, Horney fled to Switzerland.

In 1952, after the death of her mother, famed psychoanalyst Karen Horney, Brigitte moved to America to run the institute that was carrying on her mother's work. She made a handful of movies after that but concentrated mainly on German and Canadian television. (She played Aunt Polly in a series based on the Mark Twain classics. Even though she knew English well, she was dubbed.) Late in life, she received numerous awards and accolades for her long career.

Sonya Ziemann makes Maria strong, resourceful and independent, even retaining her sexual magic in spite of being bedraggled and harassed. Maria was one of a number of serious roles for the actress whose biggest box office successes were a series of Heimatfilme made in the early '50s. In those movies, she played sweet and unassuming young fräuleins and was usually paired with Rudolf Prack. After turning to more dramatic roles, she made numerous stage appearances and, like Horney, focused on TV.

Dr. Beck was an unusually kindly role for Wolfgang Preiss, best known for portraying the evil genius of crime, Dr. Mabuse (he did so five times in the '60s series), as well as the mad doctor petrifying young ladies in *Mill of the Stone Women* (1960). He often played Nazis (General Rommel in 1971's *Raid on Rommel*) but alternated such roles with anti–Nazis (von Stauffenberg in *The Plot to Assassinate Hitler*, 1955). Preiss appears in all three films of Wisbar's wartime trilogy.

Several popular players are in the supporting cast. Well-loved character actor Günter Pfitzmann (Lt. Hovel), more popularly known as Pfitz, played in numerous TV programs from the '50s right up to 2002. Dietmar Schönherr (Gaston) likewise appeared in many TV programs as well as doing some writing, composing, directing and even hosting a talk show. Gaston the happy POW is a rather unbelievable role, like something out of *Hogan's Heroes*, but Schönherr plays him well. He also turns up in Wisbar's *Commando*.

Peter Voss, Death himself in *Ferryman Maria*, has a small role as Captain Petersen. It's implied that he goes down with the *Gustloff* but in reality, all four of the ship's captains were rescued.

Til Kiwe, who plays the snarling Gestapo chief Lothar, was a German POW (captured in North Africa) who made numerous escape attempts from camps in Arizona and Colorado, once getting as far as the Mexican border. The fact that he had studied in Baltimore before the war no doubt was a big help in his endeavors. He was an anthropologist before and after the war and went on expeditions to Africa, South America and Polynesia. He also had a minor acting career and turns up, appropriately enough, in *The Great Escape* (1963), playing a Nazi soldier.

After *Darkness Fell on Gotenhafen*, there were a number of books, documentaries and TV features about the tragedy. Wisbar returned to the story for his very last effort as a director, a semi-documentary made for German television, *Flucht über die Ostsee* (*Flight across the Baltic Sea*), which incorporates some footage from *Darkness*. Heinz Schön, the aforementioned survivor of the sinking, was reluctant to call it a wartime atrocity. After all, there were hundreds of military personnel on board as well as the refugees and there were no Red Cross markings on the boat. Questions of collective guilt, the many civilians who became "collateral damage" and the innocence of the refugees have been debated for years. Wisbar's film really doesn't deal with the "big" issues but serves as another heartbreaking example that man is wolf to man. Or in this case, to woman.

Fabrik der Offiziere
(The Officer Factory)
Deutsche Films Hansa GmbH and Co.
Released on December 29, 1960
96 minutes

Cast: Helmut Griem as Lt. Kraft; Horst Frank as Captain Feder; Carl Lange as General-Major Modersohn; Karl John as Major Frey; Erich Schumann as Captain Ratshelm; Peter Karsten as Captain Katers; Paul Edwin Roth as Judge-Advocate Wirrmann; Raymond Joob as Captain Bieringer; Max Giese as Lt. Dietrich; Johannes Grossman as Cadet Hochbauer; Walter Wiltiz as Cadet Amafortas; Marc Roger as Cadet Andreas; Lutz Moik as Cadet Kramer; Reinhard Jahn as Cadet Rednitz; Helmut Oeser as Cadet Weber; Axel Scholtz as Cadet Moesler; Folker Bohnet as Cadet Böhmke; Peter Parak as Cadet Kersten; Gisela Tantau as Elfriede Rademacher; Xenia Pörtner as Marion Feder; Margaret Jahnen as Sybille Bochner; Katharina Schmitt as Mrs. Frey; Margitta Scherr as Irene Jablonski; Miriam Spoerri, Marion Jacob, Hans Paetsch, Karl Meixner, Günther Ungeheuet.
Credits: Director: Frank Wisbar; Assistant Director: Thomas Fanti; Screenplay: Franz Höllering, Frank Wisbar; Based on the eponymous 1960 novel by Hans

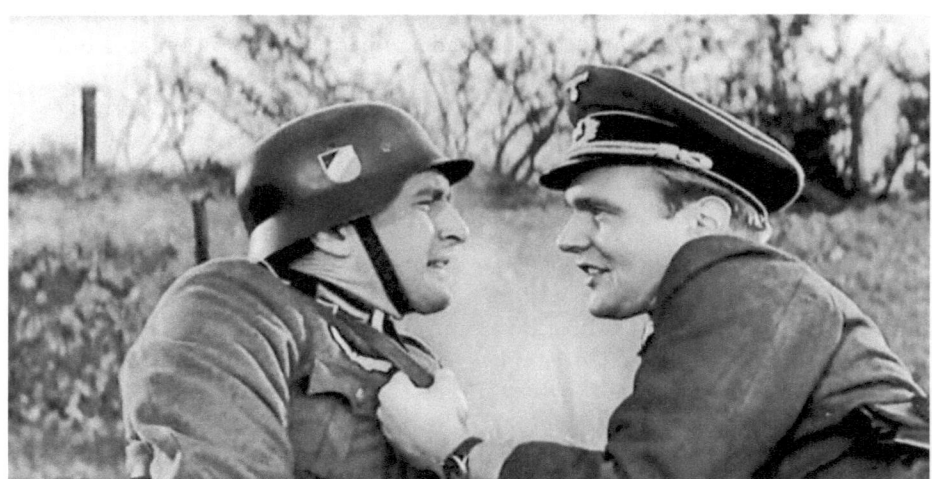

As a fuse smolders in the background, Hochbauer (Johannes Grossmann, left) confesses his crime to Lt. Kraft (Helmut Griem) in *Fabrik der Offiziere*.

Fabrik der Offiziere (1960)

This scene in *Fabrik der Offiziere* is a nicely composed shot with a slightly Expressionistic look. The General (Carl Lange) stoically awaits his fate.

Hellmut Kirst; Script Editor: Alf Teichs; Photography: Kurt Grigoleit; Camera Operator: Herbert Geier; Production Design: Walter Haag; Costume Design: Irma Paul; Editing: Martin Dübber; Sound: Heinz Martin; Music: Hans-Martin Majewski; Producer: Alf Teichs; Production: Georg Mohr, Franz Thierry, Tania Wisbar (uncredited).

The Officer Factory is the last of Wisbar's movies set in World War II. Like his other war films, the characters are strictly black-and-white, evil Nazis and good Germans and without a great deal of nuance. This is not true of the 1960 Hans Hellmut Crist novel the film is based on. The book, dedicated to the "memory of the betrayed generation and as a warning to the youth of today," offers a complex and sometimes exasperatingly convoluted picture of officers and their cadets in a training school in 1944. Crist was a Nazi party member ("I confused National Socialism with Germany," he said later) and rose to senior lieutenant during the war but his numerous postwar novels often dealt with the common soldier and his perplexity in dealing with the army. His Gunner Ash trilogy was especially popular for its trenchant satire. He is perhaps best known in America for his 1962 thriller *The Night of the Generals*, which was made into a successful film in 1967.

Crist's *The Officer Factory* sometimes seems like a dry run for *Night of the Generals* in that it's a thriller about one man's dogged search for a murderer during a time when mass murder was official policy. The book is overlong and episodic with so much backstory and so many flashbacks that the murder that drives the story often seems a subplot. Obviously, a film version would have to cut to the chase and Wisbar does just that, removing most of the secondary storylines (though oddly enough he keeps a rather silly one about a cadet who claims he was raped by three women). Wisbar also makes some serious changes to the resolution of the story that seem to subvert Crist's intent.

The film initially follows the book's plot closely. It begins at the officers' school with the funeral of Lt. Barkow, who was blown up during a training exercise. The assumption is that it was an accident but the school's commandant, General-Major Modersohn, is not so sure. An honorable officer of the old school, the general wants to know what really happened. He is convinced that Wirrmann, the judge advocate sent to investigate, has already written the matter off. The general appoints Lt. Kraft to look into the case, knowing that Kraft, though he has a reputation as a discipline problem, is not afraid to seek out the truth. A number of the other officers dislike Kraft but the cynical Captain Feder supports him.

Much of the book's satire falls by the wayside though Wisbar keeps an occasional flash of it. (One officer proclaims that Egon is not a Germanic-enough name and cannot be used any more but when he discovers it's the general's surname, he simply picks another name that is hereafter verboten.) Feder has little faith in what the school is accomplishing: "The training takes 11 weeks and we have a quota that demands that 80 percent of the cadets graduate whether they will be good officers or not. In the end, all we really teach them is that an order is an order, even if it's stupid or mean-spirited."

Kraft takes over Barkow's old section to see if he can find anyone with a motive for killing Bakow. Most of the young men in the unit are just regular fellows who want to do their duty, but cadet Hochbauer and two of his friends are fanatical Nazis who don't think their officers or fellow cadets are zealous enough.

Kraft decides to re-enact the supposed accident. While the men take shelter, Kraft prepares some explosives and lights the fuse with the assistance of Hochbauer, whom he suspects. Kraft then shortens the lit fuse and accuses Hochbauer of having done the same thing while one of his friends distracted Barkow. Kraft won't let Hochbauer take cover as the fuse sizzles. Hochbauer admits his guilt but defiantly proclaims that Barkow was a traitor and deserved to die. The explosive Kraft set is a dummy. Hochbauer tells him his confession is worthless since there are no witnesses. Neither Wisbar nor Crist really wring enough suspense out of what should be a pivotal scene.

At this point, Wisbar makes some radical changes. His sympathetic interest in Christianity replaces Crist's cynicism. In the book, Kraft knows he will never be able to convict Hochbauer of murder but instead arranges to expose the cadet's homosexual proclivities, causing Hochbauer to commit

Fabrik der Offiziere (1960)

suicide. Feder questions Kraft's methods but Kraft is content that the murderer has been punished. Ironically, he delivers Hochbauer's eulogy, which he turns into a speech against the military. He is arrested, as is the general for his support of the lieutenant. Both men are executed for treason and for undermining the morale of the school. However, at least a few of the cadets have begun to think outside of the box because of Kraft's influence. In an epilogue, we learn that Feder was hanged for taking part in the attempted assassination of Hitler.

In the book, Cadet Böhmke is a minor character, an idealist who quotes Goethe. In the film, he is the son of a pastor and admits to Kraft and Feder that he knows of Hochbauer's guilt. He is willing to testify at a hearing but then Hochbauer and his friends find a letter in Böhmke's locker from his father in which the pastor proclaims one should serve God not Hitler and the end of the Reich is at hand. Hochbauer threatens to turn the letter over to the authorities if Böhmke testifies. At the hearing, Böhmke initially equivocates but finally tells the truth. Hochbauer flees the room and shoots himself. Judge-advocate Wirrmann, a diehard Nazi, claims that Kraft unfairly persecuted the cadet. Wirrmann has Böhmke imprisoned. At Hochbauer's funeral, Kraft is disgusted by a eulogy that describes the murderer as a good German youth. Wirrmann has searched the general's desk and found papers that implicate the general in a plot against Hitler. Wirrmann offers leniency if the general will name his co-conspirators. He refuses and is promptly jailed. Kraft is furious when he hears the news and attacks Wirrmann, screaming that National Socialism has robbed people of their humanity. A guard shoots Kraft. Wirrmann wonders about "these fools" and where they find the courage.

The last scene shows Captain Feder leading the cadets in a march. As they pass the prison, they sing an army song meant to encourage the general and Böhmke (who has been beaten up by the guards). One of the cadets wonders whether they should storm the prison and rescue the general. Feder says it would do no good but they can at least let their friends know they will be remembered.

Critics were not impressed. Hans Dieter-Roos felt it was the weakest of Wisbar's military movies: "A mediocre crime story with some sentimental touches." Others opined that its characters were simplistic and not valid representations of the military under the Third Reich.

The cast is uniformly good, especially Carl Lange, who brings both Prussian dignity and poignancy to his role as the doomed general. There is more talk than suspense but that is partly the fault of the very episodic book. Wisbar captures the austere gloom of the school setting, which is made even starker by Kurt Grigoleit's cinematography. Hans-Martin Majewski's music is a bit too shrill and over-emphatic. Producer Alf Teichs, who was head of

Terra Films in 1940, had a long history with Wisbar stretching back to the '30s and *Ferryman Maria*.

Crist's book was also done on German TV as a miniseries in 1989. The miniseries apparently stayed closer to the novel than Wisbar's film.

Barbara

Aka *Barbara—Wild wie das Meer* (*Barbara—Wild as the Sea*)
Ufa Film Hansa GmbH& Co (Hamburg)
Released on November 30, 1961
96 minutes

Cast: Harriet Andersson as Barbara; Maria Sebaldt as Vupsen; Karl Lange as Bailiff Heyde; Helmut Griem as Paul; Hans Nielsen as Mikkelsen; Hans von Borsody as Andreas; Nora Minor as Barbara's mother; Erik Schumann as Dr. Nielsson; Josef Albrecht as Henry; Erika Danhoff as Sophie; Erich Dunskus as Harpunen-Olaf; Tilla Durieux as Armgart; Hans Elwenspoek as Pastor; Herbert Fleischmann as Garbriel; Günther Lüdke as Tanfloh; Hans Paetsch as Inselvogt Harme; Xenia Pörtner as Susanne; Renate Rolfs as Angelika.

Credits: Director: Frank Wisbar; Screenplay: Christian Munk; Based on the eponymous 1939 novel by Jørgen-Frantz Jacobsen; Camera Director: Klaus von Rautenfeld; Photography: Rolf Kaestel; Costume Designer: Irms Pauli; Producer: Georg Mohr; Editor: Martha Dübber; Music: Werner Eisbrenner; Sets: Kai Rasch; Sound: Knud Kristensen; Assistant Director: Thomas Fanti; Unit Manager: Willy Schoene; Makeup: Jupp Paschke, H.J. Schmalor.

> He told of a man in Goosedale who had an earth woman as a lover. She came to him during the night. The true wife knew nothing about this, but one night when she lay on the inside of the bed beside her husband she was suddenly aware of a cold hand. It was the earth woman, who had laid herself on the bed board on her husband's other side.
>
> —*Barbara*

Frank Wisbar's *Barbara* is very much in keeping with the director's fascination with the sort of mysterious and compelling women he created in *Anna and Elizabeth, The Unknown* and *Ferryman Maria*. It's his only color movie and, at least in part, it seems to hark back to the silent Nordic dramas where climate, terrain and Nature are characters in their own right and human beings are caught in forces beyond their control and act out their predestined fates against a background of storm and sea.

The story is set in the North Atlantic on the Faroe Islands, an archipelago between Iceland and Shetland. It's a place only a Viking could love. The terrain is rocky, the waters between the 18 islands often treacherous. Weeks of fog, rain and stormy weather are common. The people of this harsh environment have their own language and culture but the Danish influence is heavy. Jørgen-Frantz Jacobsen, the author of *Barbara*, had a Danish father and Faroese mother and spoke both languages. Jacobsen was a journalist and often wrote about the islands. He was stricken with tuberculosis as a young adult and suffered from it much of his life until his death at the age of 38.

Barbara, his only novel, was published posthumously in 1939 and became an international best seller. Set in the mid–1700s, it's based on an old Faroese legend, "Beinta and Peder Arrheboe," which tells of a female counterpart to Bluebeard. In the book, she marries three times (all of her husbands are pastors) and causes the death of her spouses. The title character is not really evil (Jacobsen actually based her personality on his girlfriend Estrid) though there is some talk among the gossipy islanders that she bears some kind of responsibility for the death of her second husband and there are rumors that her erotic power over men has supernatural origins. Both Barbara's husbands were pastors and she was, for a time, engaged to another pastor who finally broke it off.

The novel begins with the arrival of Pastor Paul from Copenhagen on the ship *Fortuna*. Paul is a very devout man who sees his sojourn on the islands and a hard life there as a way of renouncing the world. Though warned about Barbara, he is mesmerized by her charm and beauty and becomes her third husband. However, in spite of attempts to save her soul, he discovers that it is his own soul that is in danger. He realizes that he *expects* Barbara to be unfaithful and sees this inevitability as a kind of punishment for giving in to his erotic desires. When he is called away to minister on another island, he doubts that he will find her home and waiting for him when he returns. Delayed by the weather, he is gone for a couple of weeks during which time Barbara takes up with Andreas, a childhood sweetheart, recently arrived on the islands to write a report about the economy. A drunken Paul confronts Barbara but ends up spending the night with her. She sees no contradiction in loving two men at once. However, Paul cannot control himself and sets fire to the little house Barbara has been sharing with Andreas. Andreas decides to return to Copenhagen and promises Barbara she can come with him. Then he changes his mind and boards the *Fortuna* without her. Frantically, she heads for the dock and has some men row her in pursuit of the departing boat. She doesn't succeed in catching up with the ship and dejectedly returns to the shore to face the scorn of the onlookers. Gabriel, the mean-spirited storekeeper who has always lusted after Barbara, tells his employees to dispose of her hastily discarded luggage.

Jacobsen intended to write three more chapters but the Grim Reaper intervened. However, most critics felt that the open-ended finale was quite appropriate. Has Barbara been broken or is this just a temporary setback?

The island temptress (Harriet Andersson) and the village doctor (Helmut Griem) in *Barbara*.

Earlier we had read that the servant of her second husband, appalled at her behavior, turned her upside down into a dung barrel. If she can bounce back from that humiliation, being stood up at the dock doesn't really sound like an insurmountable obstacle to her career as the island temptress. The question the book raises is whether Barbara is a slut, a mere wanton or a free spirit rebelling at the constraints of a self-righteous and puritanical society. (A modern critic would add patriarchal to the mix.) Jacobsen seems to come down on the second side as Barbara rarely loses the reader's sympathy.

Wisbar—or the producers—did at least one thing right by shooting the film on location in the Faroe Islands. Cinematographer Klaus von Rautenfeld was a specialist in nature epics (*Im Schatten des Berges* [*In the Shadow of the Mountain*, 1940] and *Der Burg ruft* [*The Mountain Calls*, 1940]) and often worked with Luis Trenker. The photography is a canvas of brown, green and blue and captures the stark beauty of the Faroe Islands, where trees are rare and rocks and cliffs commonplace. The surf is always beating against the shore and stormy days are the norm. These are constant reminders of the islanders' struggle against the elements. And of course, serve as symbols for the characters' passions. One also thinks of the sirens in *The Odyssey* and how their song lured men to their deaths on the rocks.

The film makes two big mistakes: The story is modernized and Pastor Paul becomes a doctor. Obviously, a period piece would have been much

Seduction through the slats, *Barbara*'s best sequence—erotic and disquieting.

more expensive, requiring costumes and a clipper ship rather than the modern garb and boats we see. It's believable enough that, in the 1700s, custom might dictate that the new parson marry his predecessor's widow, similar to what happens in Carl Dreyer's *The Parson's Widow*. But such a situation seems much less likely in the 1960s, especially as Paul is now a doctor. The spiritual dilemma of the story is lost and what transpires seems dangerously close to soap opera. The script tries to make up for this by emphasizing how cut off the islands are from the "civilized" world and how the people have developed their own distinctive traditions.

Also, we see little in the way of modern conveniences. Wagons rather than cars transport the characters about and the arrival of a ship is a major event for everyone, reinforcing the isolation of the islands. "We on the Faroe Islands are the last Viking settlers in the world," says one character. "Despite radio, telephone, automobile, little has changed in the last thousand years." This is partly effective (there are references to Paul phoning but we don't actually see him do it) but that doesn't make up for the loss of the mythic dimension that is important to the story. Nevertheless, the film is very faithful to the plot of the novel.

The film begins as Dr. Paul, in the company of Judge Mikkelsen, prepares to land on Torshavn, the capital of the Faroe Islands. Paul is the new doctor on the island of Vagar and a replacement for the late Dr. Niels. "And will you be taking over the widow of your predecessor as well?" asks the judge. Paul snorts at the idea that he would marry the widow of a 60-year-old man, custom or no. The judge merely smiles.

At the main store in Torshavn, the ladies are excited about the delivery of bales of beautiful silk. Gabriel the storekeeper plans to use this to his advantage but cruelly denies any of the fine fabric to his mistress Angelika whom he treats very harshly. His co-worker Vuspen defends her. We learn that Gabriel is infatuated with his cousin Barbara, widow of Dr. Niels.

Judge Mikkelsen introduces Paul to the other members of Torshavn society, including the Bailiff Heyde (chief magistrate) Ove Harms, overseer of the Islands, and his daughter Suzanne. Also in attendance are the local priest and his wife. While Wisbar usually displays some sympathy for the clergy and a respectful interest in Christianity, here the priest is a pious windbag and his long-suffering wife mocks him to his face ("Don't you think it is reassuring to have an expert in the house who can tell us everything about sin?"). Much of the talk is about Barbara, widow of both Dr. Niels and another village doctor before him. Some of the gossip is very malicious: "A deadly nightshade; whoever partakes of the poison will be befallen by frenzy"; "She has lain in a hundred beds"; "Her very name means 'the wild one.'" Suzanne defends Barbara, her good friend, though she has no objection to her being described as a "merry widow."

Barbara arrives on the scene. She is currently living in Torshavn, at her mother's house. but agrees to accompany Paul and Mikkelsen to Vagar to handle the agreement about her late husband's cottage. However, they must wait for more favorable weather.

Gabriel tells Barbara to come to his store that night to inspect the new dresses and silk from Copenhagen. Barbara agrees but, knowing Gabriel's real motives, asks Suzanne to join her later. In the book, the two women have fun with the frustrated storekeeper, parading in a state of semi-undress as they try on different outfits. In the film, Gabriel is an even more swinish character and attacks Barbara, who angrily fights him off.

Paul has a couple of pleasant encounters with Barbara and a less agreeable one with Gabriel, who bitterly insults his cousin and warns Paul of her wiles. "He caught a mermaid by her hair," Gabriel recites. "She was caught in the net on the rim of the boat and she was naked as a stone. 'Come with me and I'll be yours in the deep.'" Paul ignores the storekeeper's drunken rant and insists that he has no intention of falling in love.

Later, the little town is abuzz with excitement: A Spanish ship has docked because of engine trouble and a dance is being prepared in the town hall, with the captain and his crew attending. The women of Torshavn are enthralled at the prospect of meeting new men. As the drinks flows plentifully and the women flirt, the judge makes a little speech about the islands:

Our islands in the North Atlantic are only small dots in the great Atlantic Ocean—far away from your sunny, southern homeland. Our land is sparse, our existence hard. The summer is short even though the sun does not set. In winter, we are without sun, the howling storms of the Atlantic Ocean about us, in months of darkness. But we nevertheless understand to enjoy our existence. That is shown to you by this gaiety.

Some of the women and the sailors pair off. Gabriel notes with a smirk that Suzanne has left with one of the Spaniards. Barbara goes to a nearby stable with a sailor but when he gets passionate with her, she opens the sheepfold, releasing the bleating sheep that then surround them. The Spaniard is bewildered and angry but Barbara mocks him: "You thought you only have to crook your finger and we'd go obediently into the hay. Idiot!" The next day, the Spanish ship leaves port.

The weather has finally settled down so Paul, the judge and Barbara set off for Vagar. Their boat breaks down, forcing them to land on another island. As rain pours down on them, they make their way to a farmhouse. Barbara tells Paul she dreams of escaping the islands, perhaps to Paris or America or India. In the course of their playful discussion, Barbara asks Paul if he has ever seen a snake. "Well," he responds, "it was wearing a kerchief and walked on two legs."

At the farmhouse, Paul and the judge sleep in a storeroom with Barbara bedded down in an adjoining room. The judge, exhausted and a little drunk, passes out while Paul observes Barbara undressing in silhouette. Soon after Paul goes to bed, he feels a hand touching his own; it is Barbara reaching through the slats that barely separate the rooms. As the wind whistles faintly in the background and the music becomes a whisper, Barbara and Paul embrace. It's a particularly well-directed scene, both erotic and slightly sinister. In the book, the passage about the earth woman quoted at the beginning of this essay precedes Barbara's seduction of Paul, making the encounter even more ominous.

Paul falls in love with Barbara in spite of her warnings that she is "not dependable and full of unrest," and they agree to marry. Back in Torshavn, other lives are changing as well. Vupsen and Suzanne and two other women are pregnant by their Spanish lovers. "The midwife will be able to build a new chicken coop," snickers one of the townsfolk. Concerned about the situation, Suzanne's father approaches Gabriel with the suggestion that he marry Suzanne. Gabriel consents but makes the condition that he will succeed his future father-in-law as overseer. He agrees. Suzanne, despairing of the return of her Spanish paramour, unhappily consents.

Paul meets with the doctor who was once engaged to Barbara. The man warns Paul that this match puts him in danger. Paul shrugs off his colleague's objections and announces that his wedding to Barbara will take place as planned. The wedding reception is attended by Andreas, nephew of Chief Magistrate Heyde. Andreas has just arrived on Torshavn to do an economic report for the authorities in Copenhagen. Andreas and Barbara were former lovers and Paul notes with alarm that the handsome young man and his bride seem quite attached to each other. He brings Barbara home early over her objections.

The winter on Varga is especially hard on Paul. "I can't sleep any more. I don't know whether it is night or day," he exclaims with the ever-howling wind suggesting the end of the world and slowly driving him mad. Barbara reminds him that this is a normal winter for the islands and the people are used to it. This sequence is a bit short; we only once see Paul standing at the rocks before he begins complaining to Barbara. Rather than simply hearing about it, a montage of scenes showing the harshness of the winter may have been more effective in conveying Paul's increasing desperation and sense of being an outsider. In general, the film seems on the talky side and one yearns for the silent passages of Wisbar's best '30s work.

Spring finally comes and Paul's spirits improve though Barbara seems increasingly lazy. He gives her a playful spank and she bristles, warning him never to do that again since it reminds her of her mother's strict discipline. The mail arrives, bringing the news that Suzanne has given birth and wants Barbara to be the godmother. Barbara is excited at the prospect of going to Torshavn but when Paul finds out that Andreas is to be the godfather, he insists that they stay home. Barbara accuses Paul of acting like a tyrant and says she will go to Torshavn anyway. She throws a tantrum, smashes a mirror and storms out of the cottage. An ear-witness to the argument, Paul's servant Kristoffer, not fond of Barbara, picks her and drops her in a water barrel (better than a dung barrel at least). Paul is indignant but Barbara surprisingly is not. In spite of her earlier objection to physical chastisement, the dunking suddenly makes her cooperative and she tells Paul she will do whatever he says.

The couple's period of bliss is brief. Paul is called away on a medical emergency to another island. Just before he leaves, Andreas shows up claiming he must do a report on health conditions on Varga. Paul is not happy to see him but departs on his mission anyway. Andreas loses no time trying to seduce Barbara but she resists. Meanwhile, Paul is delayed on the other island as more patients turn up. When Paul is able to return to Varga, he finds that Barbara, having given in to Andreas' advances, has left with him for Torshavn.

In spite of dangerous weather, Paul insists on going to Torshavn. Judge Mikkelsen obliges him and their boat safely maneuvers the turbulent waters. All the townspeople are attending a play titled *The Child Murderess* (no doubt a reference to all the unexpected pregnancies after the departure of the Spanish ship). The pastor is scandalized by the notion of an unwed mother drowning her baby being played for humor, but the audience finds the play very amusing.

Drenched and half-mad with longing for his wife, Paul arrives at the play but Barbara quickly spirits her distraught husband to her mother's house. Barbara tells Paul she will never be a good wife but the doctor insists she is the only woman for him. The two make love. When the exhausted Paul awakens from a long sleep, Barbara is gone. Barbara tells Andreas she must leave the islands or Paul will be utterly destroyed. Andreas invites her to go with him to Copenhagen. Barbara is enthused about the prospect: "I shall be free for the first time in my life." Won't she miss the islands? "Has the convict any longing for his cell?" is her response.

Frantic and drunk, Paul, searches for Barbara. Gabriel encourages him to be violent when he catches up with her. Paul finds that the cottage Barbara shares with Andreas is empty. Unlike in the book, he doesn't set the place ablaze but is content to burn Barbara's fancy clothing.

Andreas' uncle and Mikkelsen are angry at the scandal Andreas has caused and they insist he leave for Copenhagen immediately. They warn him that his dalliance with Barbara could ruin his government career. The two men find Andreas' promise to take Barbara with him absurd: "Within four weeks, she'd end up in a whorehouse. Barbara belongs here." When Barbara wakes up at her mother's house, her mother tells her that Andreas has left her and is already aboard ship. Barbara throws a coat over her nightgown and, barefoot, runs to the dock. The ship has already gone. Gabriel, watching the ship's departure with the crowd, sneers at Barbara's humiliation.

Barbara and Paul make a half-hearted attempt at reconciliation but both realize there is no hope for them. The film ends much as it began with a new doctor arriving on a ship to take over the practice at Varga. Judge Mikkelsen is also on board and tells the physician that his predecessor, after an unhappy marriage, divorced his wife and went to Greenland. When the new doctor snickers at the notion that he might take the cast-off wife for himself, the judge responds: "In the solitude of our island existence, this woman is a ray of sunshine. An amusing person but not without danger. Her name is Barbara." The last shot shows Barbara on the cliffs, looking directly at the camera, appearing self-assured, triumphant, and mistress of all she surveys. The cycle continues and there seems little chance the new doctor will avoid the fates of Barbara's three husbands.

Barbara's longing to escape the islands is more pronounced in the film than in the book where her love for Andreas seems to be the motivation for leaving her homeland. The notion that she belongs in the small society of the Islands makes sense given that she would just be one of many in Copenhagen instead of the object of so much attention—good and bad—in her native land. The last shot of the film seems to indicate that she knows where she belongs and what her role is.

Barbara is different from Sybille Schmitz's siren in *The Unknown* in that her sexuality is innocent. Madeline in the earlier film is cynical but comes to recognize her destructive power over the opposite sex. When she falls truly in love, she kills herself to prevent the ruination of her beloved. Barbara likewise is aware of how men fall under her spell and realizes that Paul will be destroyed if they stay together. However, Paul is not Barbara's soulmate; he's merely one among many though she entered into marriage with him with a sincere heart as no doubt she did with her earlier spouses. There's no reason to think her love with Andreas would have been sustained in the long haul either. Barbara in some ways is more like Lulu than Madeline: She has a great experience of love and always succumbs to its call. This does not mean that she's loose; her behavior with Gabriel and the Spanish sailor demonstrate that.

Wisbar was fascinated by Sybille Schmitz's face and the camera lingers on her lovingly throughout *The Unknown*. Sybille's look was exotic, strange and almost asexual while Harriet Andersson's beauty is more natural and robust. Wisbar can't seem to look away from Andersson and when she's not on screen, she still dominates the action. The viewer too is anxious to get back to her and away from the backbiting islanders and all their chat.

Andersson is famous for her appearances in Ingmar Bergman's films. The first film for which she drew attention was Bergman's *Summer with Monika* wherein she played a kind of Barbara-in-the-making role as a young woman who rejects the conventional. The movie begins and ends with Monika looking directly at the camera with a defiant expression that dares the viewer to judge her (a bit different than *Barbara*'s somewhat suggestive final shot of its heroine). There were other memorable Andersson portrayals in *Smiles of a Summer Night*, *Cries and Whispers* and as the mentally ill daughter of *Through a Glass Darkly* ("God is a spider!"). She also played in a few duds: the bizarre *Dogville*, the thus-far-unseen Jerry Lewis movie *The Day the Clown Cried* and Robert Siodmak's final film, the campy *The Last Roman*.

Jacobsen once wrote that Paul was based on himself—not the priest part, obviously—but rather in his yearning for the unattainable. Helmut Griem does a good job of conveying the lovelorn doctor's basic decency but falls short in suggesting the intensity of the character's self-destructive (or masochistic) obsession with Barbara. This is one of Griem's early films and the good-looking actor became something of a matinee idol.

Barbara has a solid supporting cast. Hans Nielsen, whose stage and film career stretched back to the '30s, makes the judge humane and believable, a fundamentally upright man but not without flaws. Nielsen played a variety of parts during the Third Reich, perhaps most notably in the anti–British

Titanic (1943) where he portrayed a fictional German officer who tries to prevent the tragedy. In his later years, Nielsen often played authority figures: judges, prosecutors and priests.

Herbert Fleischmann (Gabriel) was a radio actor prior to making his film debut in *Barbara*. His portrayal of Gabriel as a self-righteous, hypocritical and greedy lecher makes an appropriately unpleasant impression. Fleischmann won the Ernst Lubitsch Press award for playing the clown in 1971's *Das Freudenhaus (The Bordello)*. A good character actor, he also appeared in Wisbar's last theatrical film, *Breakthrough Locomotive 234*.

Hans von Barsody's Andreas is the same attractive but ultimately shallow character he was in the book. Von Barsody can also be found in Wisbar's *Commando*. Tillia Durieux scores as Aunt Armagh, a feisty old lady who has an opinion (often dubious) on everything. Durieux's own life would give Barbara a run for her krona. Her second husband committed suicide outside the courtroom granting their divorce and her third spouse died in a concentration camp. Durieux was a great beauty in her youth and even posed for Renoir. A fixture in the wild Berlin nightlife of the '20s, she was also a Reinhardt actress, appearing with Paul Wegener in *Oedipus* (playing Jocasta) and was the first to interpret Oscar Wilde's *Salome* on the German stage. She was also fiercely anti–Nazi and joined the Yugoslav resistance during World War II. Her postwar years were considerably more sedate as she focused on the stage while making the occasional film.

Barbara received mediocre reviews. A second version of Jacobsen's novel appeared in 1997. A Danish film, it was directed by Nils Malmros and returned the story to its original period.

Commando

Original title: *Marcia o crepa/March or Die*
Midega Film/Monachia Zeynfilm/Tempo Film
Released in Italy on November 14, 1962
98 minutes (American release)

Cast: Stewart Granger as Captain Le Blanc; Dorian Gray as Nora; Maurizio Arena as Dolce Vita; Ivo Garrani as Colonel Dionne; Fausto Tosci as Brascia; Riccardo Garroni as Paolo; Carlos Casaravila as Ben Bled; Peter Karsten as Barbarossa; Hans von Barsody as Fritz; Rafaael Luis Carlo as Kappa-kappa; Dietmar Schönnher as Petit Prince; Leo Anchóriz as Garcia; Guillermo Carmona, Pablito Alonzo, Jaimie de Pedro, Francisco Cornet.

Credits: Director: Frank Wisbar; Assistant Directors: Antonio Linares, Wieland Liebski; Script: Giuseppe Mangioni, Mino Guerrini, William Denby, Milton Krims, Frank Wisbar, Eric Bercovici, Arturo Tofanelli; Producer: Willy Zehn; Photography: Cecilio Paniaqua; Art Director: Enrique Alacón; Editor: Mario

Serandrei; Music: Angelo Francesco Lavagnino; Production: Enzo Napoli, Ramón Plana, Martín Sacristán, Garbiele Silvestre, Carnilla Teti; Costumes: Demofilo Fidani; U.S. Distributor: American International Pictures.

Commando is a fairly suspenseful action film with well-paced direction by Wisbar and one of the very first movies to use the Algerian War as a background. That long, bloody and bitter fight of Algerian revolutionaries to throw off French colonial rule had actually just come to a conclusion shortly before *Commando* was made. The film, unlike *The Battle of Algiers* and *Lost Command*, both from 1966, doesn't take any kind of political stand. Wisbar's interest is in the soldierly virtues of the heroes: courage, perseverance and group loyalty. There is skepticism about the conflict itself and whether it's worth anyone's life, regardless of the right or wrong of things, and doubts are cast on the character of the higher-ups who are more interested in their chess-like battle maneuvers than the lives of the men under their command. In this respect, the film is not unlike *Dogs, Do You Want to Live Forever?* and *Sharks and Little Fish*.

Captain Le Blanc of the French Foreign Legion is a hard-drinking cynic but an accomplished soldier. His commanding officers have a difficult assignment for him: capture and bring back alive FLN rebel leader Ben Bled so he may be tried and executed as a public example. Intelligence has determined that Ben Bled is going to attend a dinner with friends in a little village and is not expected to have his usual heavy entourage of bodyguards. Le Blanc is to quickly put together a team, parachute under cover of darkness into the village deep in hostile territory and later rendezvous with a rescue helicopter with their prisoner.

Le Blanc swiftly assembles his squad of 12. They're not quite the Dirty Dozen but they are mostly a crude, loutish bunch (we see several of them at a café amusing themselves by tormenting a belly dancer with a slingshot). One of Le Blanc's choices is Paolo, who has to be sprung from jail where he's awaiting trial for rape. Whatever their moral defects, they have great combat skills and are fiercely loyal to Le Blanc.

The first part of the mission goes according to plan: The commandos swoop down on the village, storm the house where Ben Bled is visiting and capture him. Two of the commandos are killed, as are Ben Bled's friends and bodyguards. The group makes it to the rendezvous point accompanied by Nora, a Frenchwoman who begs to be taken with them lest she be killed in retaliation. The *AFI Catalog* describes her as a prostitute but in the English-language version—the one we're basing our synopsis on—it's not clear who she is supposed to be or why she is there in the first place. Clutching her makeup kit and without a hair out of place, she spends most of the film pleading or shrilly complaining, annoying both the other characters and the viewer.

Of course she is present to save the film from the box office curse of having an all-male cast.

The capture of Ben Bled is skillfully directed. The tension is increased by the lack of music and the barking of the village dogs. Indeed, the howling grows even louder as the commandos leave as though the beasts themselves are in pursuit. The sequence has a curiously modern resonance in these days of Navy SEAL operations and the mission to get Osama bin Laden. Ben Bled though is not a bin Laden; indeed, the portly figure in a business suit seems more like a diplomat or businessman than firebrand revolutionary. Even though he's the enemy, Ben Bled is not really a villainous figure. Of course, since he's continually being trussed up, gagged, verbally abused, threatened and dragged around in fetters, it would be hard not to feel a little sympathy for him.

The helicopter sent to rescue the commandos gets shot down and the group is forced to take refuge in a deserted church. Inside they find an Arab boy whose parents were executed by the rebels. Ben Bled seems moved by the boy's suffering but an angry Le Blanc makes the insurgent leader bury the corpses. Before long the church is surrounded by the rebels who can't storm the building for fear of killing Ben Bled. While the commandos are distracted, Ben Bled destroys their radio. There is a second helicopter scheduled to go to another rendezvous point the following night but Le Blanc has no way of communicating their situation to headquarters. Garcia, Le Blanc's aide-de-camp, volunteers to go to the rendezvous site and instruct them to land nearer to their current location.

Some of the action scenes are a bit reminiscent of 1934's *The Lost Patrol* wherein the Arab opponents are not seen as they pick off the British patrol one by one. Wisbar opts for a similar unseen menace approach until later in the film where the shootouts are handled in the usual cowboys-and-Indians manner.

Garcia succeeds in escaping. While the other commandos spend a tense and vigilant night, Paolo attempts to rape Nora but she is saved by Le Blanc. The men discover a truck in the garage but the distributor is broken. However, some of the rebels are in a Jeep over the hill. If the commandos can get the Jeep, it's possible that its distributor might fit the truck. A couple of the commandos attempt to do this by lobbing grenades at the vehicle and its occupants (not very logical considering they need the Jeep for parts). They get the distributor and make it back it to the church. The distributor fits the truck.

Garcia has succeeded in making the rendezvous and contacting headquarters but, disobeying Le Blanc's orders, he attempts to return to the church. He is captured and, in full sight of his comrades, tied to some brush which is then set aflame. Le Blanc refuses to trade Ben Bled for Garcia and shoots

Garcia to spare him the agony of the flames (rather like in *Drums Along the Mohawk* and the 1992 *Last of the Mohicans*).

Le Blanc decides that some of his men should escape via the truck while displaying a decoy Ben Bled and draw the insurgents to pursue. Meanwhile, Le Blanc and the others will steal away on foot with the real Ben Bled. The scene is a bit confusing and it's not clear why the Arabs will think an obvious scarecrow is really their leader. In any case, they end up opening fire, indicating that they now find Ben Bled expendable. Even though the commandos are killed, their ruse has worked and Le Blanc and company manage to escape to the rendezvous site. Along the way, Nora, in a rare unselfish moment, is shot trying to protect the Arab boy. She still has her makeup kit and dies happy, not realizing that the jewels she has hidden under the makeup had been stolen earlier. The helicopter arrives but only Le Blanc, the Arab boy and Ben Bled have survived to board it.

An ironic surprise awaits Le Blanc back at headquarters. The political situation has changed in his brief absence and peace talks are underway with Ben Bled being chosen to represent the FLN. Instead of the gallows, he's headed for Paris to help negotiate. Le Blanc is disgusted that all his men have died for nothing. He angrily turns his back on his superiors but, in a sentimental coda, appears to adopt the Arab lad (who has not said a word through the entire picture).

Kevin Thomas of the *Los Angeles Times* (March 13, 1964) was not impressed, calling *Commando* "mediocre" with a "timely subject matter reduced to the level of a formula western." Thomas also took the opportunity to complain about international productions: "Dubbing on one hand produces a hodgepodge of accents and confused storylines. Attitudes, on the other, are blurred by trying not to offend national sentiments."

Most of the actors in *Commando* were not familiar to American audiences but they turn up repeatedly in the '60s in spaghetti westerns, spy thrillers, German krimi mysteries and hanging out with the sons of Hercules. They rarely spoke English so dubbing, which usually destroyed the acting, was commonplace. (Subtitling was usually reserved for more sophisticated films, not ones in which action and sex were the principal elements.) The dubbing in *Commando* is no better or worse than in similar films but it's certainly a detriment.

The best-known actor in *Commando* is Stewart Granger, playing Le Blanc, the French captain with an English accent. In the '50s, Granger inherited the Errol Flynn swashbuckler mantle and appeared in big films like *Scaramouche* and *The Prisoner of Zenda*. He brought intelligence and craggy good looks to his heroic portrayals but his movies went downhill in quality as the decade wore on. In 1981, Granger penned his autobiography *Sparks Fly Upwards* but ended the book in 1960. That's perhaps understandable as most of his '60s films were like *Commando*, international concoctions with a veritable United Nations of actors, writers and directors and rarely rising above routine fare. It was a lucrative business, though, and Granger later claimed he made—and spent—more than $1.5 million. Granger retired to Spain and went into real estate but later said, "I've never been so bored in my life." In 1978, his friend Richard Burton lured him back in front of the cameras for *The Wild Geese* but this was followed by only a couple more movies, the sort of things he did in the '60s but on even lower budgets. Granger did get some TV work including playing Prince Philip in *The Royal Romance of Charles and Diana*, a title that certainly seems ironic in retrospect.

The only other performer of note in *Commando* is the strangely named Dorian Gray (née Maria Luisa Mangini). She had appeared in supporting roles in Fellini's *Nights of Cabiria* (1957) and Michelangelo Antonioni's *Il Girdo* (1957) but by the '60s was more likely to be found in films like *Colossus and the Headhunters*. She retired in 1965 and died a suicide at age 83.

Commando may not have broken box office records but the theme music by Angelo Francesco Lavagnino was later orchestrated by Ken Thorne and became a hit in the U.K. It can be found on YouTube under the film's U.K. title *The Legion's Last Patrol*.

Commando, like many of its ilk, found its nook in American TV of the '60s, turning up on late shows and Million Dollar Movie matinees. However, the coming of cable ended all that and *Commando* disappeared from view, like so many others. Judging by the user comments on IMDb, the film was fondly remembered by many who saw it in its original release.

Durchbruch Lok 234
(Breakthrough Locomotive 234)

Porfil-Film
Released on August 14, 1963
88 minutes

Cast: Erik Schuman as Harry Dölling; Maria Körber as Ilse Dölling; Rainer Eggers as Arno Dölling; Ingo Eggers as Helmut Dölling; Olaf Eggers as Dieter Dölling; Eva Fiebig as Oma Dölling; Helmut Oeser as Max Schober; Heidrun Kussin as Alice; Hans Paetsch as Professor Pollnow; Anne Marie Böhme as Mrs. Pollnow; Angelika Thieme as Rosel Pollnow; Joseph Offenbach as Krause; Karl Heinz Gerdesmann as Mieke; Katharina Mayberg as Mrs. Mieke; Georg Lehn as Vogel; Herbert Fleischmann as Dr. Konetzki; Peter Lembrock as Train policeman; Silva Simon.
Credits: Director: Frank Wisbar; Screenplay: Gehard T. Buchholz; Producer: Frank Tietz; Music: Bernd Adamkevitz, Peter Laurin; Photography: Bert

Meister; Art Director: Wilhelm Vierhaus; Assistant Director: Thomas Fantl; Sound: Karl Tramburg; Production Managers: Luise Doering, Wolfgang Jung, Joseph Thuis; Camera Operator: Peter Forster.

The Berlin Wall may be just a vague memory of the Cold War for many Americans but it's far from forgotten in Germany. The Wall was constructed in 1961 due to Russian frustration at so many East Germans leaving the workers' paradise of the GDR for the capitalist fleshpots of the German Federal Republic (as many as 1000 a day were crossing over to the west). The Wall put a stop to that though not to people attempting to leave. Over 100 were shot dead trying to escape until the Wall became inoperative in 1989. People wanting to get out used a variety of methods, some quite ingenious. One particularly daring escape occurred in 1962 when 29 East Berliners tunneled under the Wall to freedom. *The Tunnel*, a documentary on the escape, played on NBC in 1962. Around the same time there was a fictionalized version, *Escape from East Berlin*, directed by Robert Siodmak.

Wisbar's last film is likewise taken from a true incident and is well acted and fairly suspenseful—though in no way memorable.

This synopsis is based on a viewing of the movie:

Harry Dölling drives a train in East Berlin. He's an average sort of guy who has a wife, Ilse, and three sons. His mother also shares their modest apartment. He does his best to get along, has an occasional night out bowling with friends and is generally well-liked. However, he is not an admirer of his communist government. When one of his colleagues gets arrested for watching West German TV, Harry is shocked to learn that his 11-year-old son Arno is responsible since he innocently answered his teacher's leading question about whether he knew anyone who tunes in to West German stations. A furious Harry slaps Arno repeatedly. Harry calms down and later, tenderly watching his boys while they sleep, remarks to his wife that they need to rescue them from "the things that they did to us in our youth," thus equating the communist rule with the Nazis and the Hitler Youth.

Despondent over their situation, Harry begins to drink heavily. Soon he discovers that the Albrechtshof station is very close to the Berlin East-West border and there's an unused track that goes right into West Berlin. Of course, the Wall is right there and there are guards but only a small barrier blocks off the track. Harry hits upon a plan but he needs to act quickly as the Albrechtshof route is going to be changed.

Harry's good friend Max, a stoker, and his girlfriend Alice wish to come with him. A number of other people also want to participate, including an elderly professor and his wife and daughter. Krause, Harry's partner on the train, is not in on the plot and falls ill the day before the planned escape. Max visits him and gives him a bottle of wine, urging him to stay in bed one more day. After Max and Alice leave, Krause, suspicious of their motives, says to himself, "Not a bit of it."

Vogel, Harry's demanding boss, is out sick and his temporary replacement allows Max to replace the absent Krause. On the day of the escape, however, Krause also shows up; he wants to get away as well. Harry's family and the other participants in the plot are all on board but, while his daughter has made it, the professor and his wife just miss the train. However, the kindly Dr. Kontezki offers to drive them to a station where they can catch the train en route. It's obvious that he knows what they're up to and even tells them he'd like to go with them but can't because his patients need him, especially as medical care in the East is substandard.

Various dramas unfold as the train heads for the border. The security guards on the train are especially watchful and suspicious. This causes one of the would-be escapees to panic and consider blabbing but his girlfriend talks him out of it. The professor's daughter, not seeing her parents, gets off the train. However, they get on at the next stop. The engine begins to overheat but Harry, Krause and Max are able to keep it going.

Vogel returns to work and is very suspicious about Max replacing Krause. He calls the authorities near the Wall, but one of them, sympathetic to what might be going on, delays notifying his superiors. On the train, Arno's pet squirrel escapes and jumps on an old lady who complains to the guard. The guard insists on seeing what's in Ilse's bag and discovers that there's extra linen in it, something he finds suspicious if they're just going to nearby Albrechtshof. Just at that moment, Harry speeds up the train, bypasses the station and barrels for the border. The security guards yank on the emergency brakes but Harry has sabotaged them and the train roars on. As the locomotive smashes through the border gate, the guards at the Wall spray the train with machine gun fire but passengers and crew are unharmed and the Lok 234 stops safely inside West Berlin.

Harry, his family and their friends head for the nearby lights of West Berlin. Some of the passengers not in on the escape plan start back for East Berlin. The professor, knowing that his daughter is still in the East, decides to return as well, leaving behind the books and papers he has lugged with him, knowing that that hauling them back would be suspicious in the eyes of the authorities. Krause bids a tearful farewell to his beloved engine and joins the others.

The real-life escape happened largely as the film describes it, though the guards did not fire on the train. There were 31 people aboard and 25, many of them in on the plot, remained in the west while a few returned. The East German government, furious, called the escape a criminal act as well as dangerous because of the train's high speed at the border. The tracks in question were promptly dismantled.

While Wisbar is no Alfred Hitchcock, he manages to bring some tension to the dash to the finish line. The action sequence of the train surging forward while the guards fire is certainly exciting enough. The last scene, with the characters marching through the dark toward the lights of West Berlin, is moving. Though Wisbar's anti-communist leanings are obvious, their triumph somehow seems a bit low-key, as though uncertainty as well as freedom lies ahead of them.

The performances are all believable enough, though none of them stand out. Eric Schumann (Harry), who worked with Wisbar a number of times, has the same rugged good looks as John Ireland. The character loses a bit of viewer sympathy when he manhandles his son, even allowing for the circumstances. Herbert Fleischmann, so convincingly vile in Wisbar's *Barbara*, is here equally persuasive as the good-hearted Dr. Kontezski. Popular TV star Joseph Offenbach brings the right comic touch to Krause without overdoing it.

In some ways, this is an unsatisfying swan song for the man who made *Ferryman Maria* and *Ann and Elisabeth* but it's consistent with the more realistic-though less interesting subjects that he found compelling in the last phase of his career.

West German TV

For the last two years of his life, Frank Wisbar worked on doing TV programs for the Federal Republic. These films were done for ZDF; this second German national broadcasting system started in 1963 and focused on entertainment while the older network ARD concentrated more on the news. Wisbar must have found it a refreshing contrast to the hectic days of early American television and *Fireside Theater*. The latter was often derided by critics but now Wisbar, with bigger budgets to work with and a more leisurely schedule, could direct the *Playhouse 90*–type of production that won so much critical acclaim in the '50s. Here is a first-hand look at two of Wisbar's German TV movies.

Onkel Phils Nachlass (*Uncle Phil's Legacy*)

Broadcast on December 22, 1965
55 minutes

Cast: Willi Maertens as Uncle Phil; Ilsemarie Schnerring as Mrs. Grigson; Horst Beck as Mr. Grigson; Herta Fahrenkrog as Una Flemming; Helmut Oser as George Flemming; Linda Fulda as Joyce Grigson; Wolf Franck as Steve Grigson; Peter Musaüs as Mr. Brown; Alf Stocks as Kurt Klopsch; Trude Adam as Mrs. Smith; Mita von Ahlefeld as Mrs. Pringle; Gerda Gmelin as Mrs. Cunningham, Gerdamaria Jürgens as Mrs. McCarthy; Heinz Piper as Oberst Gregg.

Credits: Director: Frank Wisbar; Teleplay: Niclaus Richter; Based on the 1953 short story *Uncle Phil on TV* by J.B. Priestley; Photography: Robert Kerndorff, Claus Winnikes; Makeup: Herbert Grieser, Heinz Furhrmann; Editor: Gela-Marina Runne; Assistant Director: Katja Fleischer; Sound: Karl Tramburg; Costumes: Anne; Production Designer: Herbert Kirchoff; Produced by ZDF (Zweites Deutsches Fernsehen).

Haunted or threatening household electronic devices—televisions, phones, computers—have become standard plot elements in horror and science fiction. There's *Poltergeist, Videodrome, The Twilight Zone,* the *Ringu* movies, the novel *The Circle* and most recently the excellent British series *Black Mirror* which is scary enough to make you want to throw your computer out the window and move to a cabin in the wilderness. What makes such

Onkel Phils Nachalss—even a 1965 state of the art television can't exorcise the ghost of the cantankerous Uncle Phil (Willy Maertens).

machines unsettling is that you have brought them willingly into your home where you are at your most vulnerable. Are you watching the television or is it watching you?

Perhaps the earliest attempt at finding something sinister in commonplace media devices was the 1942 short story *The Twonky*, about a radio that is actually a dangerous robot-like machine built by a man from another dimension. The radio becomes a television for the 1953 film adaptation. The machine ends up killing its owner. Nineteen fifty-three was also the year J.B. Priestley wrote his short story "Uncle Phil on TV."

Even though television in Britain had been around since the late '30s, it was very slow to catch on. By 1950, relatively few people owned a set. That would change when it was announced that the coronation of Queen Elizabeth was going to be on the tube, causing the telly to quickly be transformed into a standard household item. Priestley was fond of TV and frequently appeared on it but *Uncle Phil* pokes gentle fun at the medium and the viewers who were enraptured by it.

By the time Wisbar did his version of the story, TV was hardly a novelty but *Uncle Phil's Legacy* captures the feel of the early '50s and what it must have been like for families to gather around the tube the way cavemen circled around a fire. Wisbar's first-hand experience in the formative days of TV no doubt put him in good stead.

Mr. and Mrs. Grigson live above their family business, a grocery store. (This is different from the short story where the men all work in a shop.) Mrs. Grigson's older brother Phil resides with them along with Grigson's daughter Uma and her husband George. Completing the household is the younger Grigson daughter Joyce and her brother Steve. Joyce likes rock music while the introverted Steve prefers to read.

What all the family members have in common is that none of them have any use for the curmudgeonly Uncle Phil. Phil insists on helping in the store, much to Mr. Grigson's exasperation as the old man often makes sarcastic remarks to the customers and is careless with the merchandise (at one point he drops a whole crate of eggs). Joyce is constantly irritated at her uncle's insistence that she turn down the volume on her radio and the blowhard George doesn't like competition in the know-it-all department. Uncle Phil also has heart problems and is dependent on pills to keep him healthy.

Wisbar takes a slightly tongue-in-cheek look at family life before the tube. After dinner and when they take a break from bickering, the Grigsons hang out in the living room and do things like read the paper, sew or play board games. Uncle Phil falls asleep in his chair and Mrs. Grigson shushes the other family members so the old man won't be disturbed. Then there's a clever cut to rows of black umbrellas on the somber, rainswept day of Phil's funeral.

Uncle Phil was insured and the family now has a legacy of £150. Everyone likes George's suggestion of buying a television set, an item few of their neighbors could afford. The latest model TV is delivered and the dealer instructs the family how to use it. The first day, when the men are downstairs working, Mrs. Grigson and Uma decide to preview the new wonder and cautiously turn it on. There's an old western playing. They watch for a few minutes and then Mrs. Grigson is disturbed by one of the actors, an older man. He's only seen from the back but there's something strangely familiar about him. They turn the set off and go to prepare dinner.

That night the TV is given a proper debut. An extra couch is brought in to accommodate all the family members comfortably. The proper rituals are observed, including turning down the lights to get a better picture and the great premiere commences. There's a sporting event and then a variety show. Suddenly, Mrs. Grigson bolts from the room. When Uma follows her into the kitchen to see what the matter is, Mrs. Grigson tells her that she was sure one of the people on TV was Uncle Phil.

Soon, no matter what kind of program is playing, Uncle Phil inevitably makes a cameo appearance though initially not all the family members see him. Uma tries to convince her mother that it's all in her imagination but when they turn on the set to watch a mountain-climbing program, there's a close-up of one of the climbers and it's Uncle Phil. He turns directly to the camera and says, "Do you think it was easy living with the Grigsons? Climbing is child's play next to that." Uncle Phil's TV appearances become more and more hostile. During a tennis match, Uncle Phil turns up again: "If you ask me, tennis is relaxing next to always fighting with the Grigsons." He accuses Mr. Grigson of being an incompetent grocer, says that George is a fortune hunter, and demands that Steve return money that he took from him. Soon the entire family is seeing him and George's attempt at some sort of rational explanation falls woefully short.

Joyce brings some friends to the house to watch TV and there is a detective show playing. As the detective bends over a body (which has a dagger sticking in him), the corpse becomes Uncle Phil and addresses Joyce directly: "I'm the victim. The Grigsons are my murderers. They looked forward to me dying. And finally, my niece helped make it happen. She hid the box with my pills." Joyce screams a denial and hurls a stool at the TV, smashing the picture tube.

The short story ends with Mrs. Grigson trying to get a refund from the TV dealer. He gives them only a little of their money back since they have destroyed the picture tube.

Wisbar adds a brief coda. It's a few years later; Joyce is married and the family gathers for a celebration at their wealthy son-in-law's home. He unveils a new machine: a flat screen wall television complete with video recorder.

Mrs. Grigson doesn't want him to turn it on but he insists. After a brief moment, Uncle Phil is back and addresses the family in his usual manner: "I never thought it possible that there would be such a fool in the whole country of England to marry this snotnose."

The cast seems to be having fun, especially Willie Maertens as Phil the grumpy ghost. Maertens had earlier worked with Wisbar in *Darkness Fell on Gotenhafen*. TV sports anchorman Wim Thoelke has an uncredited bit as the announcer during the tennis game and comic actor Ernst H. Hilbich, also *sans* billing, turns up as the game show host.

When people refer to ghosts in early television, they are usually talking about the double image that sometimes appears when the reception is poor or the TV antenna needs to be adjusted. However, the story of the haunted Grigsons had a real parallel according to a 1954 article in *Television Digest* (as reported in the book *Haunted Media*). The Mackeys of Indianapolis were subjected to the unwelcome TV appearances of the wife's dead grandfather, always garbed in the suit in which he had been buried a few months previously. Mrs. Mackey was driven to distraction and eventually deposited the haunted set at the local police station.

At least the spectral grandpa didn't make rude comments.

Willkommen in Altamont (Welcome to Altamont)

Broadcast on November 21, 1965
85 minutes

Cast: Wilhelm Borchert as William Rutledge; Albert Lieven as Reeves Jordan; Günther Schramm as Henry Sorrell; Kurd Pieritz as Joseph Bailey; Alexander Golling as Preston Carr; William Ray as Dr. Johnson; Catana Cayetano as Annie Johnson; Heidrun Rieckmann as Helen Neely; C.F. Goodwater as Amos Todd; Bruno Dietrich as Lee Rutledge; Charlotte Schellenberg as Mrs. Rutledge; Herbert A.E. Böhme as Colonel Grimes; Franz Rudnick as McIntyre; Reinhold Nietsch as Hutchings; Peter Dickerson as Dan; Ulysses D. Jenkins, Robert Owens, George Goodman, Claude Thomas, Ernst G. Schniffner.

Credits: Director: Frank Wisbar; Teleplay: Susanna Rademacher; Based on the 1923 play *Welcome to our City* by Thomas Wolfe; Camera: Horst Fehlaber, Wolfgang Schallon; Editor: Gela-Marina Runne; Assistant Director: Ruth Althaus; Costumes: Anne Schmidt; Sound: Eduard Kessel; Set Designer: Erich Kettelhut; Produced by ZDF (Zweites Deutsches Fernsehen).

In 1923 when Thomas Wolfe was at Harvard, he took a stab at writing plays. One of them, *Welcome to Our City*, was performed by the 47 Workshop at the college. It had ten scenes and ran three and a half hours, much to the exhaustion of the invited audience. He was told that if he ever had any hope of having the play done professionally, he would have to shorten it. Instead Wolfe revised it to make it even longer. Not surprisingly, it has very seldom been staged. One such occasion was in 1962 in Zurich where Susanna Rademacher did the translation into German. I do not know whether she used the original version or Wolfe's longer one.

Three years later, Rademacher adapted the play for Wisbar and ZDF. It was considerably shortened but the gist of the very grim story was there. Wolfe based the city of Altamont on his hometown of Asheville, North Carolina, and delivered a merciless satire of small town parochial life in the vein of Sinclair Lewis and H.L. Mencken. The play climaxes in a race riot, something that certainly never happened in Asheville. Perhaps one other reason why the play is seldom performed is that even though Wolfe is solidly against the white Establishment and very sympathetic to the exploited black population, the latter is often depicted in a very stereotypical fashion.

I don't know what drew Wisbar to the play. He had lived in America

Willkommen in Altamont—college boy Lee Rutledge (Bruno Dietrich) wouldn't dream of acknowledging Sally Johnson (Catana Cayetano) on the street but a private tryst is a different story.

and Eva Wisbar and their daughters had settled in Virginia. Wisbar's third wife Dolores was also from Virginia but Wisbar is not likely to have been much exposed to small town life in the deep South. He was certainly familiar enough with racism, given his history during the Third Reich; and of course domination of the poor by the rich knows no racial or national boundaries. No doubt the civil rights movement in America and the resulting political strife gave the play relevance even though it was set in the 1920s.

Real estate developers in Altamont, led by Henry Sorrell and his flunky Joseph Bailey, have big plans for their city. (Interestingly, Wolfe's mother was a successful real estate agent.) They're going to tear down the slums and turn the ghetto into a thriving commercial and residential district. (This is rather like the "gentrification" trend of the '70s.) Most of the black people living in that area are renters and will be easily dispossessed. The only two Negroes who own property there and have to be bought out are old Amos Todd, who has a shoe repair shop, and Dr. Johnson, who lives in a big house that was owned by the Rutledge family during the Civil War. The Rutledges subsequently fell on hard times and the house went through several owners. Judge Rutledge is eager to reclaim his family home and feels especially chagrined that it has fallen into the hands of a Negro.

The city fathers and the various politicians, including the governor, are all on board with Sorrell's plans. Old Amos, passive and subservient, is easily persuaded to sell and is more worried about his nephew Sam and the rough crowd he hangs out with. The proud Dr. Johnson initially refuses but eventually begins to cave in under pressure from all sides. Rutledge's son Lee is home from college and pays a secret visit to Dr. Johnson's pretty daughter Sally. Johnson interrupts their tryst and the two men scuffle. Later Dr. Johnson shows up at the Rutledge home to return the hat Lee lost in the fight and angrily tells Judge Rutledge that he will never sell.

Things begin to get tense in the black neighborhood. A minstrel show is coming to town and a black activist from Boston denounces it and tries to persuade the crowd of men hanging around to boycott it. Dr. Johnson arrives on the scene and urges the crowd to resist being put out of their homes. The group seems responsive but when the sound of music from the minstrel show is heard, the crowd abandons the speakers and goes to listen.

With the seed of rebellion sown, the ghetto becomes restless. Sorrell and the city fathers would prefer to avoid bad publicity but then a riot ensues. Judge Rutledge suffers both a failure of nerve and a guilty conscience and no longer cares about reclaiming the family homestead. It's just as well because in the melee, the house gets burned down.

The National Guard is called to restore order. Old Amos refuses to leave his shop and is shot dead (a startling moment as the bullet hole appears in the window as he stares out). Dr. Johnson, armed with a pistol, is also shot. Rutledge arrives on the scene just as Johnson dies. The judge is left alone to contemplate the madness of it all and now realizes that the past can't be recaptured.

This is pretty much just a filmed stage play and Wisbar makes no attempt to open it up even though the last scenes certainly have cinematic possibilities. (Of course, the budget probably wouldn't have allowed showing a full-scale riot.) The street where the black population hangs out is no different than what you might see on stage. The set, done by the great Erich Kettelhut, is serviceable but nothing more. (There's a curious anachronism: The theater poster is from *The Love Parade* which didn't get released until six years after Wolfe wrote his play.) Wisbar seldom goes beyond what would be the norm for a TV film in terms of set-ups and camerawork. It is competent but little more.

Notable in the cast is Albert Lieven, the star of Wisbar's *Hermine and the Seven Upright Men*, here playing Reeves Jordan, a journalist who wants to rent in Altamont but is shunned when it is revealed he has tuberculosis. Somewhat surprisingly, he then disappears from the action in the original play. The character is given additional scenes in this production, possibly from Wolfe's longer version of his play.

Altamont also contains one of the rare film appearance of Catana Cayetano, who makes an appropriately sexy Annie Johnson. Cayetano was born in Guatemala to a poor family but as an infant was adopted by a wealthy German couple living there. She attended Cambridge University expecting to embark on a career as an international interpreter but she had an interest in dramatics as well and did a number of plays and a handful of movies, most notably a 1965 adaptation of *Uncle Tom's Cabin* (playing Eliza) and the 1969 horror film *Cardillac* (based on an E.T.A. Hoffmann tale). Cayetano later returned to the academic life and settled in the U.S. where she wrote her autobiography *Split at the Root: A Memoir of Love and Lost Identity*.

Wisbar directed three other movies for ZDF. The 1965 *Der Feuerzeichen* (*The Fire Sign*, 1965) is an adaptation of Catholic anti–Nazi novelist Werner Bergengruen's eponymous 1949 book. *S.O.S. Moro Castle* (1966) is a recreation of a forgotten tragedy of 1934 where an ocean liner caught fire, resulting in 135 deaths (passengers and crew). Wisbar's final TV film was 1967's *Flucht über die Ostee* (*Flight on the Baltic Sea*), a docu-drama on the *Wilhelm Gustloff* tragedy, a subject Wisbar had earlier addressed in *Darkness Fell on Gotenhafen*. *Flight* is mostly concerned with "Operation Hannibal," the desperate attempt of the German military to evacuate thousands of people from East Prussia before the onslaught of the advancing Russian army. Clips from *Darkness* depicting the sinking of the *Gustloff* are incorporated into *Flight*.

Wisbar worked on the scripts for two 1968 TV films that were not released until after his death: *Johannes dur den Wald* (*Johannes in the Forest*), the story of Germany's most notorious outlaw Schinderhannes, and *Der Kinder von Geltenhausen* (*The Children of Gelenhausen*).

Bibliography

Beyer, Friedemann. *Schöner als der Tod: Das Leben der Sybille Schmitz*. München: Belleville, 1998.
Cinzia, Romani. *Tainted Goddesses: Female Film Stars of the Third Reich*. New York: Sarpedon Publishers, 1992 [English translation].
Cole, Lance. *Secret Wings of World War II*. Barnsley, South Yorkshire, UK: Pen and Sword Books, 2015.
Cooke, Paul, and Mark Silberman. *Screening War: Perspectives on German Suffering*. Rochester, NY: Camden House, 2010.
Doherty, Thomas. *Hollywood and Hitler*. New York: Columbia University Press, 2013.
Everson, William K. *Classics of the Horror Film*. Secaucus, NJ: Citadel Press, 1974.
Fallada, Hans. *A Stranger in My Own Country*. Cambridge UK: Polity Press, 2015.
Grass, Günther. *Crabwalk*. Orlando, FL: Harcourt, 2002.
Haining, Peter. *Agatha Christie: Murder in Four Acts*. London: Virgin Books, 1990.
Jürgens, Curd. *Und kein bisschen weise, Munich*. Munich: Droemer Knaur, 1976.
Kirst, Hans Helmut. *The Officer Factory*. London: Cassell and Company, 1962.
Limberg, Margarete, Hubert Rübsaat, and Alan L. Nothnagle, editors. *Germans No More*. New York: Berghahn Books, 2006.
Mitchum, John. *Them Ornery Mitchum Boys*. Pacifica, CA: Creatures at Large Press, 1989.
Murray, Bruce, and Christopher Wickham, editors. *Framing the Past: The Historiography of German Cinema and Television*. Carbondale: Southern Illinois University Press, 1992.
Podak, Akim. *Dance with Death: The Ufa Star Sybille Schmitz*, Transit Film, 2000.
Saliot, Anne-Gaelle. *The Drowned Muse*. Oxford, UK: Oxford University Press, 2015.
Schmitz, Helmut, editor. *A Nation of Victims?* Amsterdam: Rodopi, 2007.
Schonz, Jefferey. *Haunted Media: Electronic Presence from Telegraphy to Television*. Durham, North Carolina: Duke University Press, 2000.
Snelson, Tim. *Phantom Ladies*. New Brunswick, NJ: Rutgers University Press, 2014.
Stewart, David Hull. *Film in the Third Reich*. Berkeley: University of California Press, 1969.
Tremper, Will. *Mein wilden Jahre*. Berlin: Ulstein, 1993.
Unwand, Ben. *The Collaboration: Hollywood's Pact with Hitler*. Cambridge, MA: Belknap Press of Harvard University Press, 2013.
Waldman, Harry. *Nazi Films in America, 1933–1942*. Jefferson, NC: McFarland, 2008.
Weniger, Kay. *Es Wird im die mehr genommen als gegeben*. Berlin: ACABUS Verlag, 2011.
Wolfe, Thomas. *Welcome to My Hometown*. Baton Rouge: Louisiana State University Press, 1983.
Wysbar, Eva. *Hinaus aus Deutschland, irgenwohin*. Lengwil, Switzerland: Libelle, 2000.

Index

Abbott and Costello Meet Frankenstein 133, 146
Ace in the Hole 173
Adventures of Superman (television) 127
Afraid to Live (Fireside Theater) 163
All in the Family 139
All Quiet on the Western Front (book) 168
All the President's Men 174
Alraune (1930) 90
Amadeus (film) 151, 153
The Amber Gods (Fireside Theater) 159
Amok 92
Andersson, Harriet **198**, **199**, 204
Angel, Heather 129
Anna und Elisabeth (*Anna and Elisabeth*) 2, 9, 13, 20, 21, 29–48, 87, 147, 149, 196, 212
Another Face 128
Aquacade 16
Arsenic and Old Lace (play) 103
Aubert, Lenore **144**, 146
The Awful Truth 128

The Bad Seed 111
Bagier, Douglas L. 146
Bal im Metropol (*Ball in Metropol*) 12, 94–98
The Ballad of the Buried Life 171
Barbara (book) 196, 197–198
Barbara (movie) 19, 196–205
Barrat, Robert 120
Barry, Don "Red" 149
The Battle of Algiers 206
Bauhaus, Carl 46, **32**
Baxter, Alan 145
Beebe, Ford 155–156
Behr, Carl 8
Beinta and Peder Arrheboe 197
Bellande, Edward 129
Bendix, William 161

Benkhoff, Fita 63–64, 103, 104
Bergengruen, Werner 219
Berger, Elisabeth 84
Berle, Milton 158
Bethmann, Sabine 170
Bienert, Gerhard **73**
Birell, Tala 111–112
Black Beauty 17
Black Mirror (television) 213
Blair, George 149
The Blockhouse 171
Blondell, Joan **160**, 161
Bloodlust! 153
The Blue Angel 91
Bluebeard's Eighth Wife 146
Blythe, Betty 149
Boese, Carl 7, 8, 12
Das Boot 168
Borgmann, Hans-Otto 91
Bower, Dallas 159
Braun, Eva 73–74
Brecht, Bertold 44, 47
Brent, George 163, 164
The Brute Man 139
Buchholz, Horst 175, 176
Der Burg ruft (*The Mountain Calls*) 198

Canaris 177
The Captain from Köpenick (1956) 177
Card, James 78, 117
Cardillac 219
Carlock, Dolores 18
Carnival of Souls 77
Cassidy, Ed 129
Castle, Don **138**, 139, 149
Cayetano, Catana **217**, 219
Ceiling Zero (play) 139
Cervi, Gino 151
Chandu the Magician 138

Chaney, Lon 13
Christie, Agatha 48
A Christmas Carol (television, 1951) 159
The Circle (book) 213
Classics of the Horror Film 1, 119, 120
Cliento, Diane 51
Cold Heaven (book) 35
Commando 19, 191, 205–209
Confessions of a Nazi Spy 101
Cooper, James Fenimore 140
Crabwalk 189–190
Cradle Song 43
The Criminals 78
Crist, Hans Helmut 193
Cross of Love 135
Crusade Without Conscience (Fireside Theater) 161
Cyankali 54

Dali, Salvador 127
D'Alquen, Gunter 10, 12
Dance on the Volcano 79
The Day the Clown Cried 204
Dead Men Walk 122
Death Takes a Holiday 75, 113
Delgeten, Réne 151
De Mond, Albert 149
Desert Comedy 16, 106
Dessau, Paul 47
Destiny (1921) 66, 75, 80, 97, 115
Detour 120
Devil Bat 121, 122, 127
Devil Bat's Daughter 17, 119, 120–129, 133
De Vogt, Carl 80, 81, 116
De Vogt, Karl Franz 80
Diary of a Lost Girl 78, 86
Dieterle, William 105
Dietrich, Bruno **217**
Dinty 173
Dogville 204
The Doomed Battalion 111
Doran, Ann 164
Dracula (television, 1972) 97
Dracula's Daughter 42
Dreyer, Carl 35, 66, 90
Drums Along the Mohawk 208
Dumke, Ralph 164
Dupont, E.A. 3, 111
Durchbruch Lok 234 (*Breakthrough Locomotive 234*) 19, 205, 209–212
Durieux, Tillia 205

Ecstasy 93
Edwards, Blake 120

Edwards, James 161
Elisabeth und der Narr (*Elisabeth and Her Fool*) 44
Enchanted Forest 121
Die Endlose Nacht (*The Endless Night*) 175
The Enemy Below 169
Engelmann, Heinz 170
Ephraim, Herbert 8, 24
Es geschah am hellichten tag (*It Happened in Broad Daylight*) 177
Escape from East Berlin 210
Eternal Melodies 151
Evans, Charles 145
Everson, William K. 1, 21, 75, 112, 117, 119, 120
Die ewige Maske (*The Eternal Mask*) 46

Fabrik der Offiziere (*The Officer Factory*, book) 193–194, 195, 196
Fabrik der Offiziere (*The Officer Factory*, film) 19, 170, 184, 192–196
Face of Marble 16–17
Fährmann Maria (*Ferryman Maria*) 1, 2, 3, 4, 11, 17, 20, 21, 38, 47, 65–82, 85, 90, 93, 97, 112–113, 115, 116–117, 147, 156, 182, 191, 196, 212
Fallada, Hans 44, 46
Fantomas 92
Felmy, Hansjörg 169
Ferguson, Frank 132–133
Der Feuerzeichen (*The Fire Signal*) 170, 219
The Fighting Madonna 147
Film in the Third Reich 2, 72, 92
Fireside Theater 3, 17, 18, 20, 48, 111, 122, 129, 138, 140, 146, 153, 156–165, 212
Fischer-Köppe, Hugo 103
Five Fingers 28
Five Million in Search of an Heir 12
Fleischmann, Herbert 205, 212
Flucht nach Berlin (*Escape to Berlin*) 175
Flucht über die Ostee (*Flight Across the Baltic Sea*) 20, 191, 219
The Flying Dutchman (opera) 75
The Flying Serpent 120, 122
Fontane, Theodore 94
Foreign Correspondent 139
Forgotten Faces (1936) 111
Foster, Michael 161
F.P. 1 Doesn't Answer 55, 79
Frank, Horst 169, 182, 185
Freihe Fahrt (*Full Speed Ahead*) 78
Das Freudenhaus (*The Bordello*) 205
Frobe, Gert 176–177

Froelich, Carl 8, 43, 45
Froelich, Hugo 8

Galland, Jean 87, 92
Garbo, Greta 84
Garz, Detlef 5, 7, 13
GE Theater 161
Gebühr, Hilde **50**, 53, 54
Gebühr, Otto 54
George, Heinrich 10, 60, 95, 97
Gerlich, Fritz 37
Germelhausen (*Fireside Theater*) 158
Go and Get It 173
Godfrey, Ormonde 178
Goebbels, Joseph 10, 11, 12, 16, 20, 28, 37, 38, 45, 54, 60, 72–73, 74, 79, 80–81, 92, 98, 102, 104, 150, 166, 169, 180, 190
Goetzke, Bernhard 80
Golden, Edward 13
The Golden Ball (*Fireside Theater*) 48
Goldfinger 176
Gottschalk, Joachim 190
Grabley, Ursula 28
Graff, Wilton 151, 152, 153
The Grand Duke's Finances (1934) 97
Granger, Stewart 208–209
Granville, Bonita 139
Grass, Günter 189
The Grass Is Greener (*Fireside Theater*) 164
Gray, Dorian (actress) 209
Grayson, Kathryn 151
The Great Escape 191
The Great German Films 2
Griem, Helmut **192, 198, 199**, 204
Griffin, Jay 122
Grigoleit, , Kurt 195
Grossmann, Johannes **192**
Gründgens, Gustav 78, 79, 97

Haag, Walter 182
Hadley, Reed 155
Hagelstang, Rudolf 170
Haie und klein Fische (book) 166, 168, 179, 188
Haie und klein Fische (*Sharks and Little Fish*) 19, 166–170, 184, 206
Hajos, Karl 134
Die Halbstarken (*The Holligans*) 175
Hale, Michael 125, 128
Hansen, Joachim 182
Hans Westmar 45
Hardt, Karin 60–61
Hartl, Karl 150, 153

Hatton, Rondo 139
Haunted Media 216
The Head 170
Heinz, Paul 56
Held, Martin 177
Helen of Troy (1924 film) 80
Helm, Brigitte 90
Henckels, Paul 60
Hermine und der seiben Aufrechenten (*Hermine and the Seven Upright Men*) 10, 11, 56–61, 219
Der Herr der Welt (*Master of the World*) 85
Hilbich, Ernst H. 216
Hinaus aus Deutschland-irgendwohin (*Out of German Anywhere*) 5
Hinrichs, August 100
His Sister's Secret 121
Hitchcock, Alfred 122, 127
Hitler, Adolf 5, 6, 9, 11, 12, 16, 43–44, 51, 79, 98, 103, 122, 157, 170, 181
Hitler: The Last Ten Days 51
Hitlerjunge Quex 54, 60
Hitler's Children 105, 106, 108
Hohoff, Margarete 170
Holden, Gloria 42
Hoppe, Marianne 63
Horney, Brigitte 190
Horror Hotel 117
Horror on Snape Island 135
Hound of the Baskervilles (1937) 80
House of Frankenstein 47
House of Horrors 127
House of the Seven Gables (novel) 113
House of Usher 127
Hubschmid, Paul 175
Hull, Henry 155
Hunchback of Notre Dame (1923) 119
Hunchback of Notre Dame (1939) 105
Hund, volt ihr ewig leben? (*Dogs, Do You Want to Live Forever?*) 19, 81, 170, 178–182, 184, 206

I Love Lucy 156
I Was a Teenage Werewolf 121
Ica Klang an (*I Accuse*) 46
Illusion in Moll 80
Im Bann des Eulenspiegels (*Under the Spell of the Owl Mirror*) 3, 23–29
Im Schatten des Berges (*In the Shadow of the Mountain*)
The Immortal 150
The Immortal Spring 16, 150
The Imp in the Bottle (*Fireside Theater*) 158

L'Inconnue 83–85, 91, 93
The Indiscreet Mrs. Jarvis (*Fireside Theater*) 164
Ivano, Paul 152
Ivy 129

Jacobowsky and the Colonel 28
Jacobsen, Jørgen-Frantz 197, 198, 204
Jaeger, Ernst 122
Jalna 128
James, John 129
Jane Wyman Presents Fireside Theater 18, 164
Jannings, Emil 60, 97
Jew Süss 170
Johannes dur den Wald (*Johannes in the Forest*) 219
Juarez 105
Jungle Captive 139
Jürgens, Curd 93

Karlweiss, Oskar **24**, 27–28
Katharina Knie 28
Keller, Gottfried 56
Kelly, Nancy **108**, 111
Kerst, Alexander 182
Kettlehut, Erich 170, 219
The Killers (1946) 128
Der Kinder von Geltenhausen (*The Children of Geltenhausen*) 219
Kiwe, Til 191
Klausen, Klaus **50**, 54
Klein-Rogge, Rudolph 44
Knef, Hildegard 80
Kolberg 28, 54, 60
Krach um Jolanthe (*The Fuss About Jolanthe*) 100
Kraft durch Freude (KDF; Strength Through Joy) 99–100, 183, 184
Kuhle Wampe, oder: Wem gehört die welt? (*Who Owns the World?*) 44

Laerdal, Asmund 93
The Lamb (novel) 37
Lamont, Molly 128–129
Landers, Lew 130
Lang, Fritz 3, 30, 66, 97
Lang, June 137–138
Lange, Carl 182, **193**, 195
Lansbury, Angela 164
Lantz, Adolph 85
La Planche, Louise 118–119
La Planche, Rosemary 116, 118–119, 127–128

Lassie (television) 139
The Last Command 206
Last of the Mohicans (book) 140
Last of the Mohicans (1992 film) 208
The Last Roman 204
Lavagnino, Angelo Francesco 209
Lawson, Wilfred 134–135
Lazareff, Pierre 175
Leander, Zarah 14, 81
Leary, Nolan 116, 129
Lebensborn (Nazi program) 106
Lebensborn (film) 106
Legend of Babie Doly 171
The Legion's Last Patrol see *Commando*
Leine Spiele aus Ubersee (*Little Plays from Overseas*) 165
Leonard, Sheldon 149
Lichtenstein, Herbert 24–25
Liebe, Tod und Teufel (*Love, Death and the Devil*) 190
Liebeneiner, Wolfgang **50**, 55
Der Liebeshafen (*The Love Shaft*) see *Die Werft zum Grauen Hecht*
Lieven, Albert 61, 219
Life Goes On 28
Life Is Beautiful 176
The Life of Emile Zola 105
Lighthouse 17, 134–140
Lingen, Theo 10, 25, 28
Lippert, Robert L. 146
Litel, John 139
Little Man, What Now? 44
Lockhart, June 127
The Lone Ranger (film) 145
The Lone Ranger Rides Again 145
The Lost Patrol 207
The Lottery (television) 159
Lüdke, Wenzel 174
Lugosi, Bela 121, 122
Lundigan, William 164
The Lying Truth 173

M 30, 46
Madame Du Barry 97
Mädchen in Uniform (*Maidens in Uniform*) 8, 9, 30, 31, 41, 42, 43, 45, 113
Der Mädchen von Fanö (*The Girl from Fano*) 190
Mademoiselle Fifi 119
Madonna of the Desert 16, 147–149
Maertens, Willy **213**, 216
The Magnificent Seven 176
Mahoney, Leo J. 122
Majewski, Hans-Martin 170, 176, 195

Making of a King 56
Malone, Dorothy 163
Man of a Thousand Faces 129
The Man Who Walked Alone 134
The Man Who Was Sherlock Holmes 97, 150
Man's Favorite Sport 176
Mardi-Gras (Fireside Theater) 158
Marthe Richard 92
Maurischat, Fritz 28-29
Mein wilden Jahre (My Wild Years) 4, 176
Menschen im Käfig (Caged Men) 111
Mercer, Ray 127
Michael, Gertrude 111, 163
Middleton, Charles 119-120
Milawkowski, Herman 16, 105, 106, 150-151
Mill of the Stone Women 191
The Miracle Man 147
Miracle of the Bells 147
Miss Fane's Baby Is Stolen 43
Mitchell, Thomas 163
Mitchum, John 145-146, 157
Mog, Aribert **66, 70, 73**, 77, 80, 81, 93
Moore, Brian 35
Morgenrot (Red Dawn) 166
Moser, Hans 28
Mozart, Wolfgang Amadeus 150, 151
The Mozart Story 17, 149-153
Münchausen (1943) 190
Murnau, F.W. 3, 5, 66
Muschler, Conrad Reinhold 84, 85, 91

Nacht fiel über Gotenhafen (Darkness Fell on Gotenhafen) 3, 19, 21, 170, 182, 183-192, 216, 219
Nagana 111
Nasser Asphalt (Wet Asphalt) 3, 19, 170-178
The Naughty Nineties 47
Neumann, Therese 37
Neville, John 122
Nielsen, Hans 204-205
Nierentz Jürgen, Hans 72, 81, 156
Night of the Generals 193
Nights of Cabiria 209
Nightshade 82
Nosferatu (1922) 66, 75, 116
Nosferatu the Vampyr 116

Oberwachtmeister Schwenk (Sergeant Schwenk) 62
Offenbach, Joseph 212
Olympia 81, 122

On Borrowed Time 75, 113
On Higher Orders 46
One, Two, Three 176
Onkel Phils Nachlass (Uncle Phil's Legacy) 20, 212-216
Ordet 35
Ott, Frederick 2
Ott, Wolfgang 156

paper film 8, 24-25
The Passion of Joan of Arc 90
Patrick, Gail 111
The Pearl of Great Price 134
Perry Mason (television) 111
Perschy, Maria 176
Petermann Goes to Madeira 100
Petermann ist dagegen (Petermann Is Against It!) 12, 64, 98-104, 183
Pfitzmann, Günter 191
Picture of Dorian Gray (television, 1961) 97
Pirandello, Luigi 85
Platen, Karl 97, 103
Playgirl 175
The Pledge 177
The Plot to Assassinate Hitler 191
The Postman Always Rings Twice (1946) 136
The Prairie (book) 140, 141
The Prairie (film) 17, 140-146
Prairie Chickens 119
Preiss, Wolfgang 170, 182, 191
Priestley, J.B. 214

Queen Christina 84

Rahl, Mady 170
Raid on Rommel 191
Ray of Sunshine 85
Raymond, Gene 161, 164
The Reign of Amelika Joe (Fireside Theater) 161
Reinhardt, Max 43
Reitsch, Hanna 51
Remous 92
Renzi, Eva 175
Rescue Annie 93
The Restless Night 169
Return in Triumph (Fireside Theater) 163
Richards, Addison 134
Riefenstahl, Leni 9, 16, 56, 81, 122
Riess, Curt 175
Rimfire 17, 153-156
Ritter, Carl 55

Rivalen der Luft (*Rivals of the Air*) 9, 15, 48–55
Robinson, Dewey 130
Robinson, Edward G. 136
Roselli, Johnny 138
Rosen blühen auf dem Heidgrae (*Roses bloom on the grave in the Meadow*) 82
Rossier, Joseph 50
Royal Romance of Charles and Diana 209
Rübezahl's Hochzeit (*Rübezahl's Wedding*) 103
Rühmann, Heinz 12

Sagan, Leontine 31, 43
St. Claire, Arthur 140, 141
Salieri, Antonio 151
Salome (play) 205
Salt of the Sea 189
Scared to Death 86, 128
Schafheitlin, Franz 97
Schmitz, Sybille 1, *2*, 11, 12, **50**, 54–55, **66**, **68**, **70**, 72, **73**, 80, **81**, 82, **83**, 85, 86, 87, **88**, 90, 91, 92, 93, 116, 204
Schneeberger, Hans 55
Schön, Heinz 184, 191
Schönherr, Dietmar 191
Schröter, Heinz 179–180
Schumann, Erik **184**, 212
Schumann, Harry 212
Die schwarze Maske (*The Black Mask*) 8
Scream in the Night (*Fireside Theater*) 158
Secrets of a Sorority Girl 3, 17, 129–134
Sekely, Steve 105, 110
Selpin, Herbert 28
Sergeant Sullivan Speaking (*Fireside Theater*) 161
Seven Beauties 109
The Seventh Seal 75
She-Wolf of London 127
Shock 125
Sign of the Cross 129
Silverheels, Jay 145
Simon, Simone 119
Siodmak, Robert 210
Sirk, Douglas 14
Six Characters in Search of an Author 85
Smith, Sidney 140
So This Is London 136
Sorority Girl 130
S.O.S. Moro Castle 219
Sparks Fly Upwards 208
Speelmans, Hermann 63
Spellbound 122, 127
Spira, Camilla 61
Spira, Lotte 61

Split at the Root: A Memoir of Love and Lost Identity 219
Star of Africa 169, 182
Steinert, Alexander 127, 145
Steinhoff, Hans 56
Stepanek, Karl 61
Stewart, David Hull 2, 72, 74, 81, 92
Strange, Glenn 155
Strange Death of Adolf Hitler 106
Strangler of the Swamp 1, 17, 75, 112–120, 128, 129, 136, 145, 147
Strenge, Walter 136
The Student of Prague (1935) 44
Summer with Monkia 204
Sunrise 5
Sunset Blvd. 86
Supper, Walter 10

Tasiemeka, Hans 7
Taylor, Ray **130**
Teichs, Alf 195–196
The Tell-Tale Heart (1939) 157
A Terribly Strange Bed (*Fireside Theater*) 159
The Texaco Star Theater 158
Theiss, Dorothea **32**
Thiele, Hertha 9, 31, **30**, **32** 33, **36**, 37, 38, **41**, 43, 44–45, **45**
Thoelke, Wim 216
Thorne, Ken 209
Three Russian Girls 15
Through a Glass Darkly 204
Thunder Rock 134
Thundercloud, Chief 141, 145
Time Bomb (*Fireside Theater*) 157
Titanic (1943 film) 28–29, 79, 184–185, 205
Titanic, a Night to Remember 184
Eine tolle Sache (*An Awesome Affair*) see *Under the Spell of the Owl Mirror*
Tonat, Anna 5
Tower of Terror 134
Traumulus 97
Tremper, Will 4, 6, 8, 9, 11, 13, 14, 166, 174–176
The Trial of Lucullus 47
A Trip to Tislit 5
Triumph of the Will 56, 81
The Tunnel (television) 210
The Twelve Chairs (book) 23
Two-Soul Woman 125
The Twonky 214

U-Boote westwärts (*U-Boat Course West*) 166–167

Index

The Ufa Story 61
Ulmer, Edgar G. 3
Die Unbekannte (book) 84, 91
Die Unbekannte (The Unknown; movie) 3, 5, 11, 20, 82–94, 123, 196, 204
Uncle Phil on TV 214
Uncle Tom's Cabin (television, 1965) 219
The Uninvited 113
The Untamable 125
Untenmehmen Michael (Operation Michael) 46

Valley of the Blue Mountain 18
Vallin, Rick *130*, 134
Vampire (Fireside Theater) 158
Vampyr 1, 66, 69, 75, 79
Veronika Voss 80
Via Mala (1948) 60
Via Mala (1961) 177
Vickers, Martha 164
The Vigil (Fireside Theater) 161
Vincent, Russ *144*, 145
Von Ballasko, Viktoria 97
Von Barsody, Eduard 150
Von Barsody, Hans 205
Von Cleve, Heinz 97
Von Harbou, Thea 45
Von Langen, Vera 12, 13, 15, 16, 141
Von Rautenfeld, Klaus 198
Von Reizenstein, Hans Joachim Freiherr 62
Voss, Peter *66, 70, 73, 76*, 77, 80, 191

Wagenheim, Charles 139
Waldow, Ernst 103, 104
Walker, Robert 151
Ware, Mary *131*, 134
Watkin, Pierre 131
Wegener, Paul 205
Weihmayr, Franz 47, 65, 69, 81
Weissner, Hilde
Welcome to Our City 216–217
Wen die Götter lieben (Whom the Gods Love) 150, 151, 152, 153

Wendler, Otto Bernhard 100
Die Werft zum Grauen Hecht (The Grey Pike's Wharf) 11, 62–65
Der Werwolf 65–66, 82
Westfront 1918 54
Where Are Your Children? 112
Wieck, Dorothea 9, *30* 31, 33, *36*, *41*, 42–44
Wieman, Mathias *32*, *36*, *41*, *45*, 46
The Wife of Monte Cristo 45
The Wild Geese 209
Wilhelm Gustloff (ship) 183–184, 219
Willkommen in Altarmont (Welcome to Altamont) 20, 61, 170, 216–219
Windt, Herbert 65, 67, 81, 182
Wisbar, Annemarie 7, 11, 19, 74
Wisbar, Eva 5, 7, 8, 9, 10, 11, 13, 16, 18, 45, 61, 73, 74, 98, 104
Wisbar, Frank *2*, *81*, *160*; early career 7–8, 23–25, 30–31; on film 18, 19, 20, 94, 143, 176; and the Nazis 4,-5, 6–7, 9–14, 15–16, 72, 74, 87; Senate testimony 15, 49–50, 52, 55
Wisbar, Maria 15, 16, 18
Wisbar, Mathias 18
Wisbar, Tania 12, 15, 16, 18
Wolfe, Thomas
Women in Bondage 5, 15, 16, 104–112
Women Make Better Diplomats 61
Wöss, Fritz 179
Wrather, Jack 139
Wysbar, Franz 5
Wysbar, Fritz 5

Yesterday and Today 31
Yowlachie, Chief 145

Zerlett-Offonius, Walter 28
Ziemann, Sonja 182, *184*, 191
Zucco, George 122
Zwielict (Twilight) 28
Zwölf Swischen und Viertel Eins (Between Twelve and a Quarter to One) 8

www.ingramcontent.com/pod-product-compliance
Lightning Source LLC
Chambersburg PA
CBHW032049300426
44116CB00007B/664